HELENSBURGH & RHU

THROUGH TIME

Chris Sanders

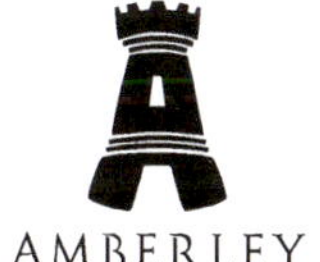

AMBERLEY

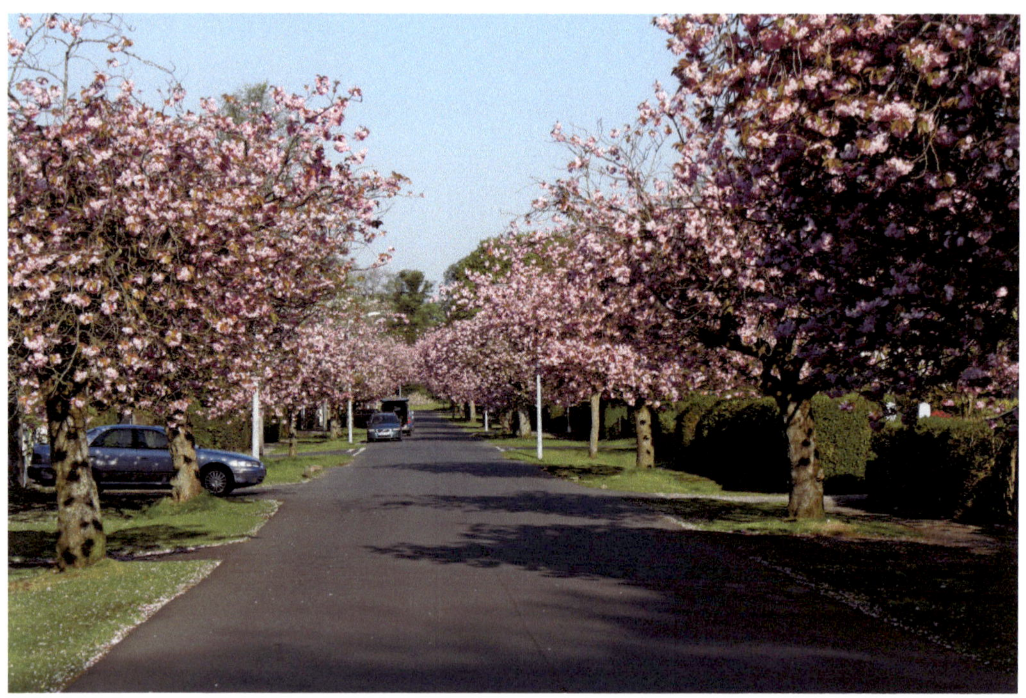

The annual blossom is very much part of Helensburgh.

This project was instigated by the late Kenneth Crawford, who provided much help and guidance throughout. The book has been produced on behalf of Helensburgh Heritage Trust using material and photographs from their website. All proceeds from the book will go to the Trust.

First published 2016

Amberley Publishing
The Hill, Stroud, Gloucestershire, GL5 4EP
www.amberley-books.com

Copyright © Chris Sanders, 2016

The right of Chris Sanders to be identified as the
Author of this work has been asserted in accordance with
the Copyrights, Designs and Patents Act 1988.

ISBN 978 1 4456 5424 9 (print)
ISBN 978 1 4456 5425 6 (ebook)

British Library Cataloguing in Publication Data.
A catalogue record for this book is available from the
British Library.

Typesetting by Amberley Publishing.
Printed in Great Britain.

Appointed GPSR EU Representative: Easy Access System
Europe Oü, 16879218
Address: Mustamäe tee 50, 10621, Tallinn, Estonia
Contact Details: gpsr.requests@easproject.com, +358 40
500 3575

Introduction

Helensburgh lies between the sea and mountains on a south-facing slope on the north bank of the Clyde, adjacent to the Highland Boundary Fault that marks the transition from the Central Lowlands to the more rugged Highlands.

Originally there were two much older settlements: the village of Row (now Rhu) in the west, where cattle were swum across the Gareloch on a drove route from Argyll to Dumbarton cattle fair (Rhu parish was created in 1648 and the first church built), and the hamlet of Milligs to the east, which surrounded a mill first recorded in 1346.

In 1705 the lands now forming Helensburgh were sold by the McAulays of Ardencaple to Sir John Schaw of Greenock who employed a surveyor, William Boutcher, to design a landscape, still traceable in the street plan of Helensburgh and the surrounding moorland; this was partially complete when Sir John died in 1756; subsequently his daughter Marion sold the land to the Colquhouns of Luss.

Sir James Colquhoun, hoping to start a weaving industry, advertised plots of land for houses and gardens in 1776, calling the new settlement after his wife, Lady Helen Sutherland. The weaving industry was unsuccessful, but the attractive site encouraged housing which spread up the hill during the nineteenth century.

Transport was always important to the development of the town. Henry Bell, the first provost, built the *Comet*, the first seagoing steam ship in the world, which started services from Helensburgh to Glasgow in 1812. Commuting was improved by the arrival of the railway from Glasgow in 1857. In the 1890s the West Highland line linking Helensburgh to Oban and Fort William was completed.

By late Victorian and Edwardian times, the town was recognised as a very attractive place to live, with a grid of tree-lined streets containing houses set in large gardens. Helensburgh became known as the Garden City on the Clyde, and a large number of important houses were built by significant architects, especially Charles Rennie Mackintosh's masterpiece The Hill House.

In the first half of the twentieth century, Helensburgh became a very popular resort for those going 'doon the watter' for a day out from Glasgow. There was an open-air swimming pool on the pier and a paddling pool and putting green developed on the promenade. There were also three cinemas in the town. Hermitage Park, which contained flower beds, rustic bridges over the Millig Burn, a bandstand and the impressive town war memorial, was created from the grounds of Hermitage House.

Helensburgh's situation on the Clyde meant that there were always close links with the navy, especially during and since the Second World War. The ship breaking yard at Faslane on the Gareloch was developed into the Clyde Submarine Base and is the home of the UK's submarines. Naval housing estates were built in the town and the base remains the largest employer in the area.

After 173 years as an independent burgh, Helensburgh became part of Strathclyde Region and Dumbarton District in 1975, and then became part of the unitary authority of Argyll and Bute, based in Lochgilphead, in 1997.

The village of Rhu, though closely linked to the town, remains a vibrant, close-knit community, with a beautiful village church, the third on that site, a large marina and the Royal Northern and Clyde Yacht Club based in a local mansion. Glenarn Garden contains a famous collection of rhododendrons and magnolias.

Towards the end of the twentieth century, as with many similar places, Helensburgh's role as a seaside resort declined, and the centre of the town and sea front became rather run down. The character of many of the shops changed, with traditional grocers and drapers being replaced by charity shops and cafés.

A number of present-day developments promise a brighter future. Argyll and Bute Council redeveloped the seafront promenade and Colquhoun Square, which is now an attractive site for markets and other events. An empty school, an early design of A. N. Paterson, has been redeveloped and extended into a new civic centre. A local church has been converted into a digital arts centre which shows live links to theatre, operas and ballets as well as first run films. Hermitage Park, which was threatened with being sold for housing, has, thanks to the efforts of an enthusiastic group of volunteers and the council, received a large grant from the Heritage Lottery Fund and will be restored. A new leisure centre is to be built on the pier, now a rather soulless car park, and several very good restaurants and café bars have opened, adding to the regeneration of the town.

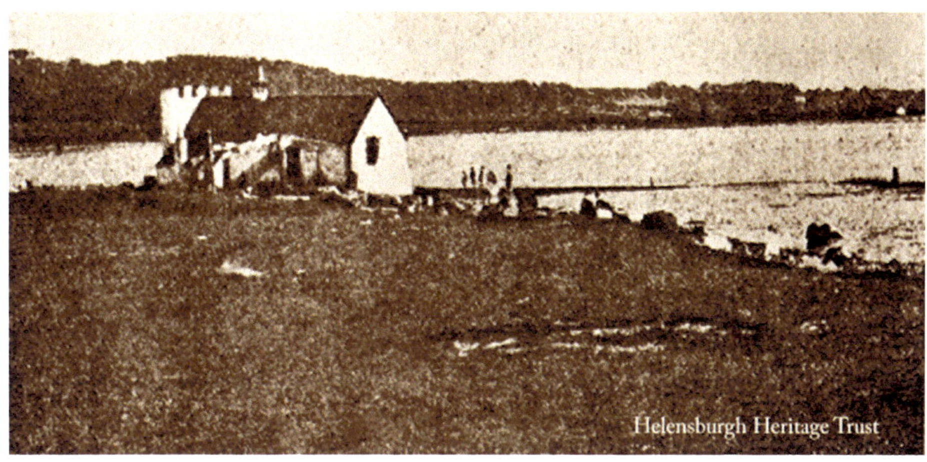

Drumfork Ferry

One of the earliest photographs taken in Helensburgh shows the long-demolished Drumfork Ferry House, which was to the east of what is now Craigendoran Station. Sheep and cattle were brought to it over the Old Luss Road, then ferried to Greenock.

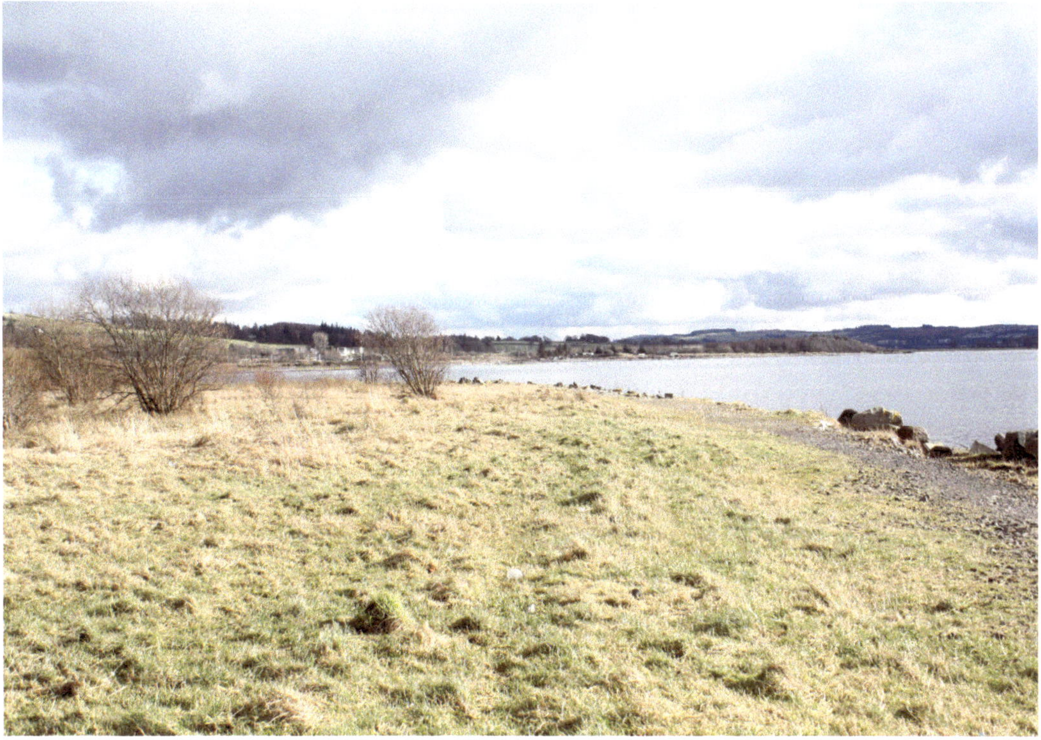

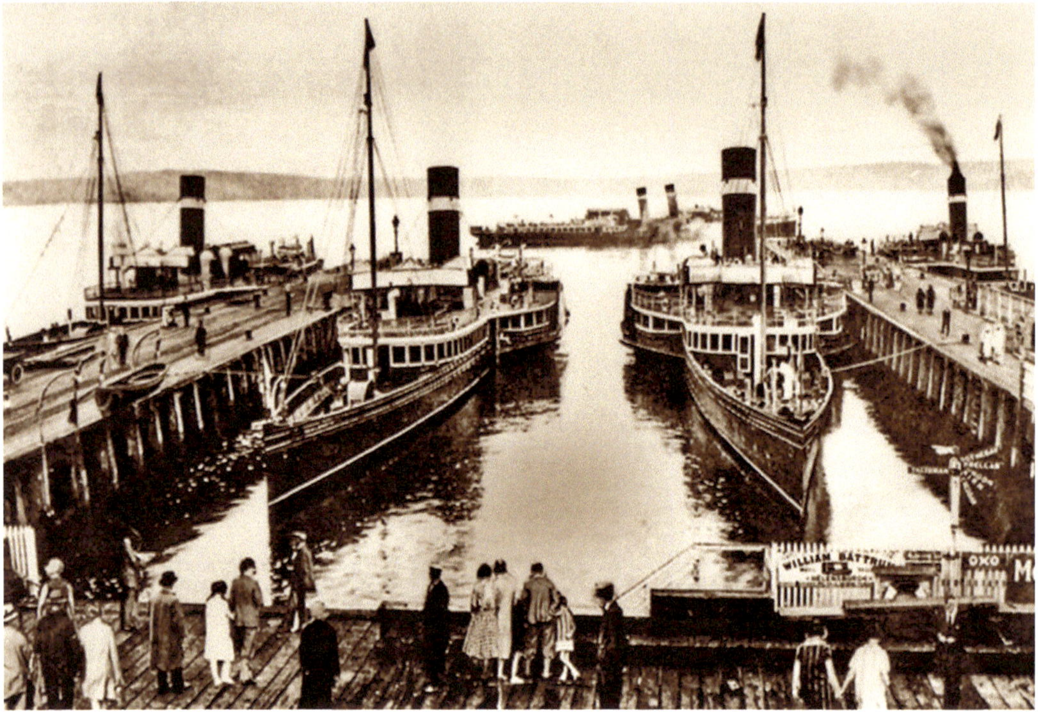

Steamers at Craigendoran

A 1933 picture of most of the LNER fleet at Craigendoran. The two that can be seen the least well are the *Lucy Ashton* and the *Jeanie Deans*, and in the centre are the *Talisman* and the *Marmion*. The steamer terminal and station opened for business under the North British Railway on 15 May 1882, and steamer services were finally withdrawn in 1972. The piers have since become derelict.

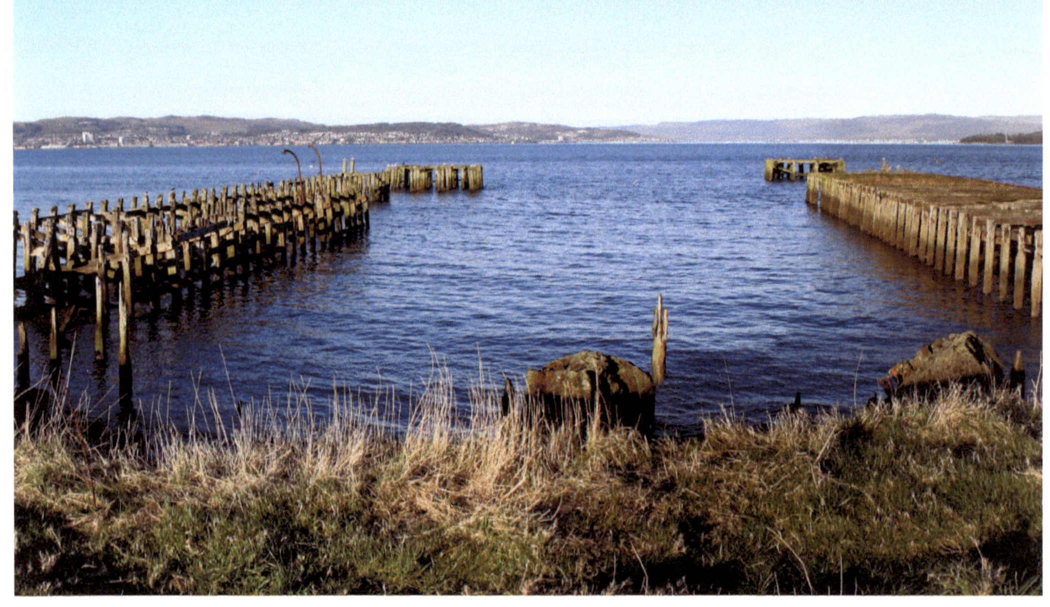

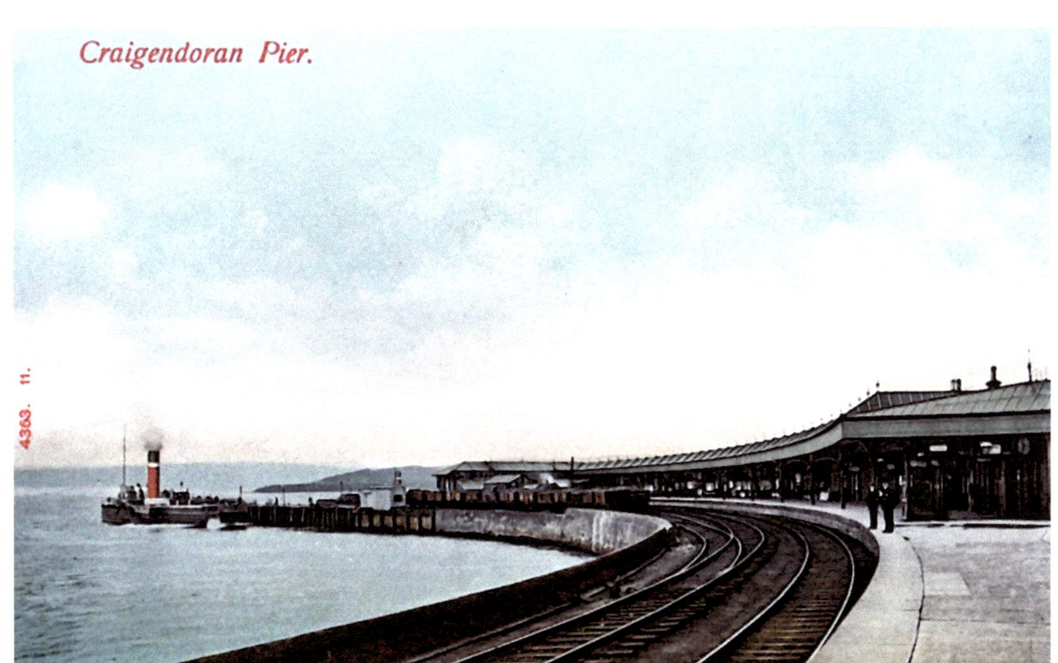

Craigendoran Pier
The platform at Craigendoran station brought day-trippers direct to the steamers at the pier (one steamer can be seen). Both the station and the pier were built in 1882 after a plan to extend the line through the town centre to Helensburgh pier fell through because of local opposition.

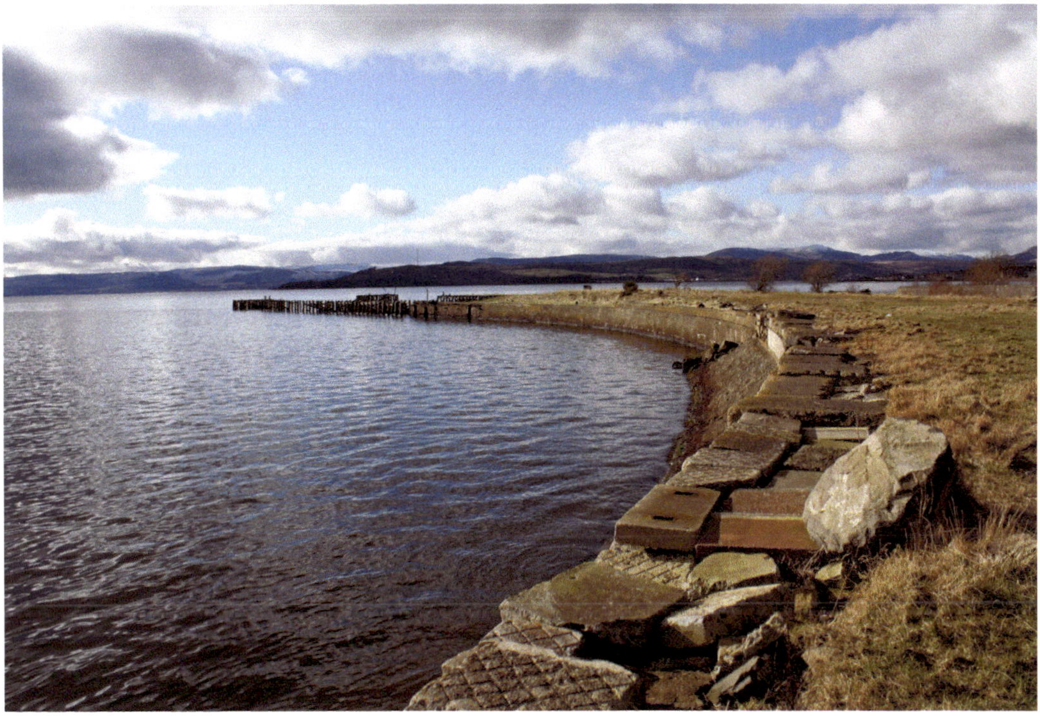

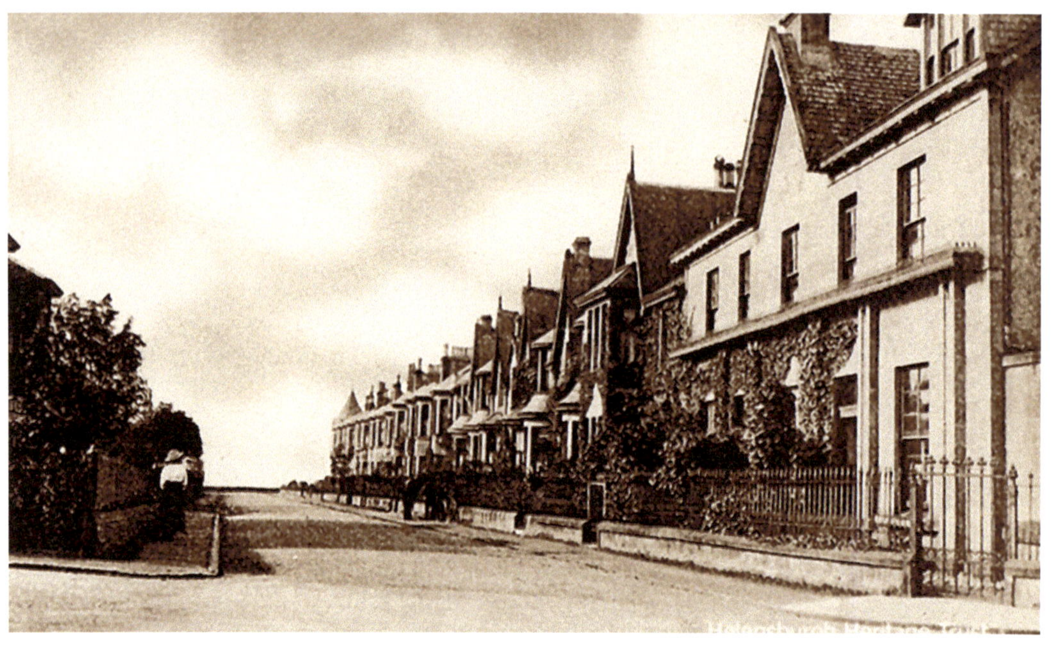

Craigendoran Avenue

The right-hand side of Craigendoran Avenue, with its row of town houses leading down to the Clyde, was built by the 1890s, the other side not completed until the early years of the twentieth century. The street remains much unchanged in the present day.

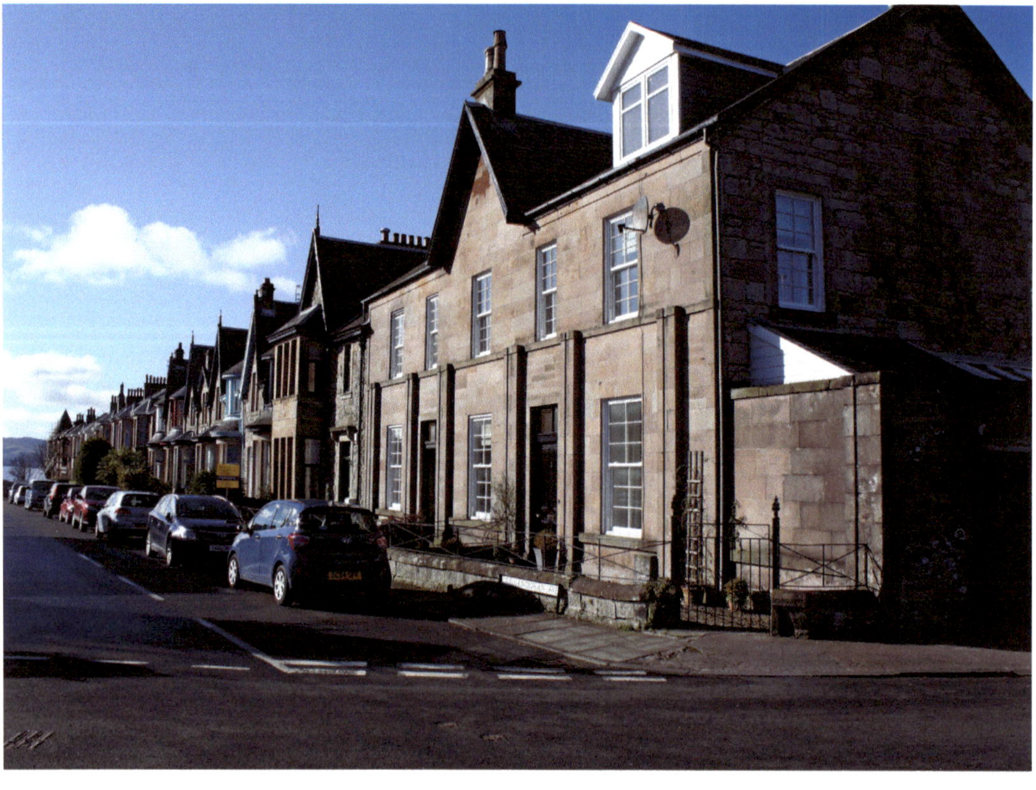

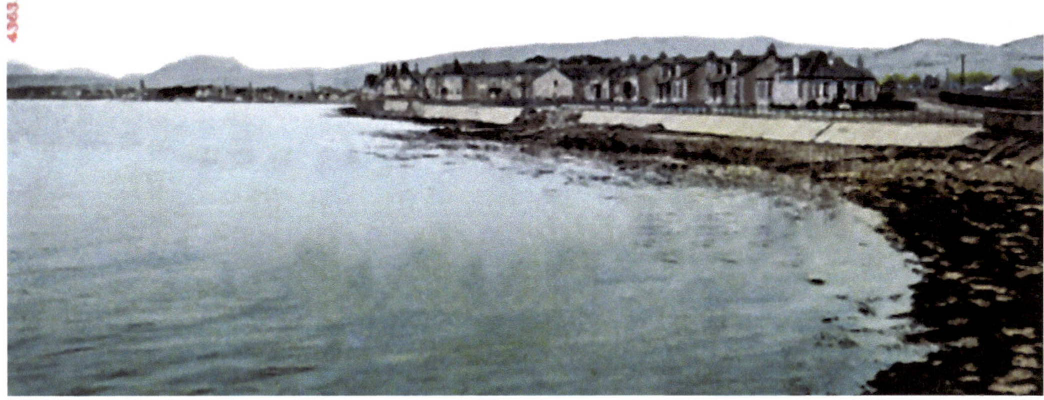

From Craigendoran Pier

This view of the new 'suburb' of Craigendoran is from the pier in the early 1900s when it was recently built. The church towers and spires of the centre of Helensburgh can be seen beyond. Although the pier is no longer in use, the park-and-ride facility at the station is well used.

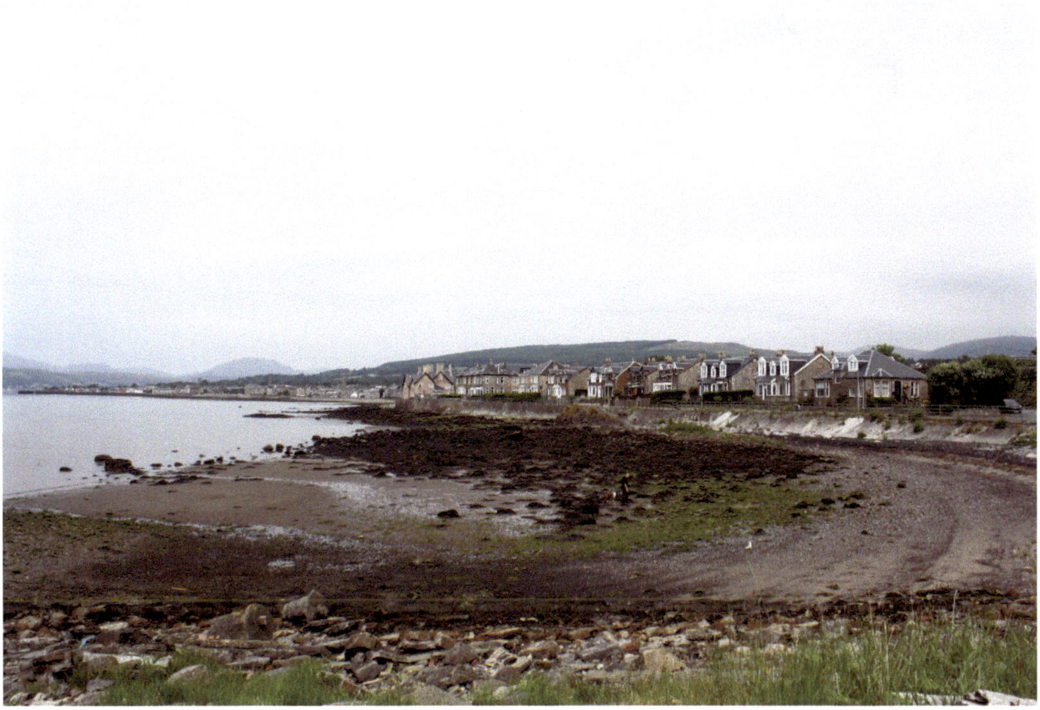

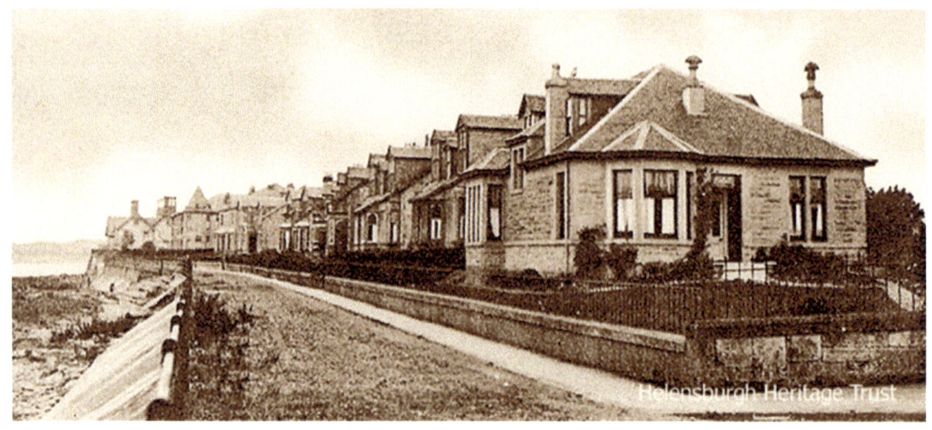

Middleton Drive

Middleton Drive, Craigendoran, beside the Clyde and west of Craigendoran Pier was built around 1900 and remains little changed today.

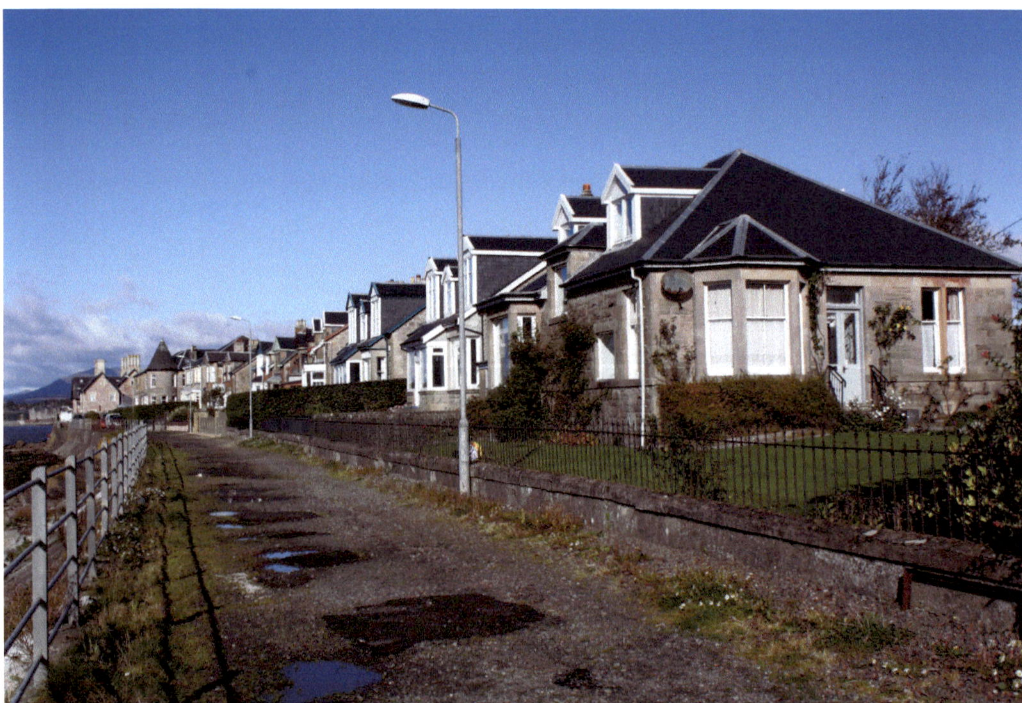

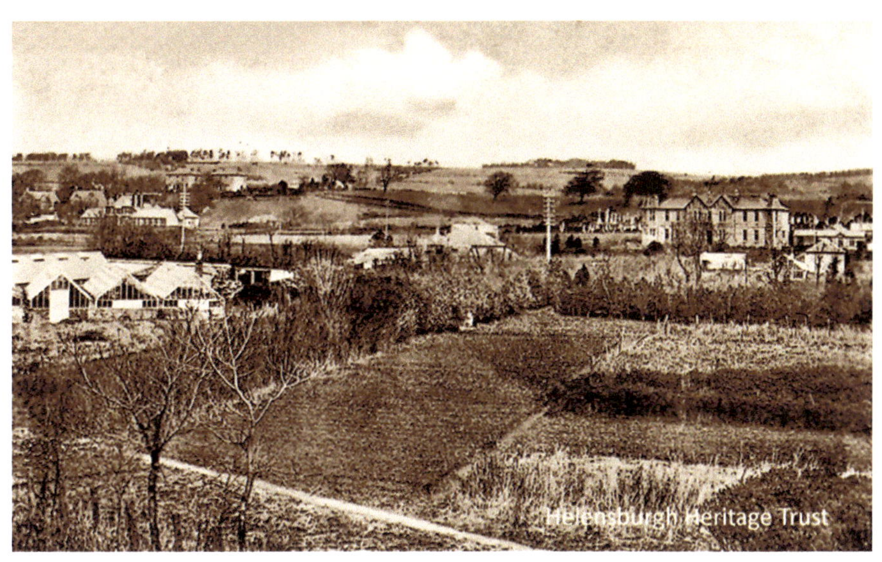

Isolation Hospital

The Infectious Diseases Hospital was in operation from 1875 to 1956. At first both general medical and surgical ailments were treated, but in 1895 the general cases were moved to the newly built Victoria Infirmary. The hospital was demolished in 1959. The stained-glass panel from the door was recently found by chance in an Edinburgh antique shop and is now displayed in the waiting room of a Helensburgh doctor's surgery.

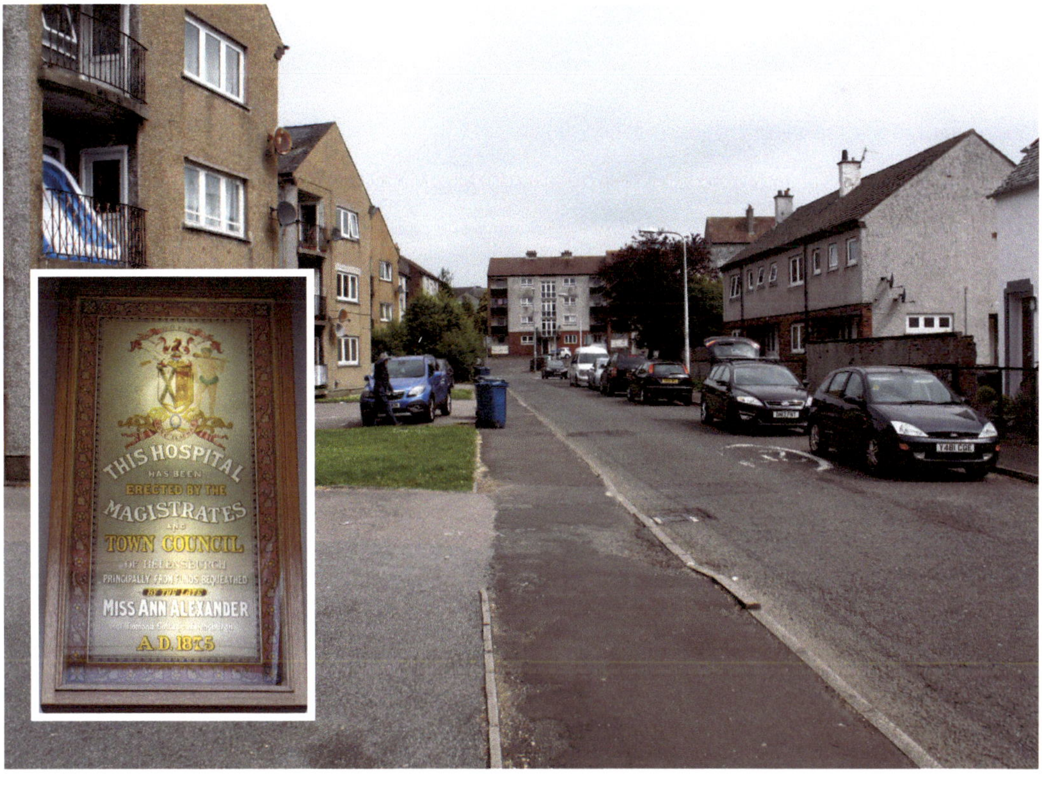

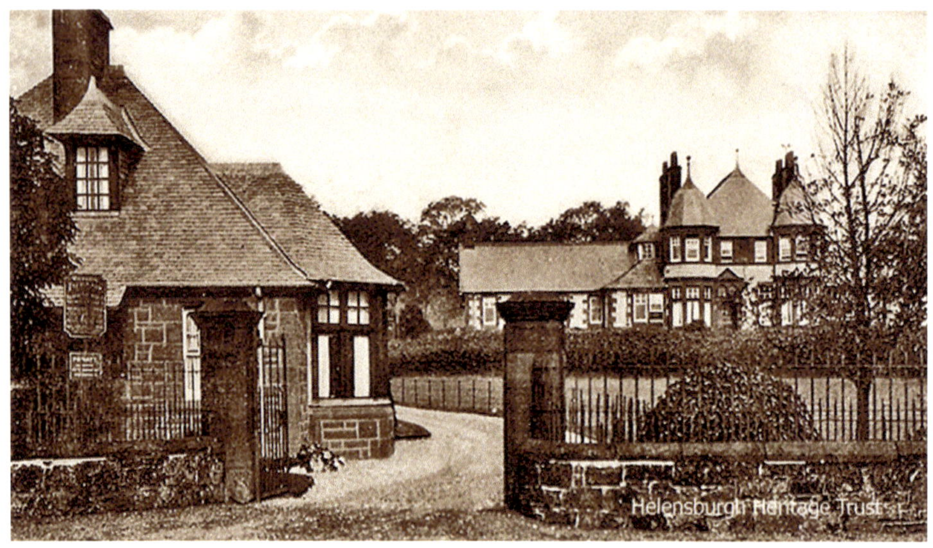

Victoria Infirmary

The hospital in East King Street was built in 1895 to the design of the celebrated architect William Leiper; the gatehouse was demolished some years ago. Now the Victoria Integrated Care Centre, it contains a number of outpatient clinics and the Jeanie Deans Centre, which covers a number of community and social issues.

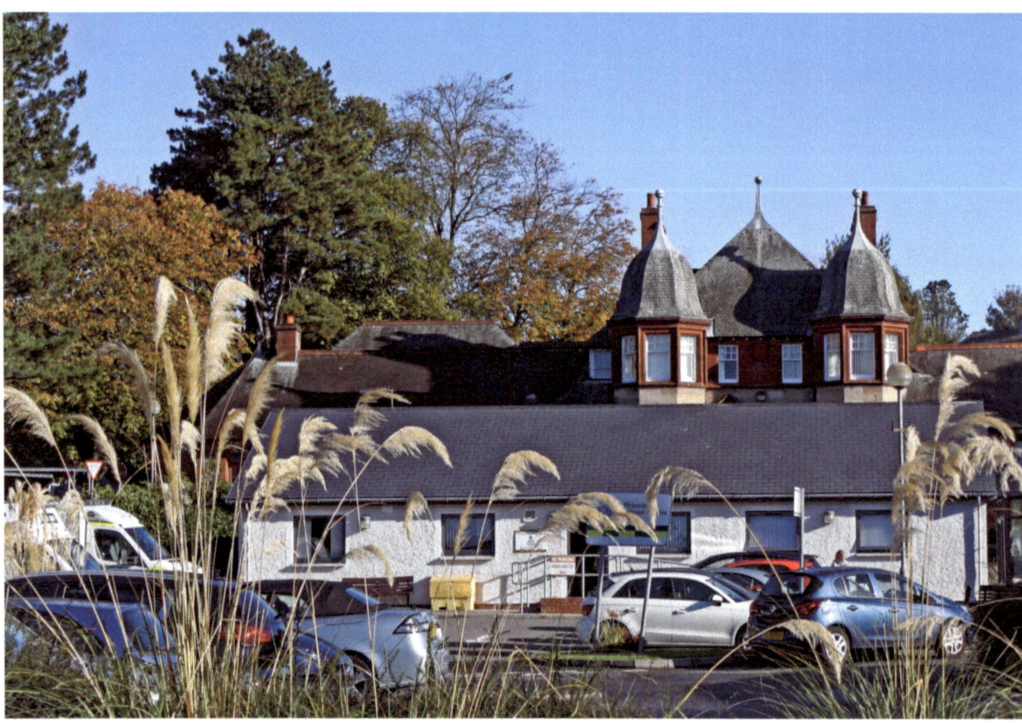

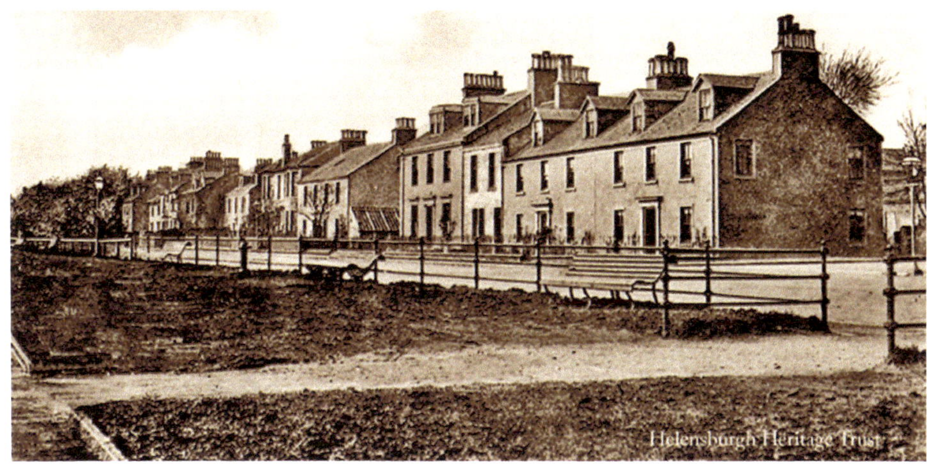

East Bay

The junction of George Street and East Clyde Street, at a time when railings separated the small East Bay Park from the road. Today, although the railings are gone, the park remains and many of the houses are unchanged.

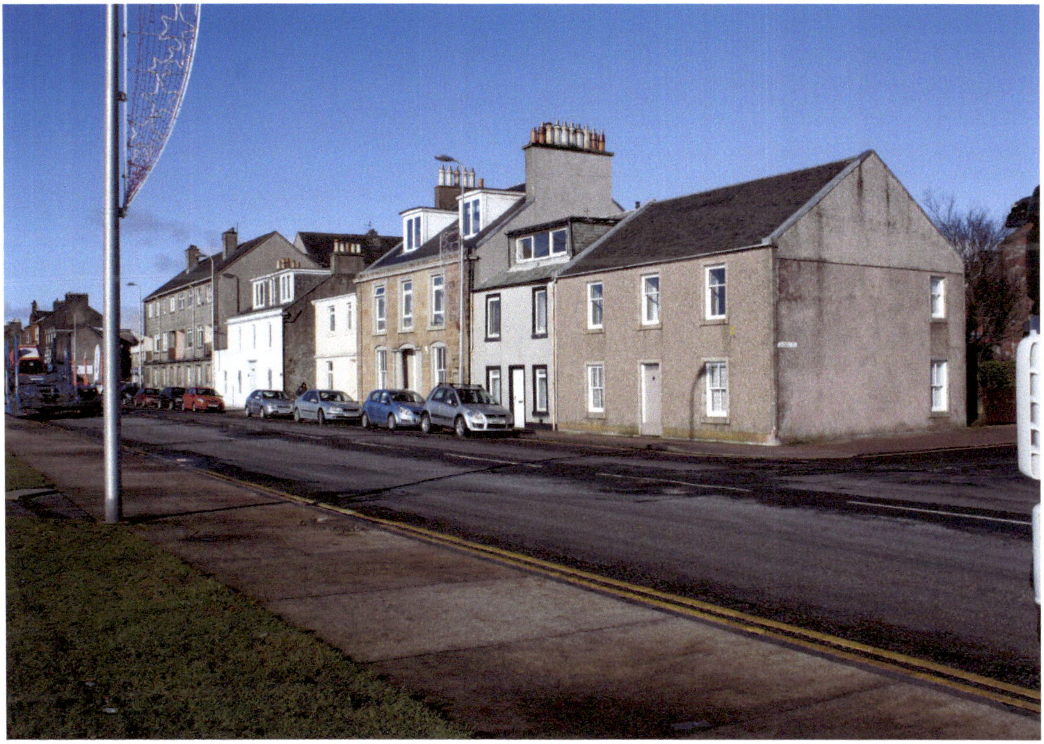

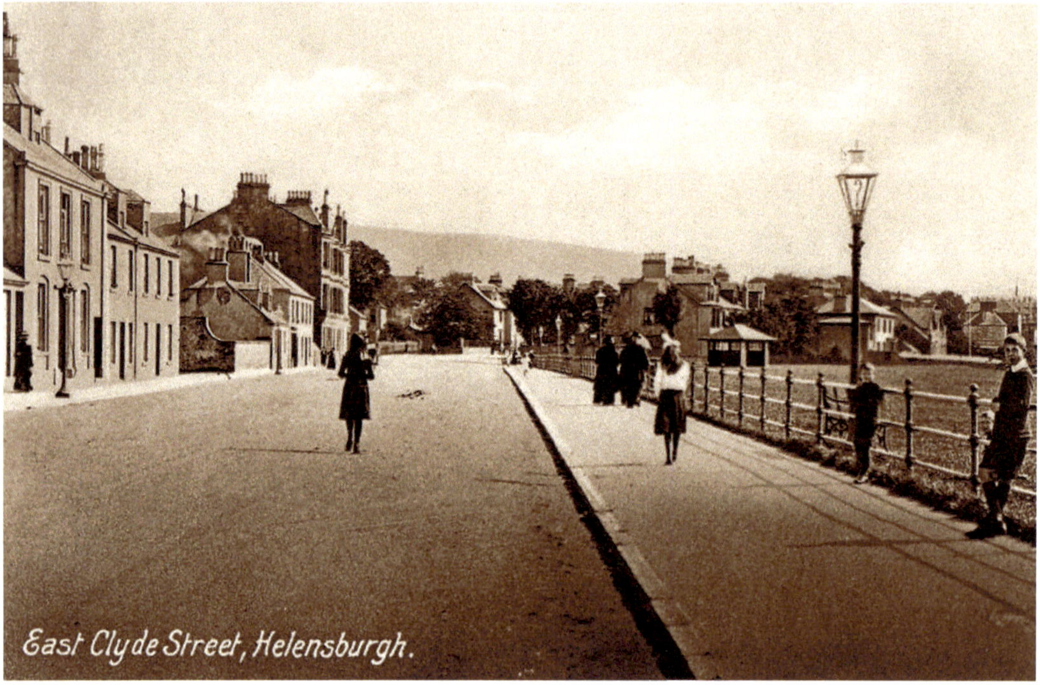

East Clyde Street

A girl strolls along East Clyde Street by the East Bay Park in Edwardian times. Now there is too much traffic for strolling in the road, and the house with a walled garden in the middle distance has been replaced by a petrol station.

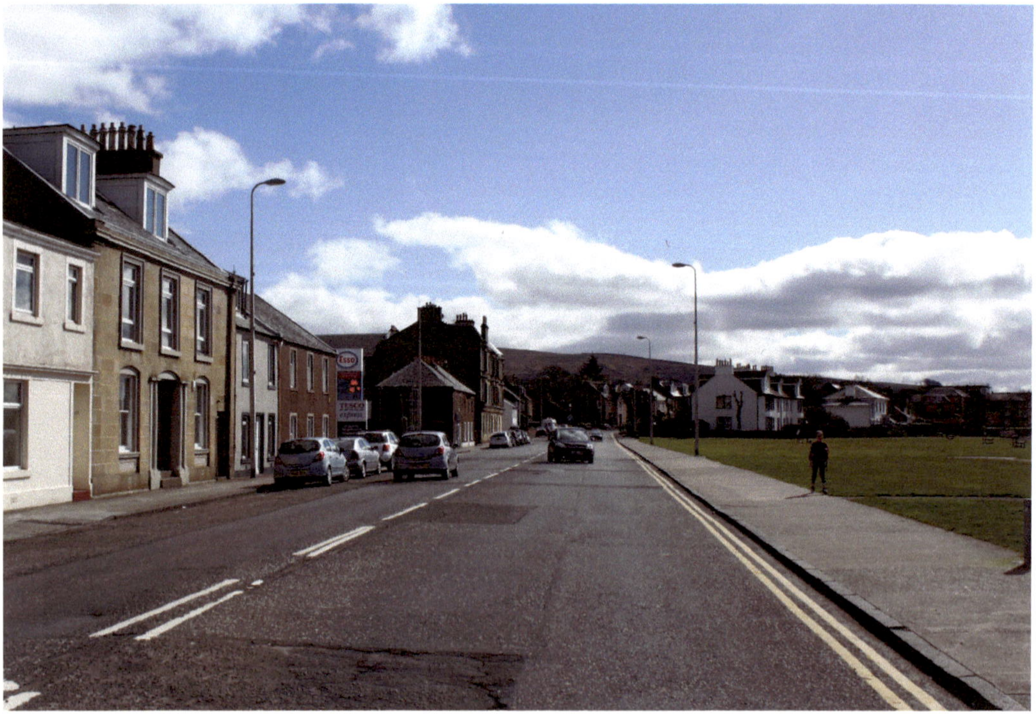

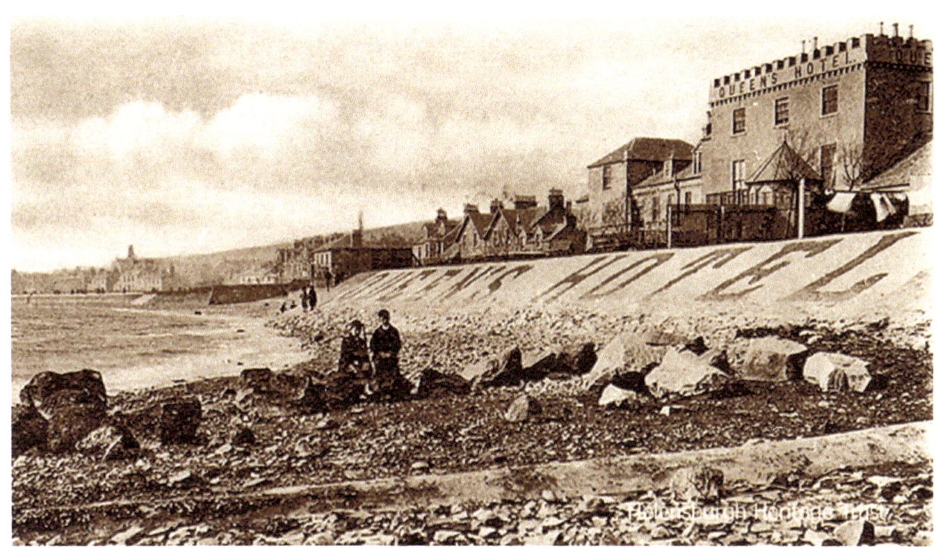

East Bay at the Queen's Hotel

A 1903 image of the East Bay, with the Queen's Hotel on the right and the centre of Helensburgh beyond. The area has been greatly developed with new flats surrounding the old hotel building.

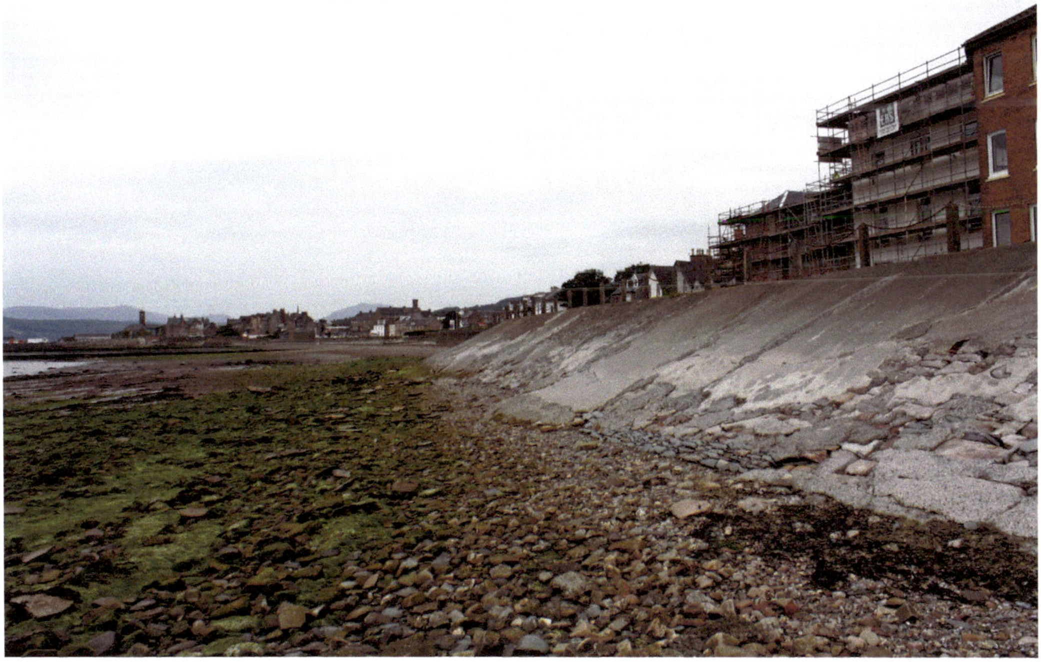

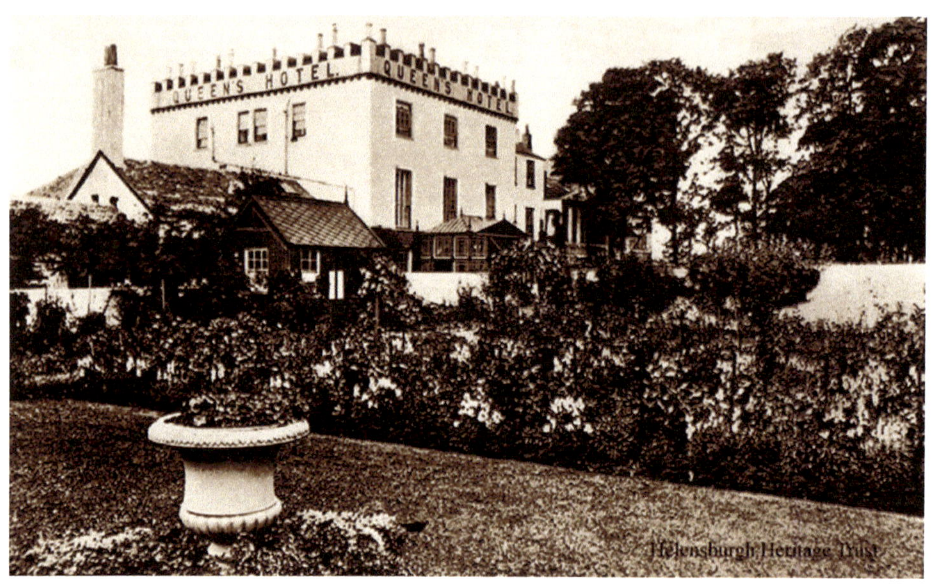

Queen's Hotel

Henry Bell, who built Europe's first commercial steamship, the *Comet*, in 1812 and was the first Provost of Helensburgh, built the Queen's Hotel, originally called the Baths Inn, in 1806. The building has had many alterations, but still stands on East Clyde Street, having been converted into flats in the 1980s. It is currently undergoing a major refurbishment.

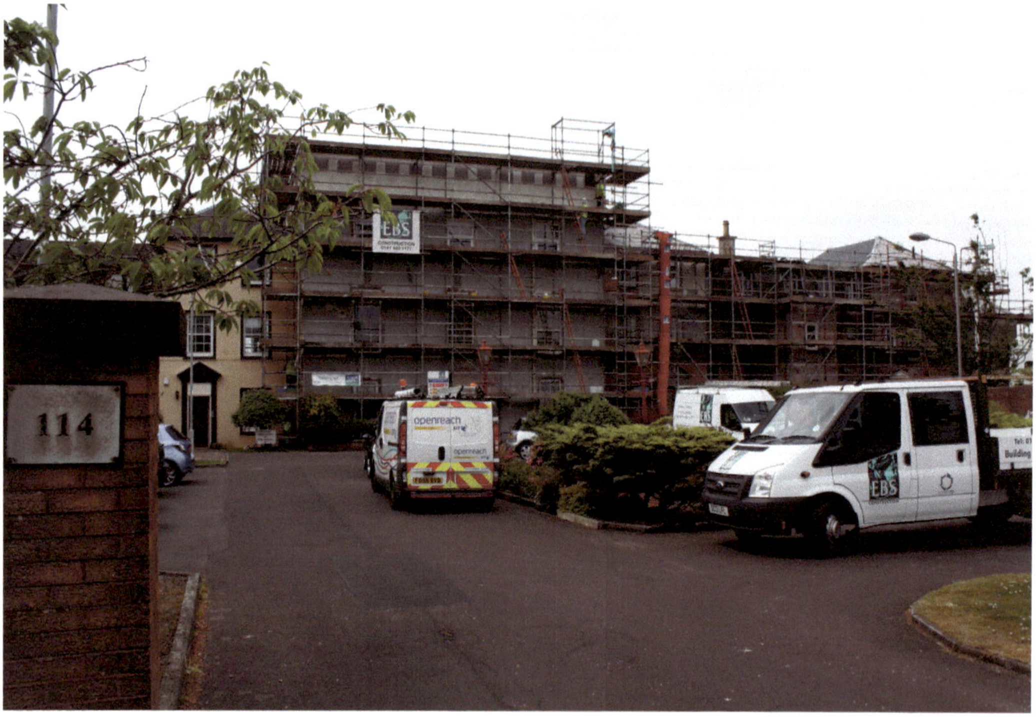

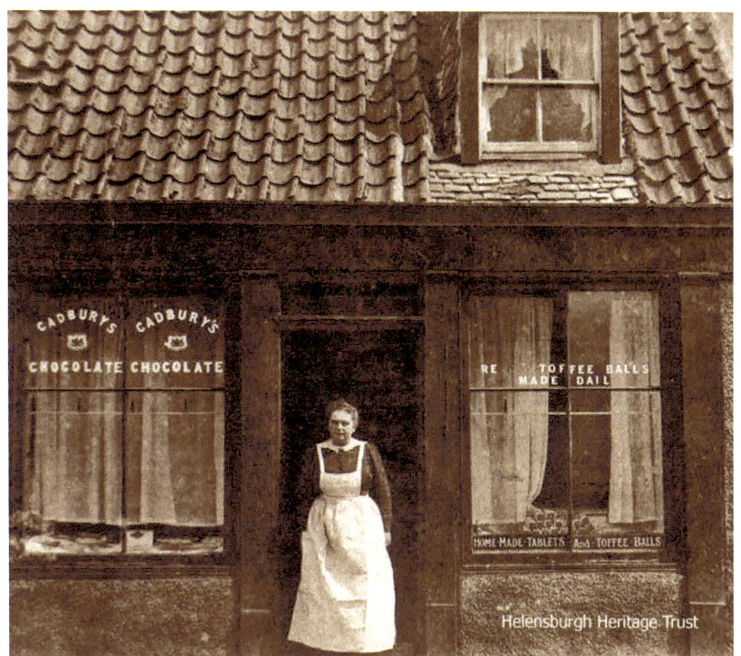

Sweet Shop

Margaret Reece is pictured outside her sweet shop, which was at the corner of Clyde Street and Maitland Street, *c.* 1910 – the sweets were made at the rear of the shop. The area was redeveloped in the 1960s, with the Spinnaker Bar on this corner until it was replaced by a food retailer in 2012.

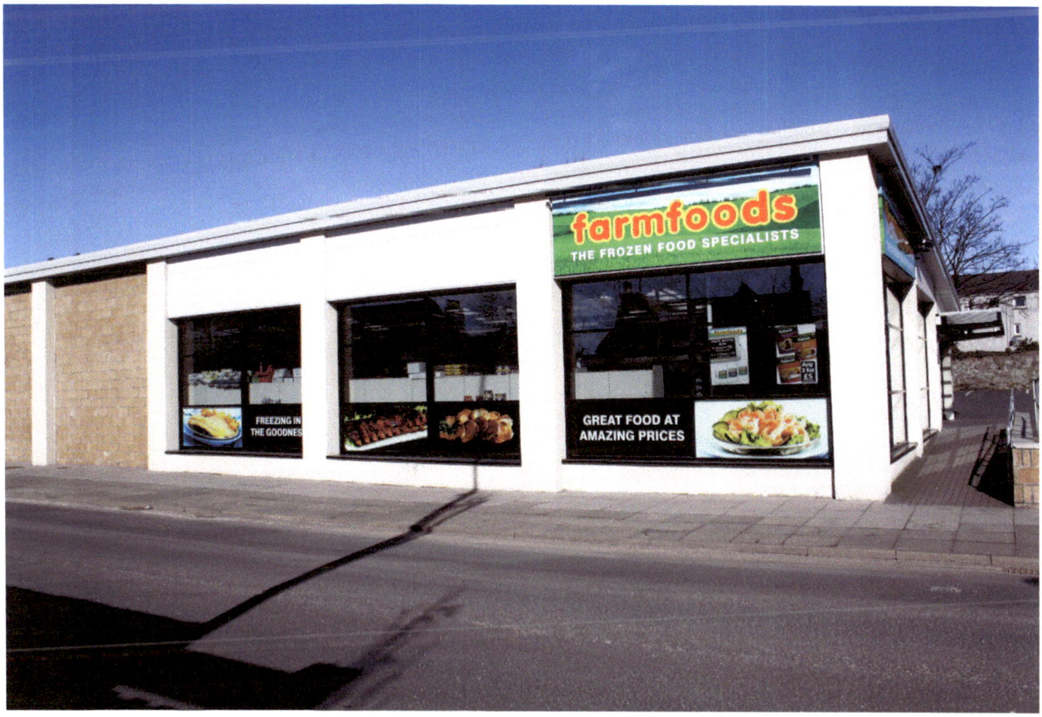

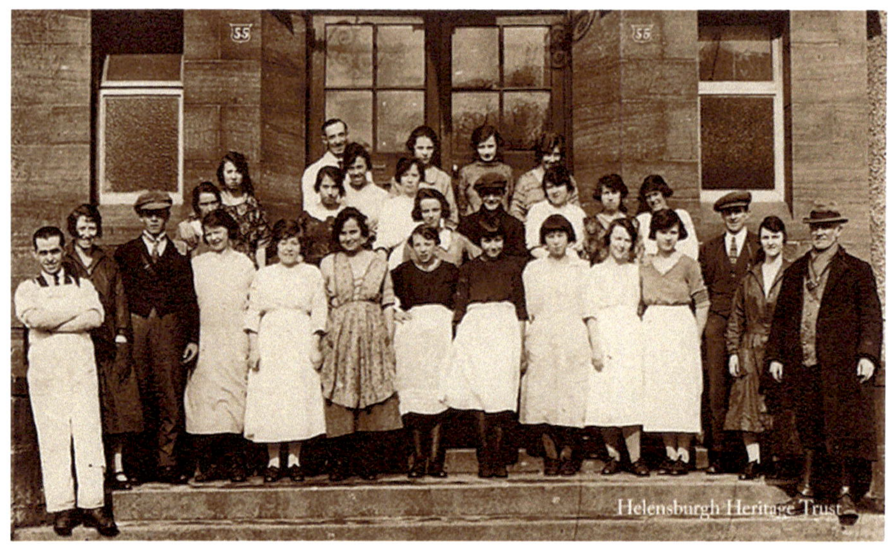

The Steam Laundry

Staff of Helensburgh Steam Laundry pose outside the front door at No. 55 East King Street. Many people in Helensburgh still remember the family laundry being sent here until it went into liquidation in 1978, replaced by an electricity substation.

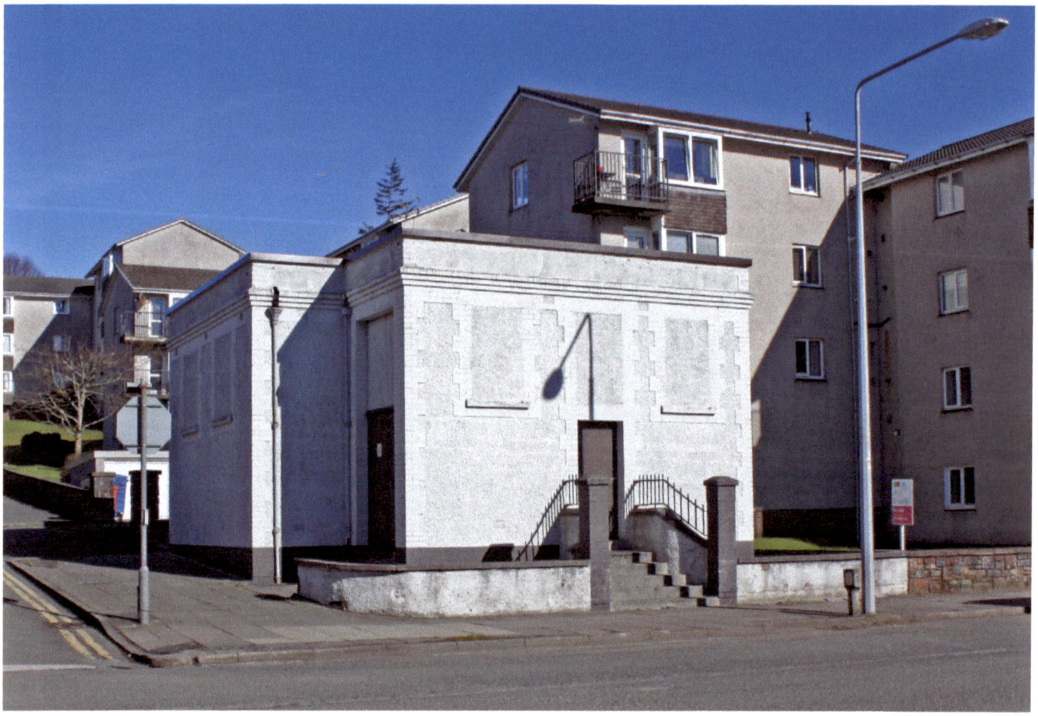

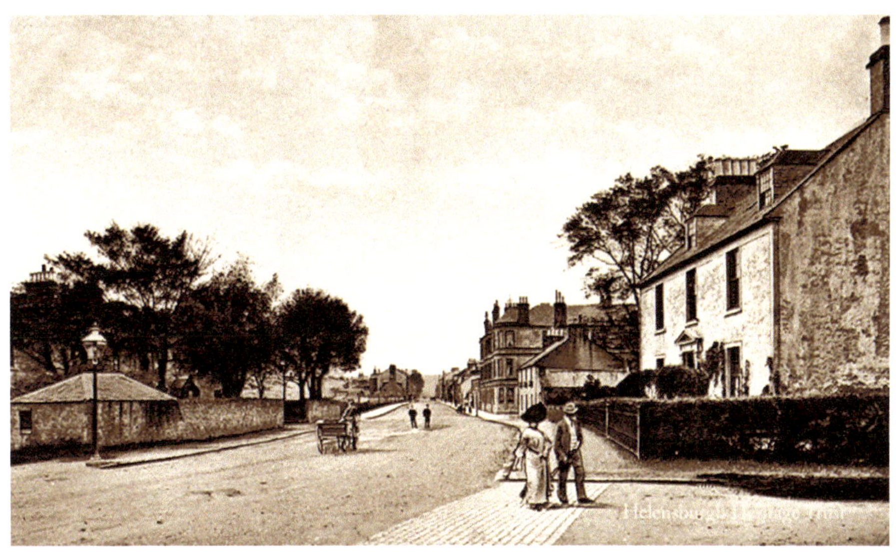

East Clyde Street

At the junction of East Clyde Street and Henry Bell Street, in 1908 an elegantly dressed couple stroll and a delivery tricycle is heading for one of the houses. The ornamental lamp post on the left marks the entrance to the Queen's Hotel.

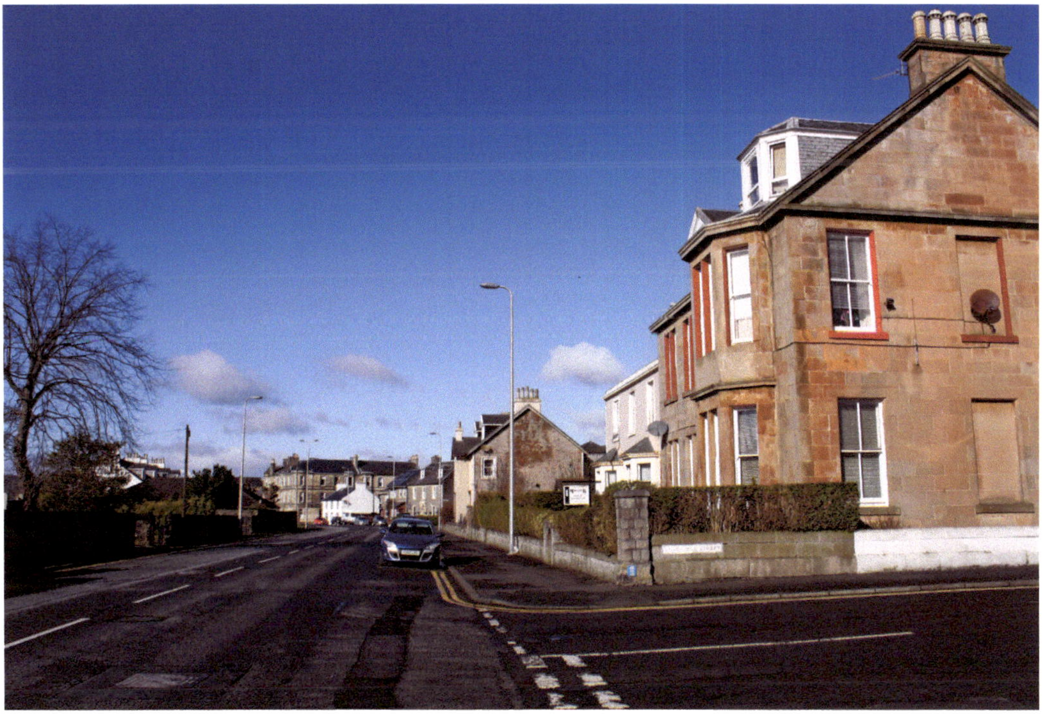

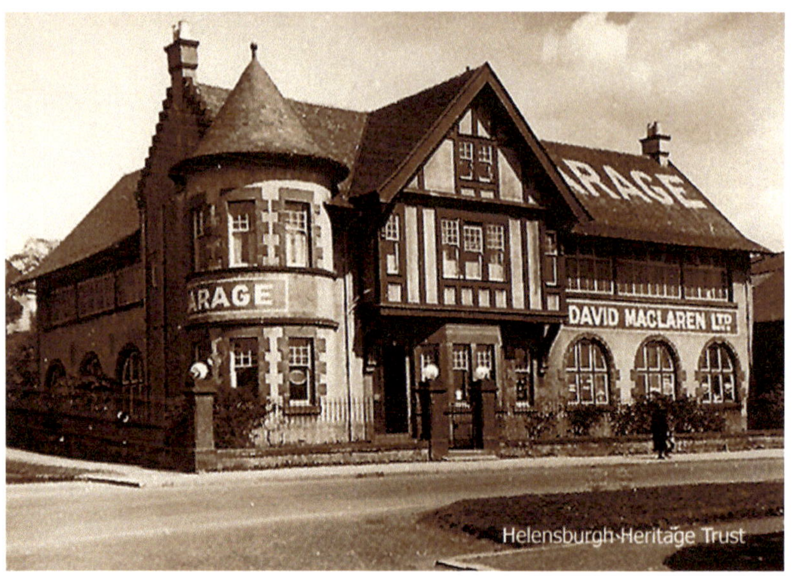

Maclaren's Garage

At the junction of East King Street and Lomond Street, Maclaren's Garage later became Phipps Motors, but was destroyed by fire in the 1970s and the present flats built.

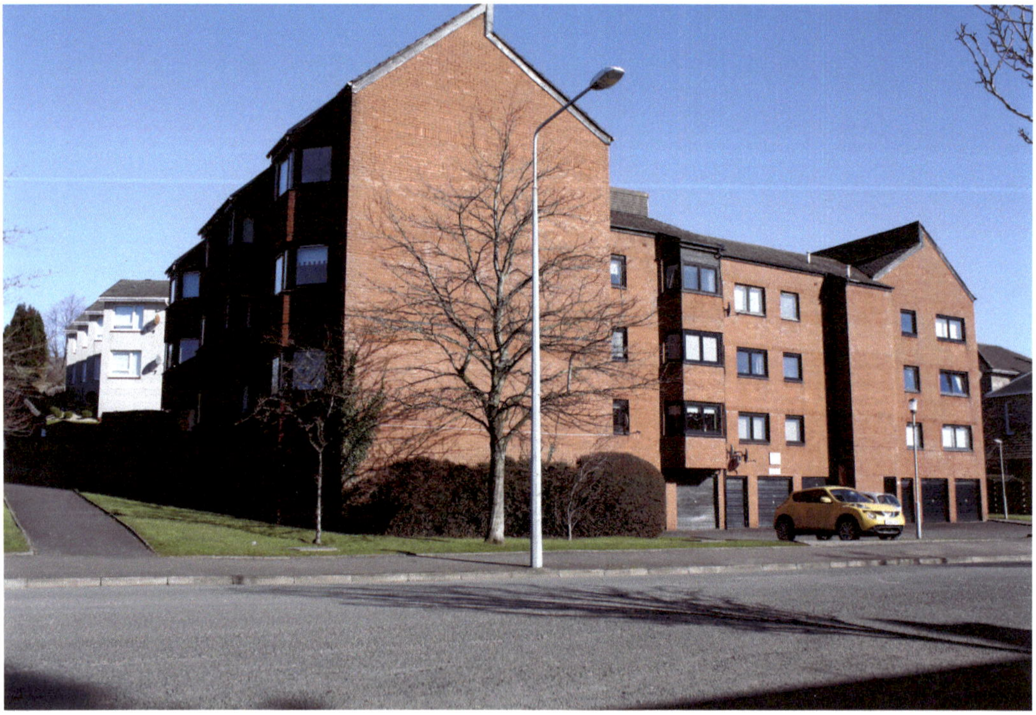

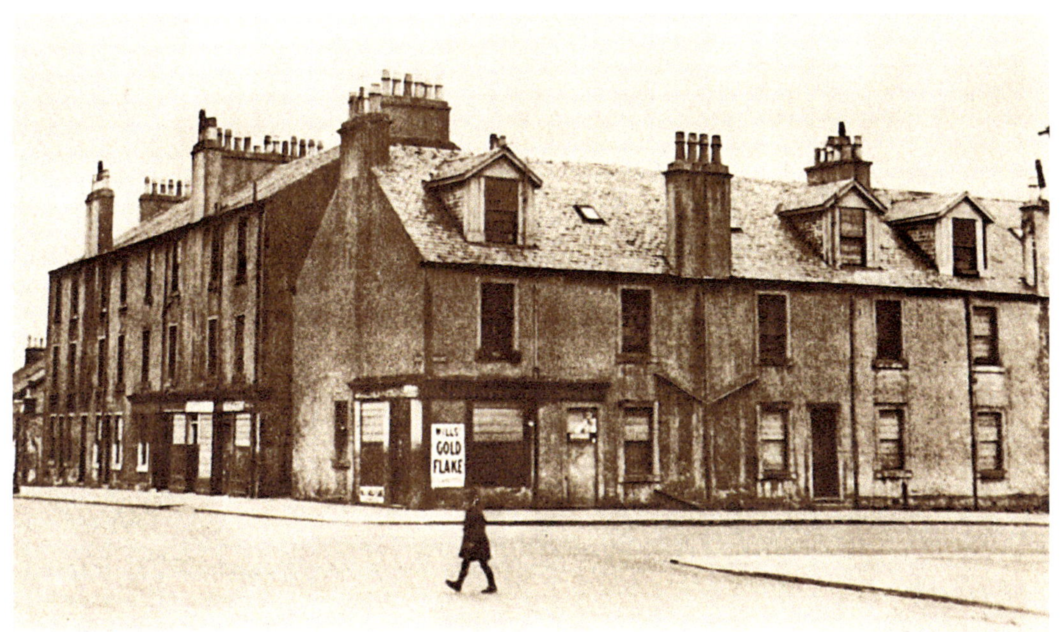

Alma Place

At the corner of East King Street and Grant Street, Alma Place, built in the 1850s, was named after the Crimean War battle. It had become run down when it was acquired by the town council and was demolished in 1935. The present council scheme was built to replace it in 1937.

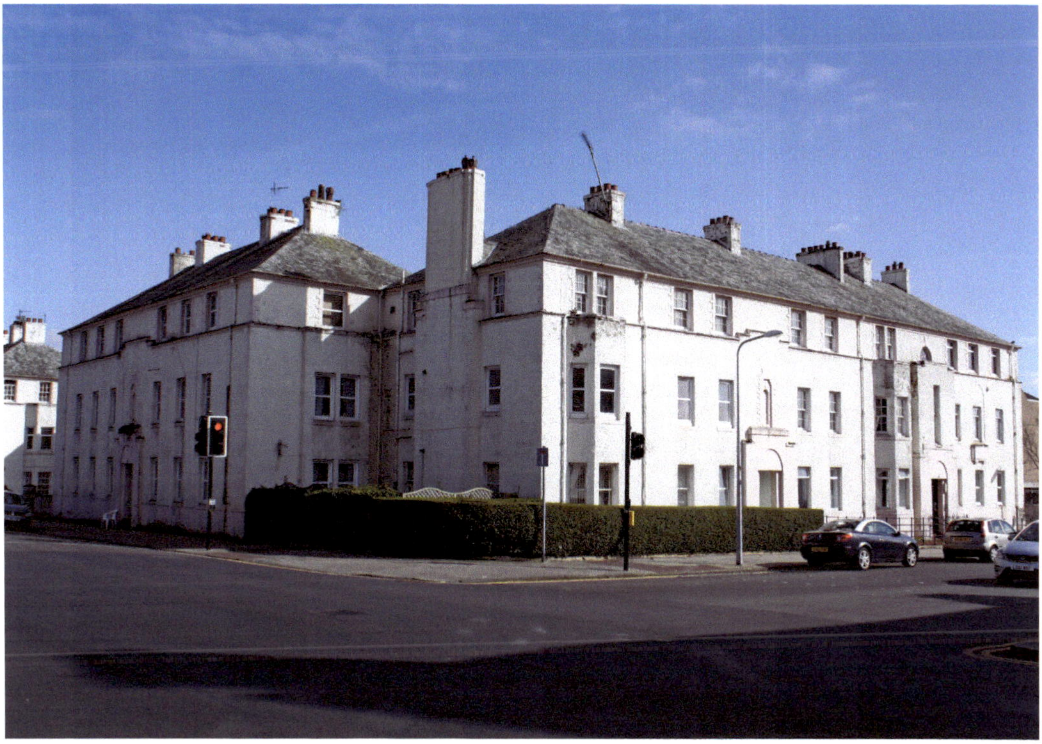

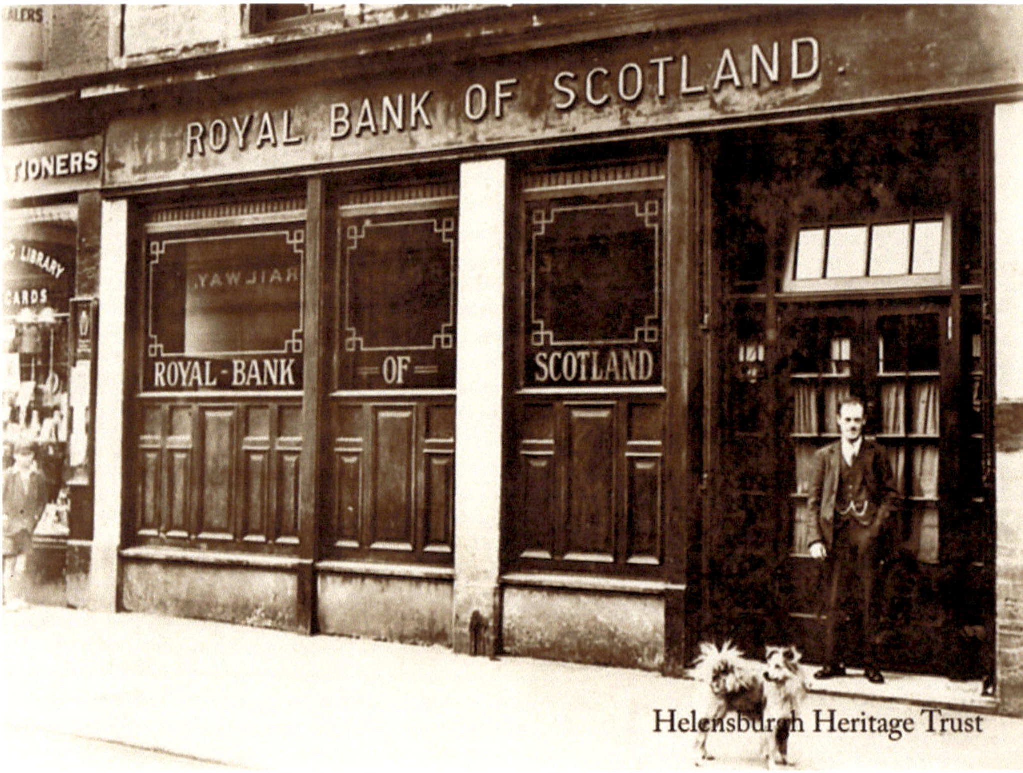

The Royal Bank

The exterior of the Royal Bank of Scotland branch, with the manager John R. Dixon, next to stationers Macneur & Bryden Ltd in East Princes Street taken in 1936. The bank is now a sandwich shop and Macneur & Bryden a licensed grocer.

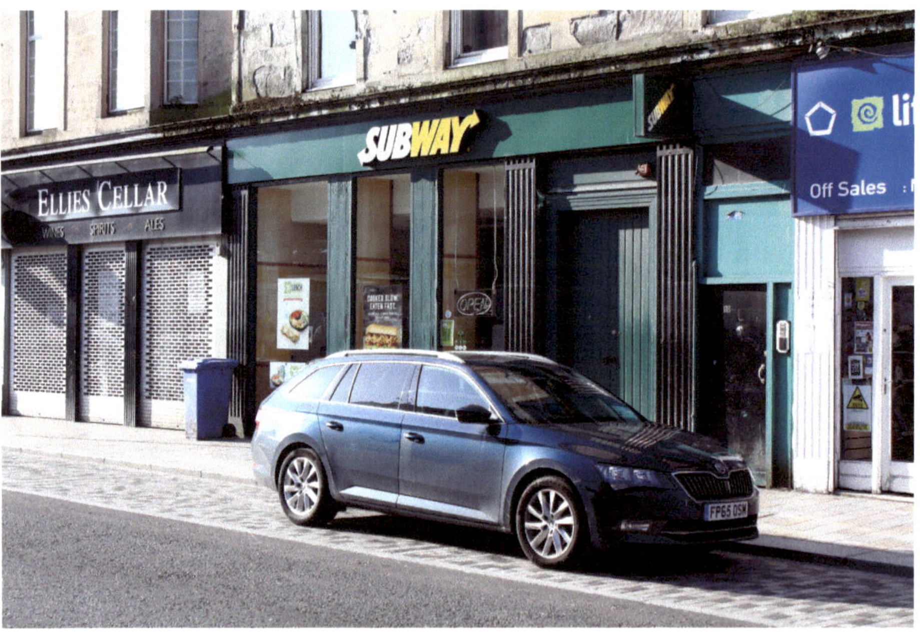

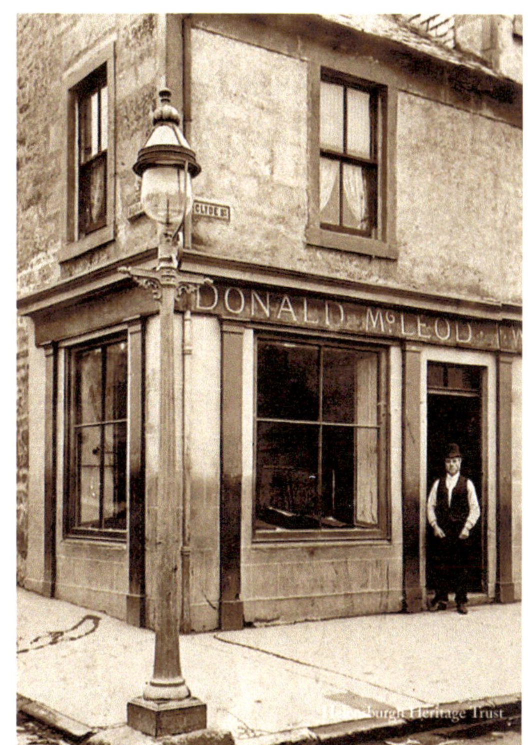

Tailor's Shop

Tailor Donald MacLeod is seen in around 1900 at the door of his tailor's shop at the junction of East Clyde Street and Maitland Street. Donald wrote *A Nonagenarian's Guide to Garelochside and Helensburgh* based on what he had been told by his uncle Gabriel MacLeod, who was the nonagenarian.

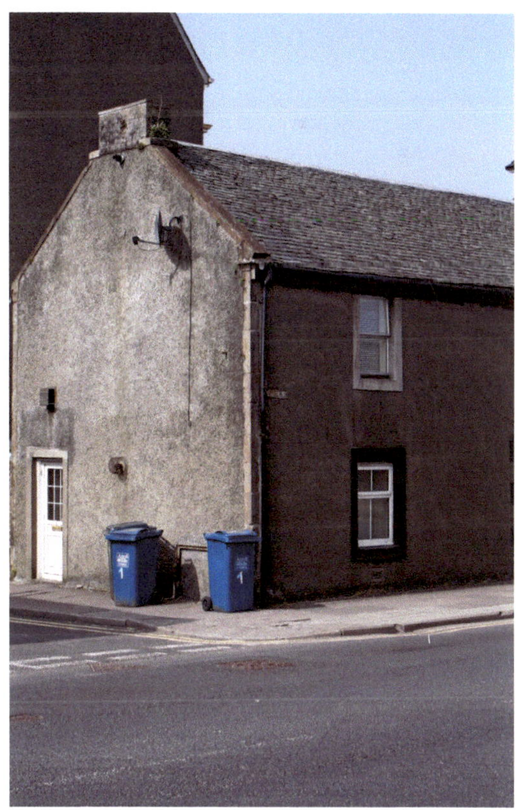

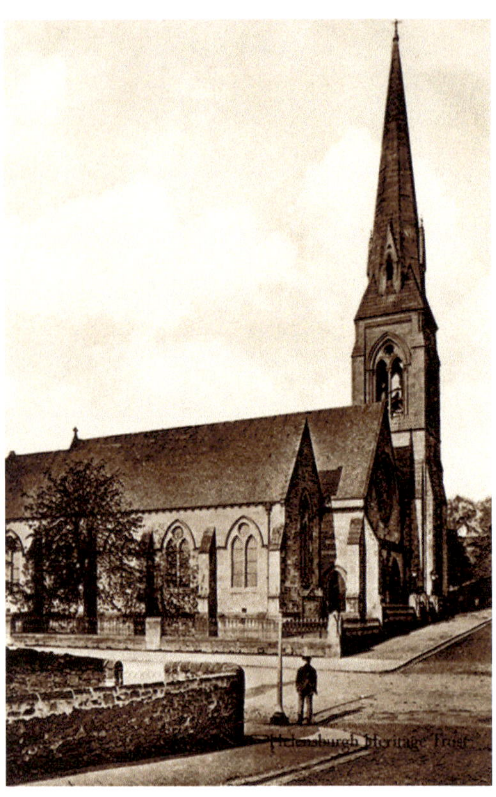

Park Church

Built in 1862 at the junction of East King Street and Charlotte Street, the East Free Church became Park Church in 1929 when the United Free Church and the Church of Scotland united. The congregation became part of Helensburgh Parish Church in 2015, and in 2016 the church building was bought by Buddhists as a Meditation Centre.

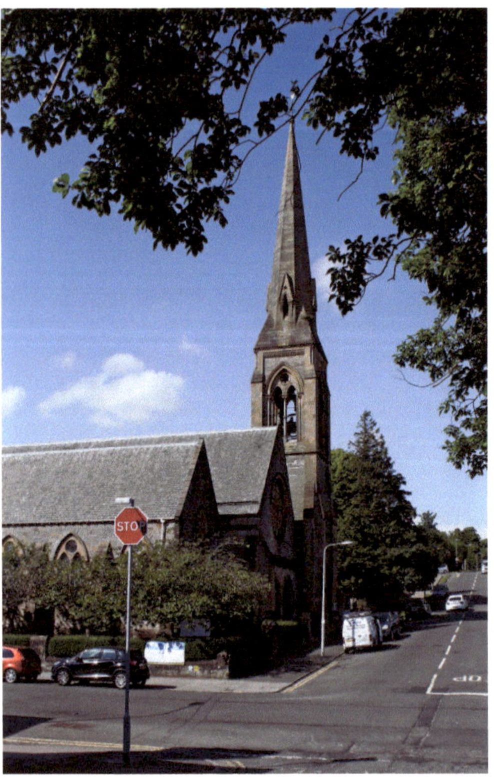

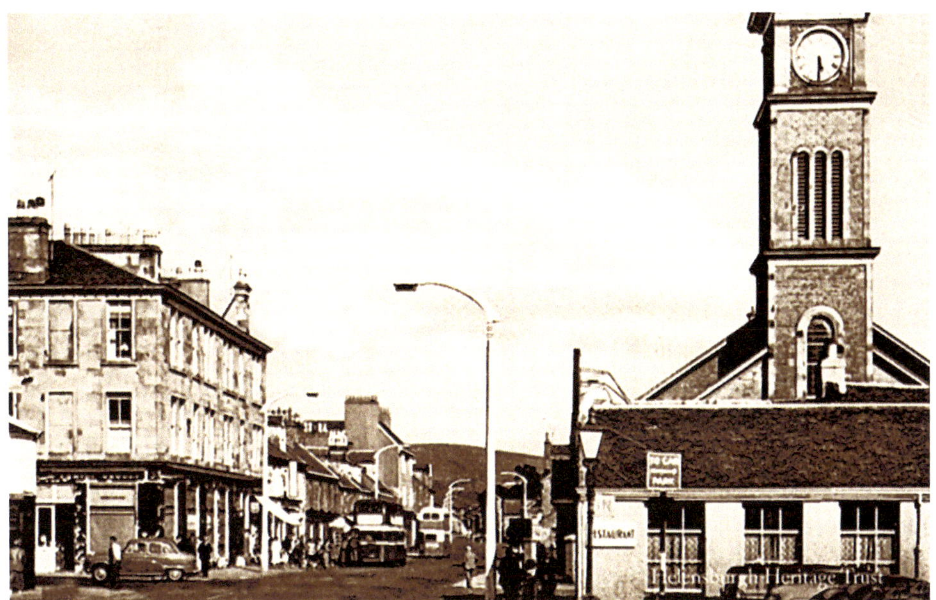

Old Parish Church

Looking east along East Clyde Street from the pier towards the Granary Restaurant and the Old Parish Church. Built in an Italianate style on the seafront in 1847, the church later became a Church of Scotland centre for servicemen and women. The church and hall behind became unsafe and were demolished in 1982, and the flats behind built shortly afterwards. The tower now contains the tourist information office.

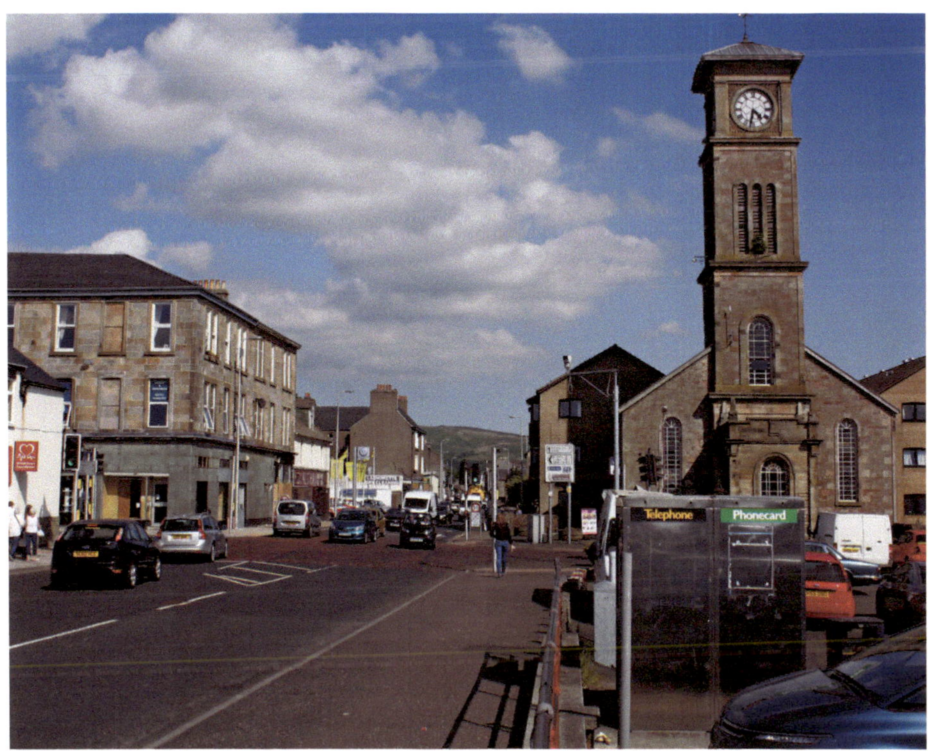

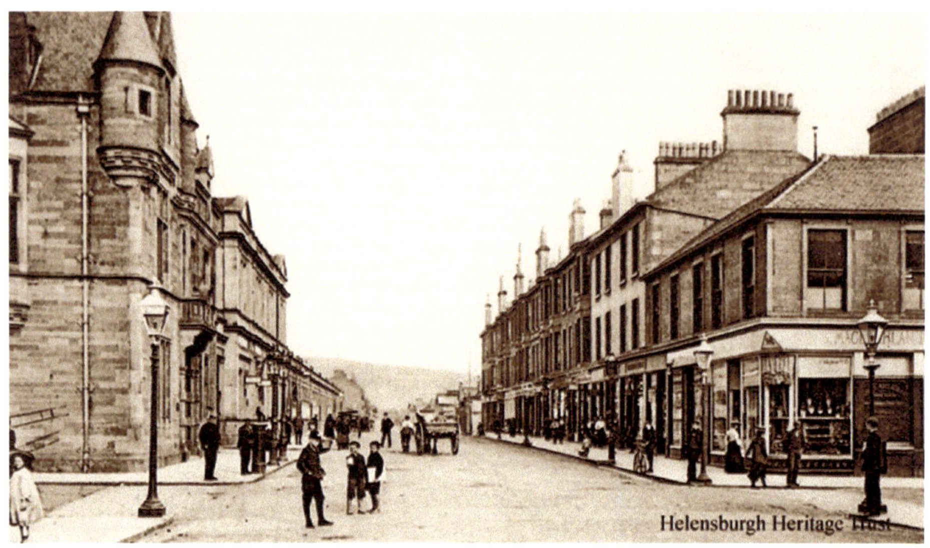

Sinclair Street and East Princes Street

Looking east along East Princes Street from the Sinclair Street junction in 1906, with a horse and cart outside the station and two small boys with bare feet by the municipal buildings. The Victorian pillar box is still there but the street lights are somewhat different.

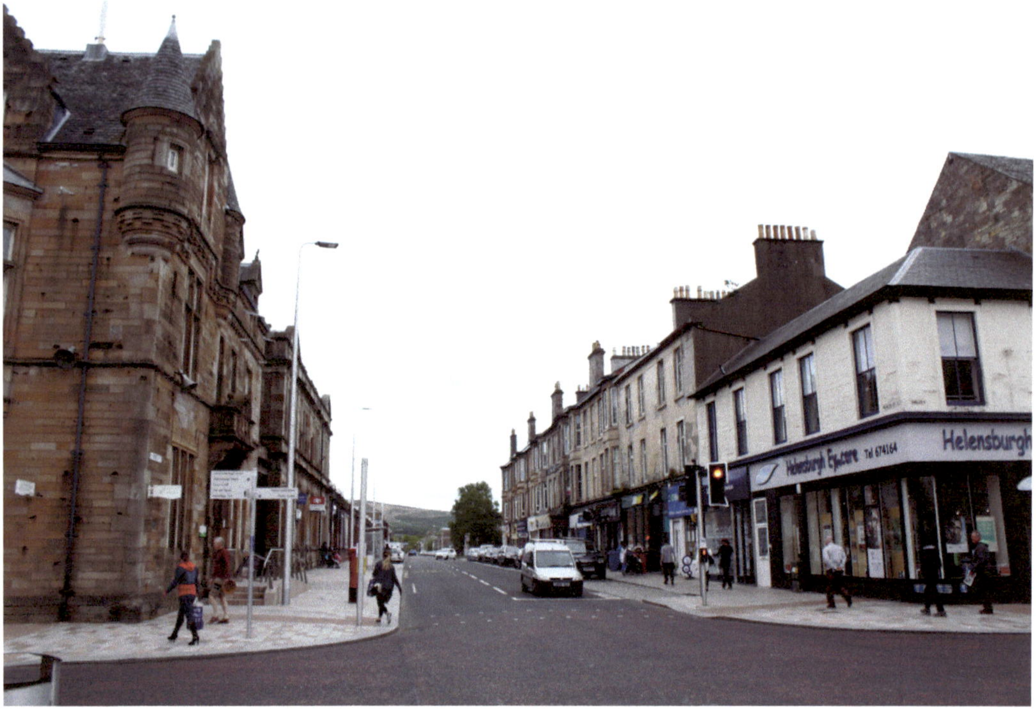

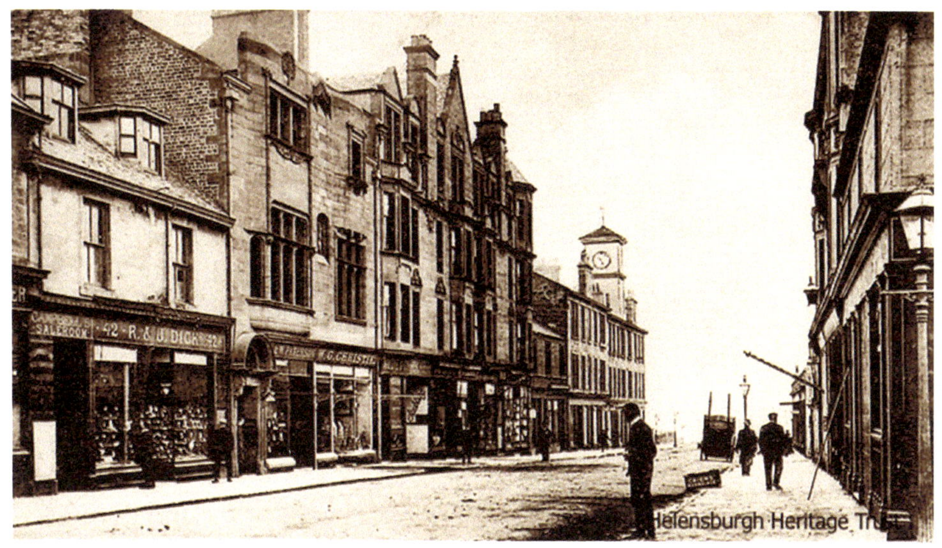

Down Sinclair Street

Looking south down Sinclair Street to the Old Parish Church tower on the seafront from the Princes Street junction, around 1910. The building on the left, with the arched entrance, was the Helensburgh and Gareloch Conservative Club, designed by Honeyman and Keppie, and is thought to be one of the first designs of Charles Rennie Mackintosh, who worked for the firm. The shopfronts have been modernised but the buildings above remain unchanged.

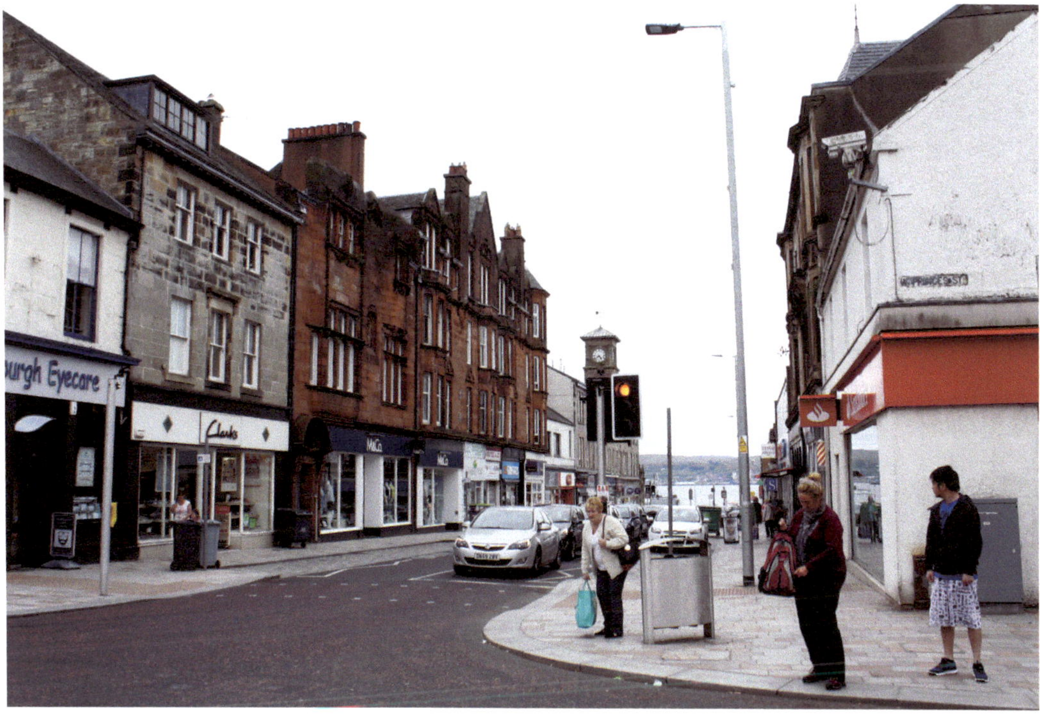

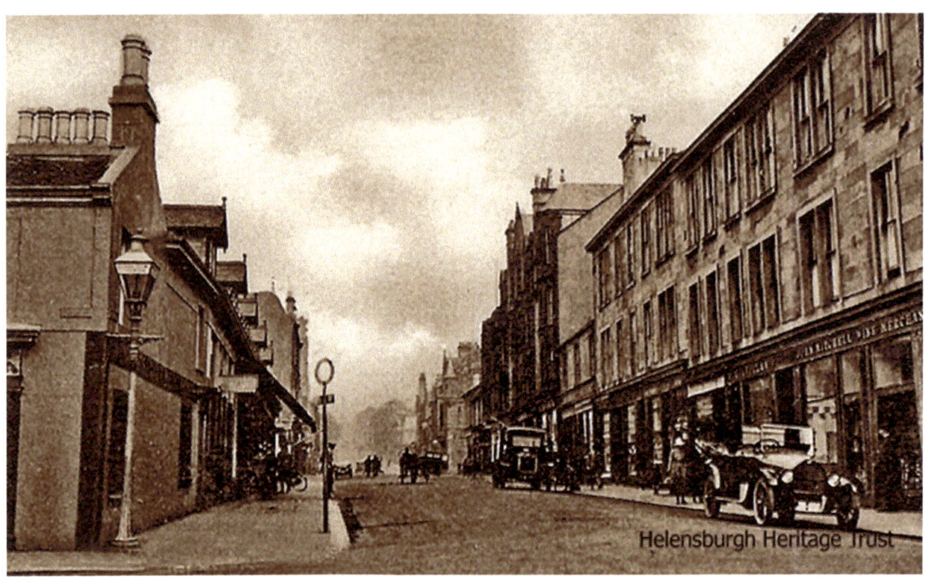

Lower Sinclair Street

Looking up Sinclair Street from the junction with West Clyde Street in the 1920s, with a contemporary car and delivery van parked outside. In the present day, charity shops are prominent and the delivery vans are much bigger.

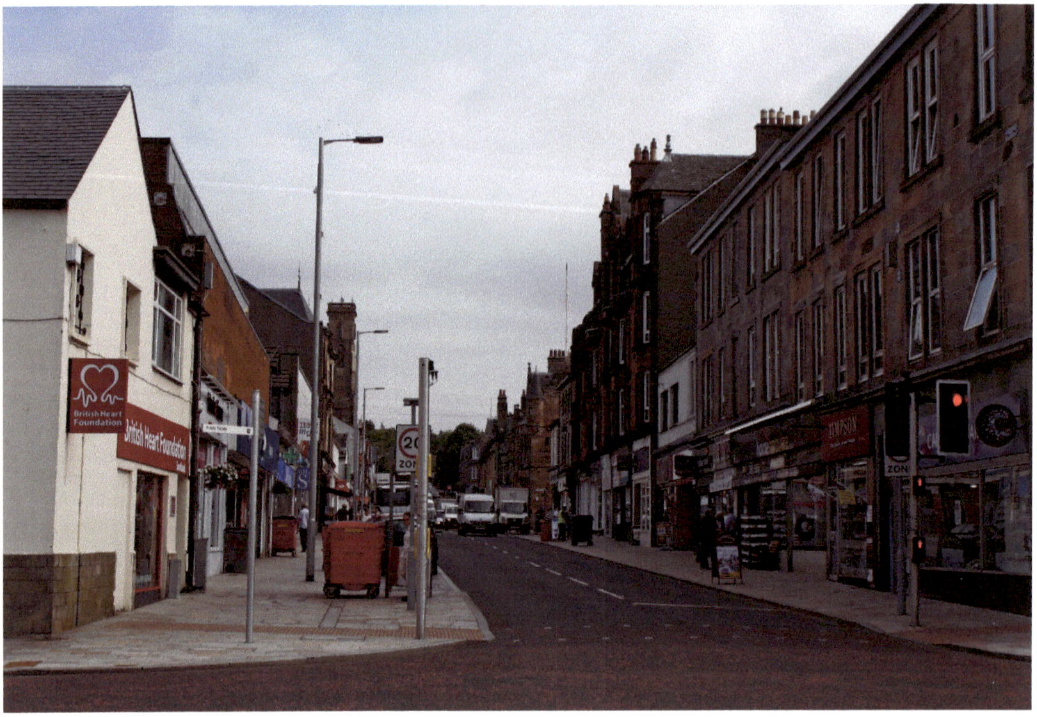

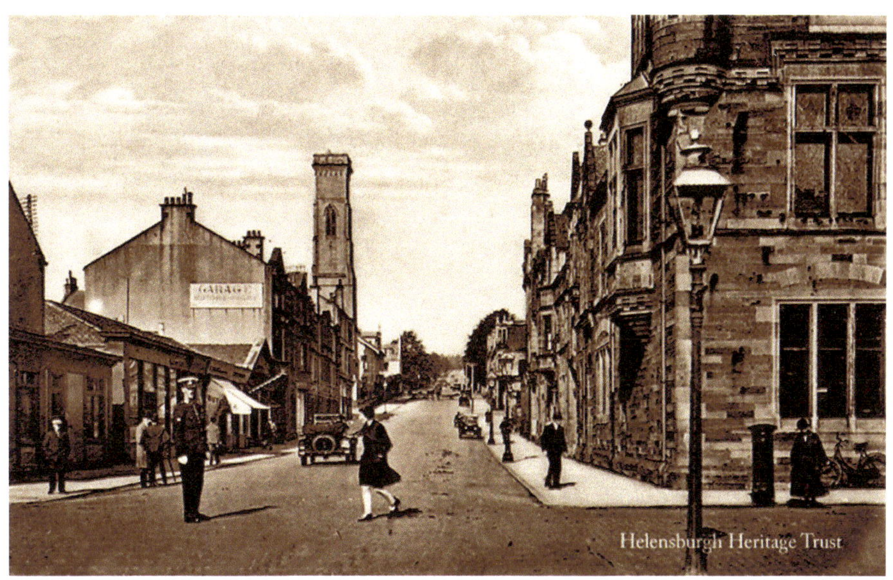

Up Sinclair Street

Looking north up Sinclair Street, from the junction with Princes Street, in the 1940s. The Municipal Buildings are on the right with the tower of St Columba church, now a very successful digital arts centre, further up the hill. Traffic lights have replaced a policeman on point duty.

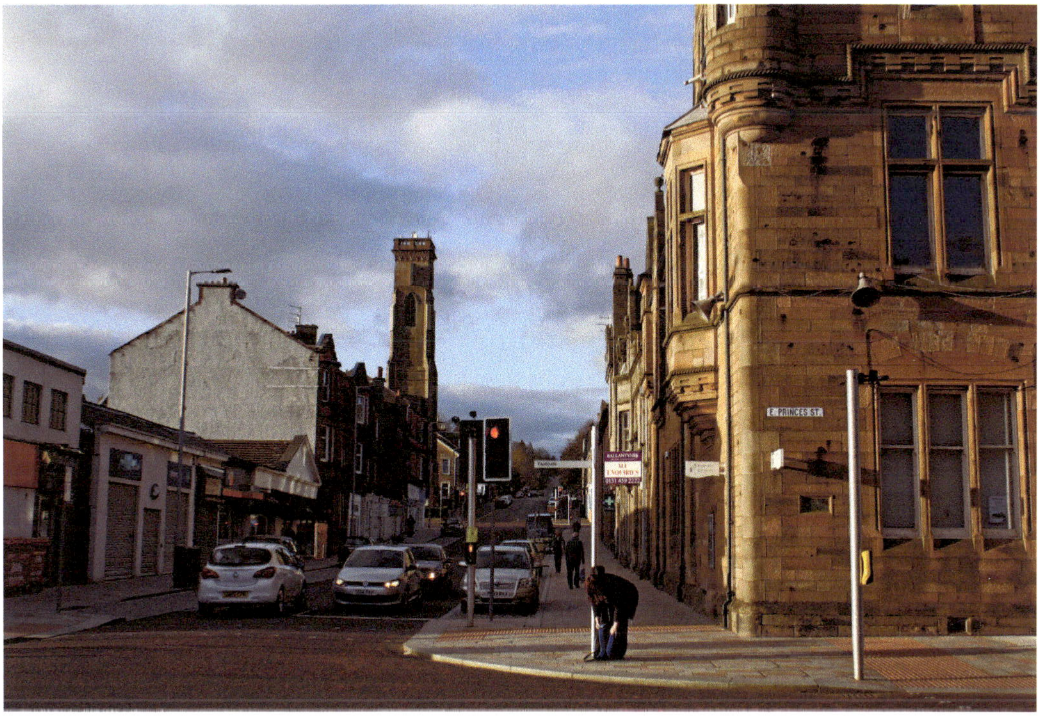

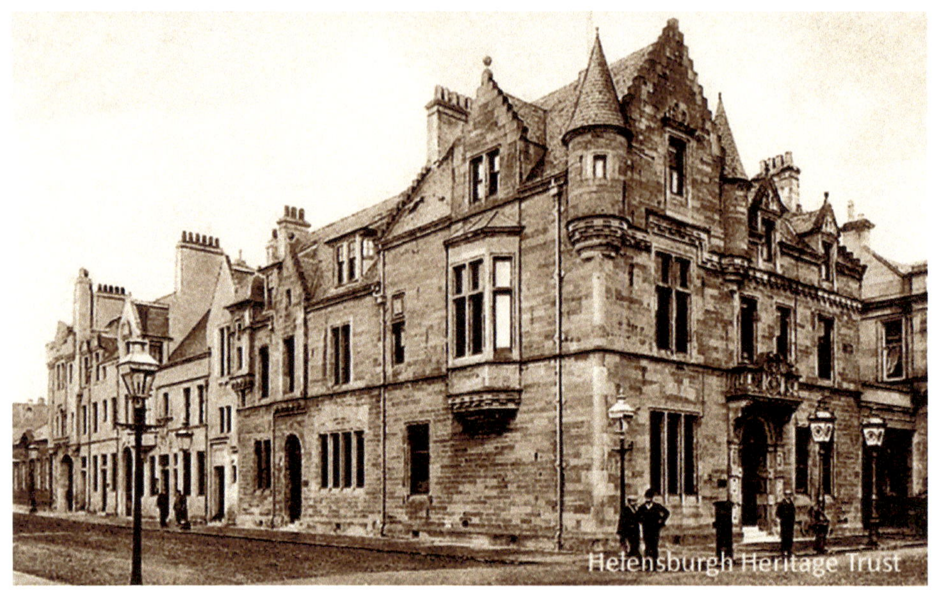

The Municipal Buildings

At the junction of East Princes Street and Sinclair Street, the Municipal Buildings were built in the Scots Baronial style in 1878 by John Honeyman at a cost of £6,000, replacing an old theatre which had also served as the Town Hall. In 1906 A. N. Paterson added the Sinclair Street extension in a more restrained Scottish style to house the police station and fire station.

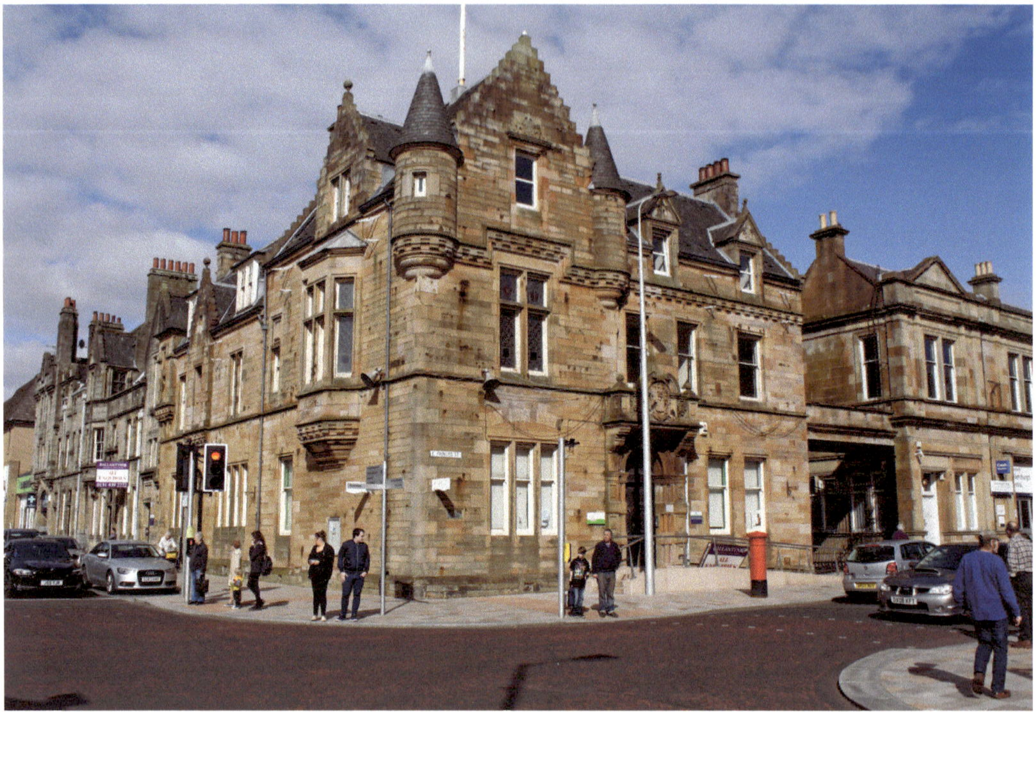

Hermitage School

The old Hermitage School in East Argyle Street was built in 1880 in late Gothic style for the School Board of Row on land formerly part of Hermitage House and made available by the Cramb family. The architect was William Spence, who also designed both the St Columba and Rhu churches. It was demolished in 1967 and replaced by Hermitage Academy at Colgrain. Hermitage Primary School was built on the same site in 1975.

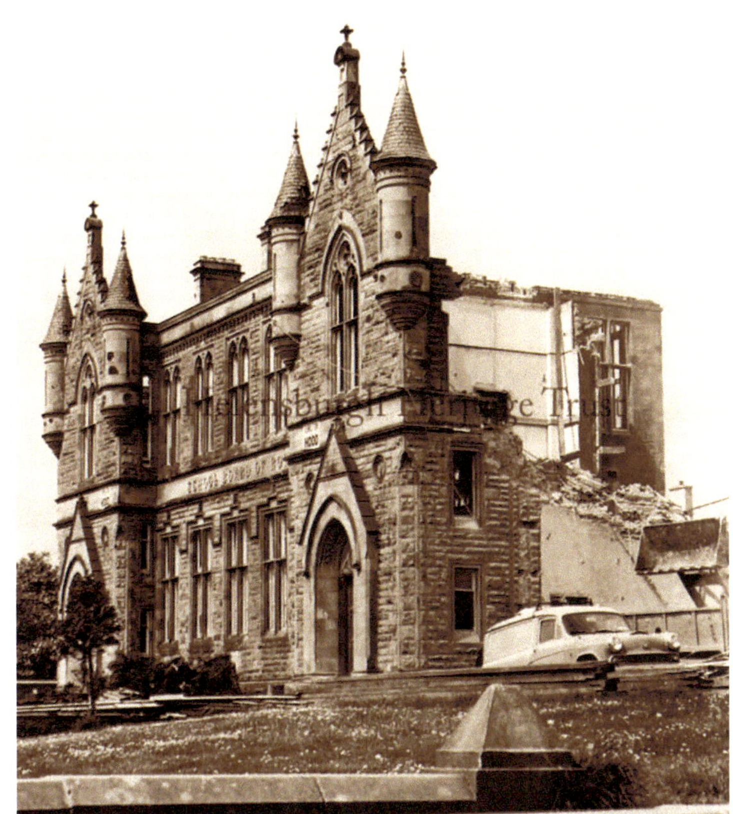

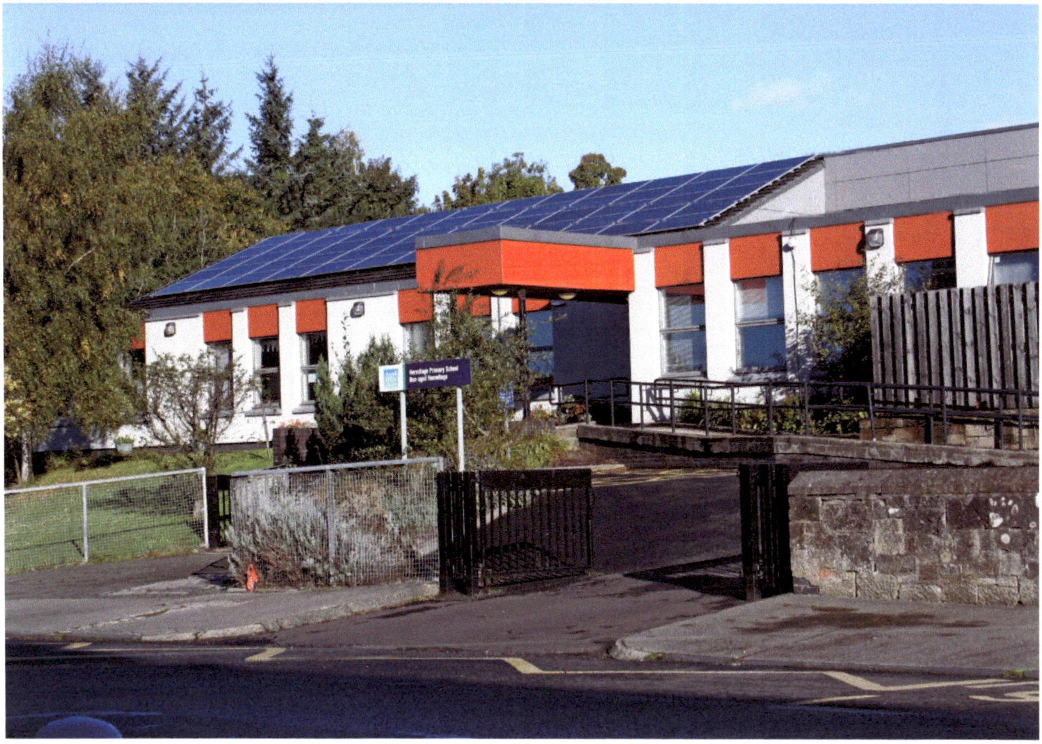

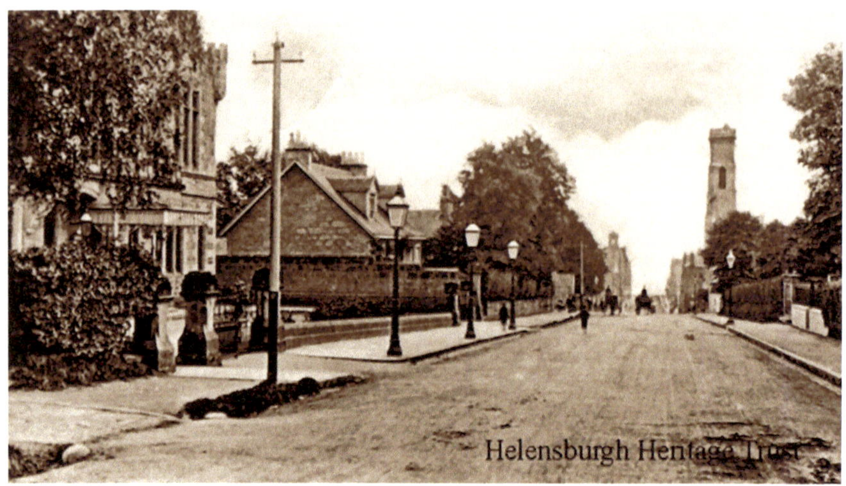

Victoria Hall

Looking down Sinclair Street with the Victoria Hall on the left and St Columba church further down on the right. Funded by public subscription in 1887 to commemorate Queen Victoria's Golden Jubilee, the hall was altered and added to by A. N. Paterson in 1899. The original metal railings in front were removed during the Second World War to help the war effort and were replaced to mark the burgh's bicentenary in 2002 after an initiative by the Friends of the Victoria Hall.

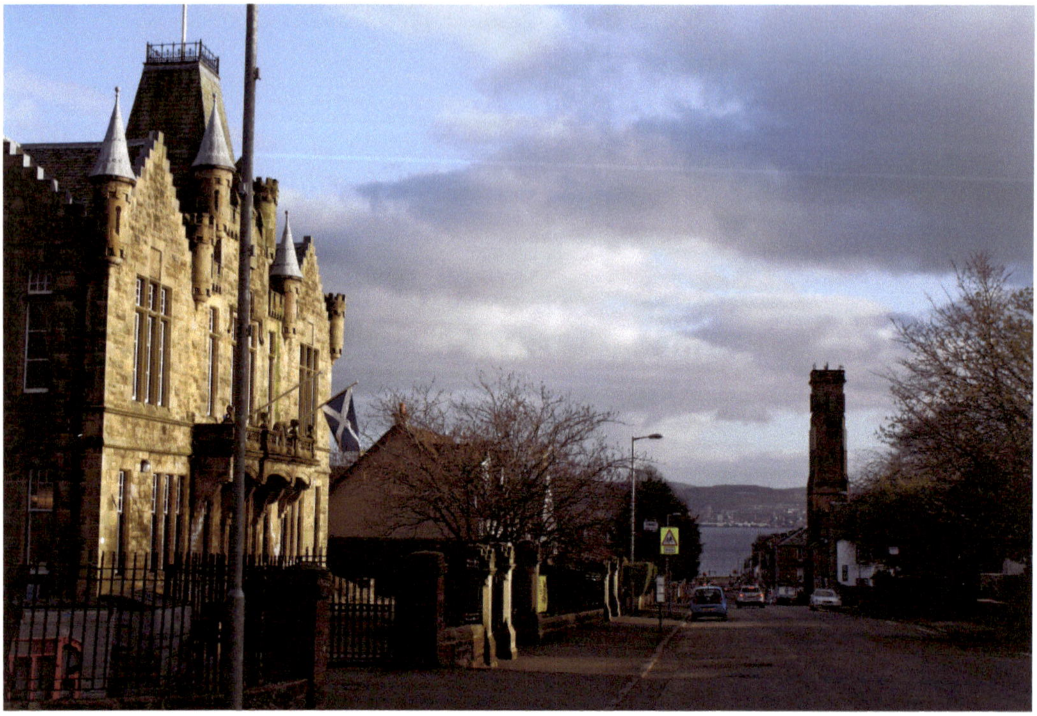

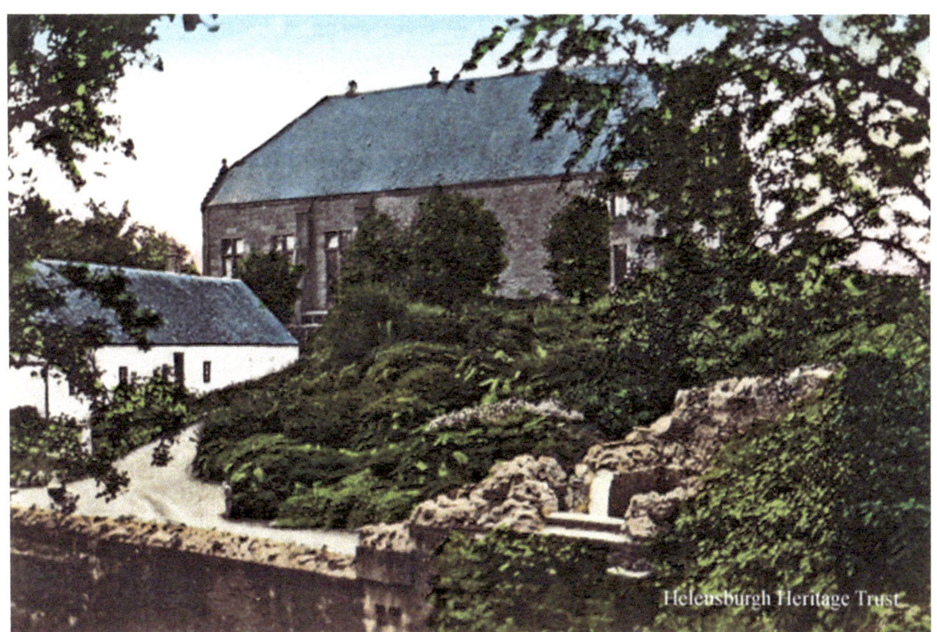

Past Industry

An unusual view of the Victoria Hall taken from the rear in Hermitage Park in 1926. At the back of the hall are workshops, which were removed later in the twentieth century, while to the right is part of the remains of the Milligs Mill which was demolished in 1922. At present, the growth of trees in the park makes it difficult to recapture this view.

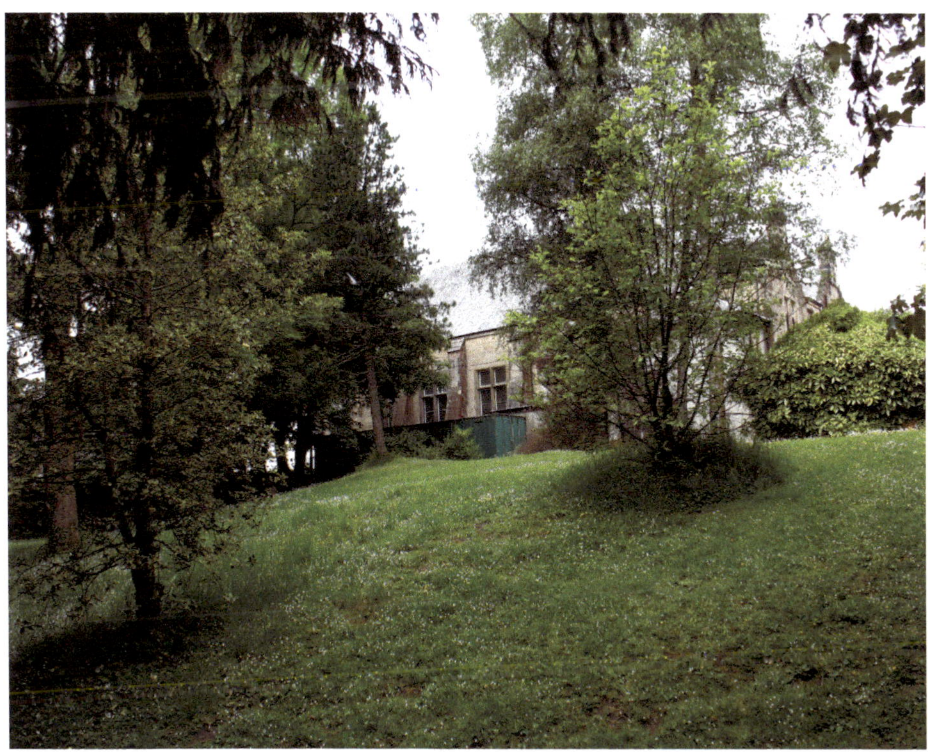

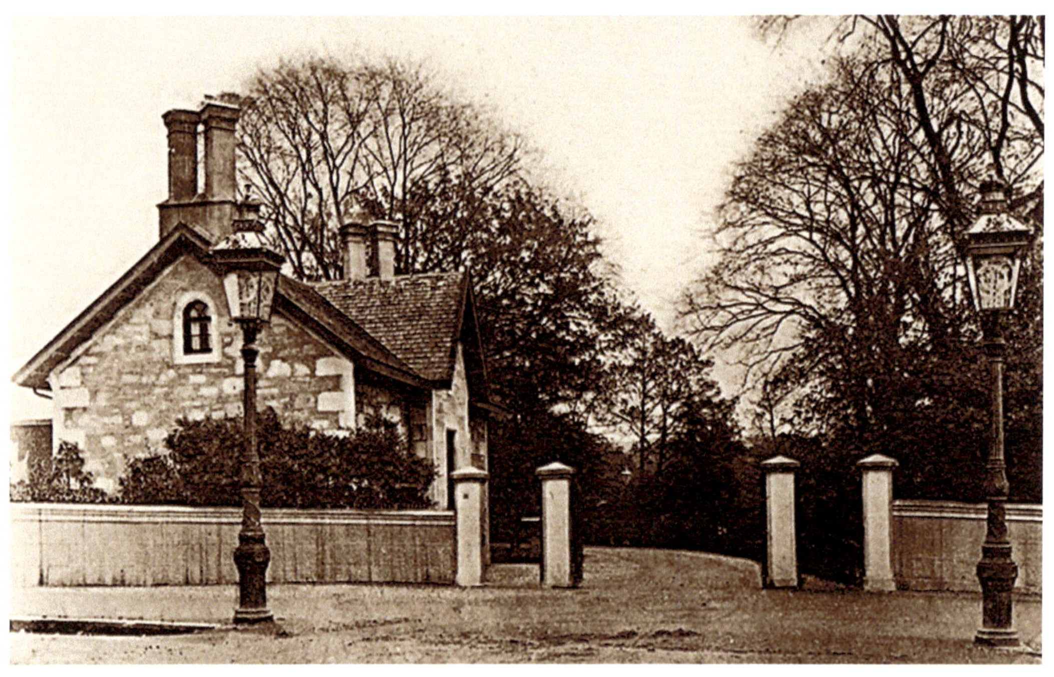

Hermitage Park Lodge

The Lodge, originally of Hermitage House, stood at the west gate of Hermitage Park for many years before being replaced by a modern bungalow further into the park, used by successive park superintendents.

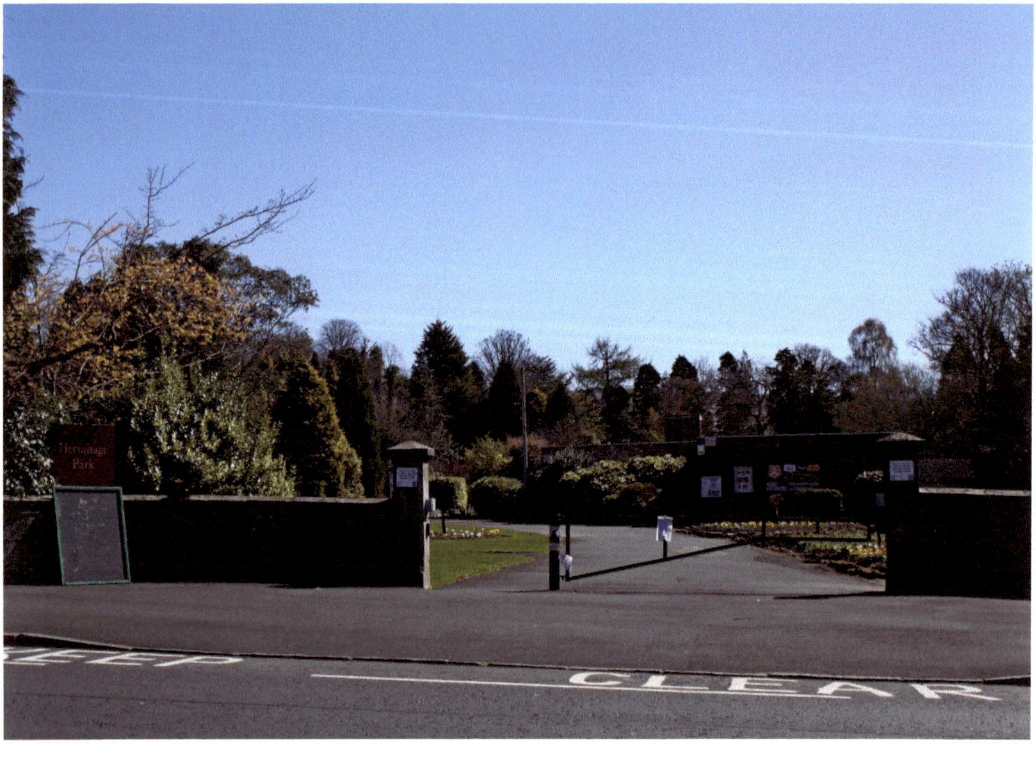

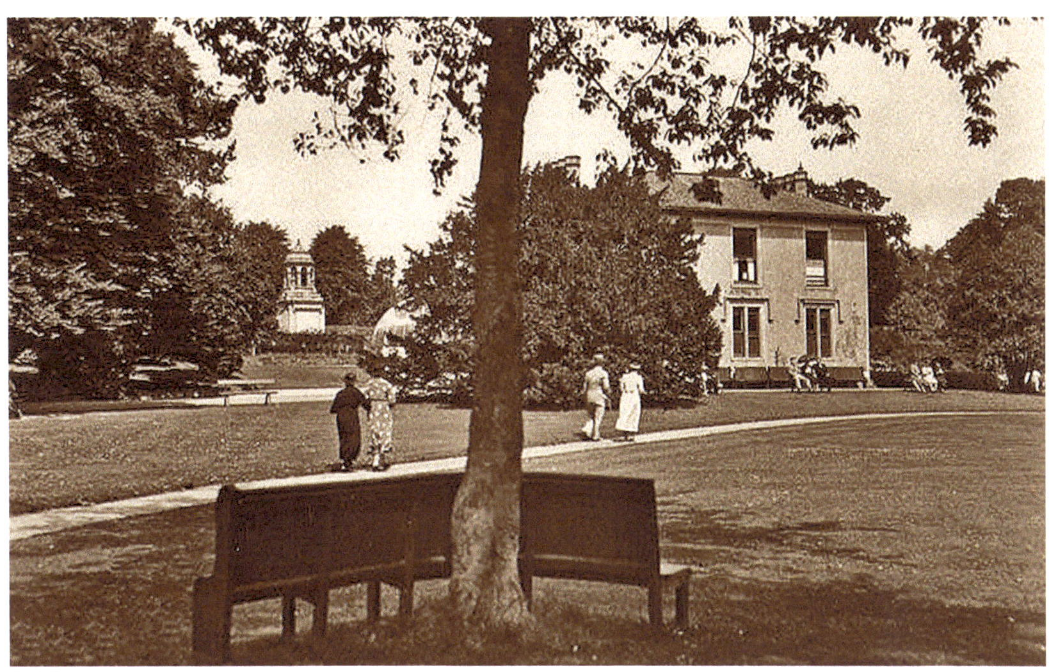

Hermitage Park

Hermitage House was built in 1840 and the house and estate were bought by the town council in 1911 to form Hermitage Park. The house was used as a hospital during the First World War but, after a number of years of disuse, was demolished in 1963. It was replaced by the current Japanese-style shelter. The park has recently received a large grant from the Heritage Lottery Fund and will be refurbished. A very successful 'Tea in the Park' is held annually.

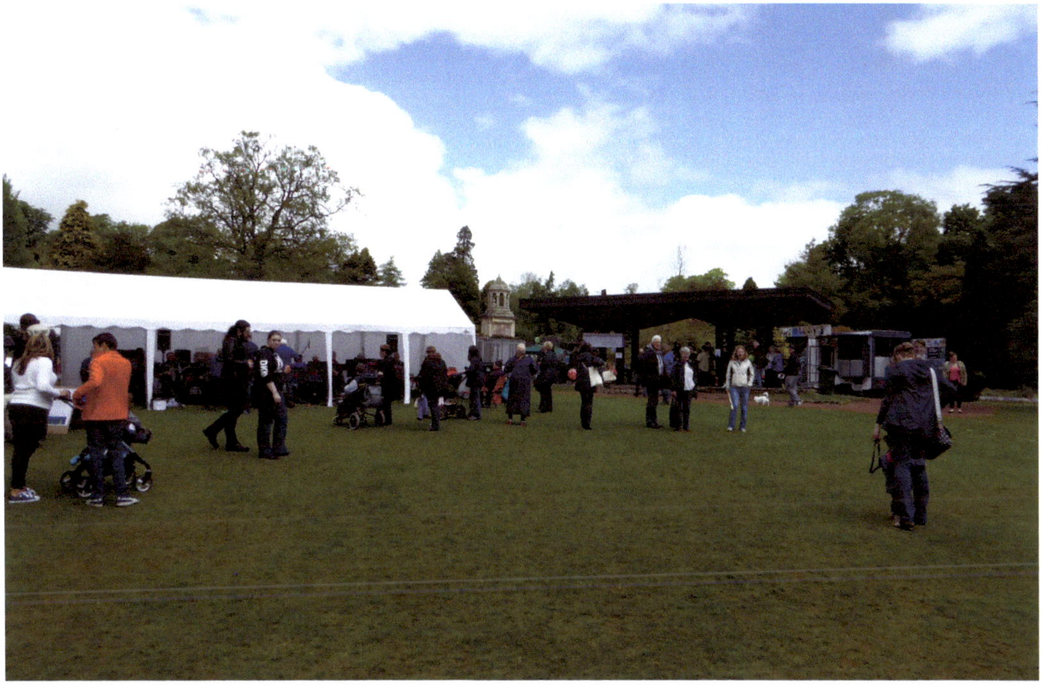

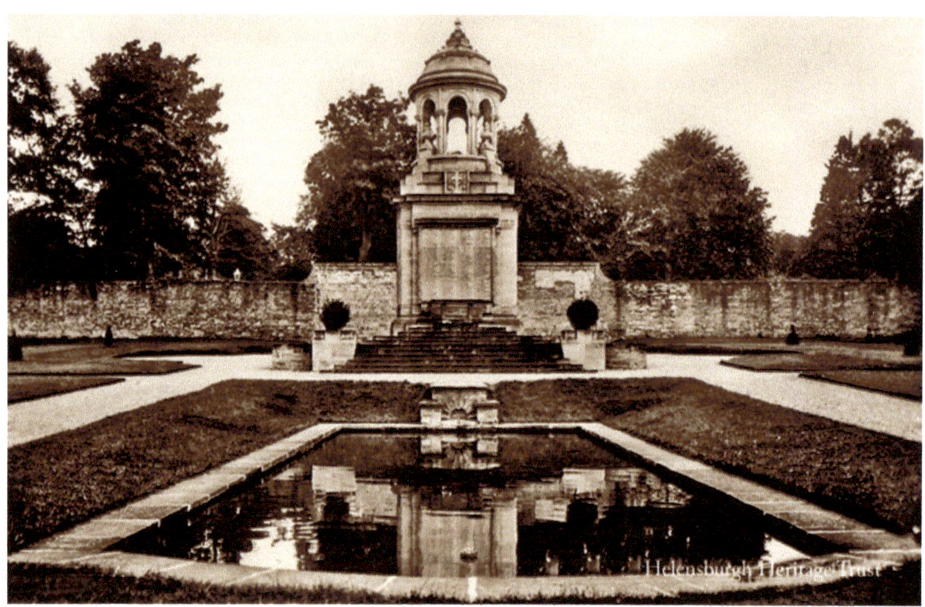

War Memorial

Designed by well-known local architect A. N. Paterson, the war memorial was completed in the old walled garden of Hermitage House in 1923. A service attended by hundreds of people is held in the Garden of Remembrance each year on Remembrance Sunday. The bench now in the foreground commemorates Colonel Findlay of Drumfork House, who was awarded the last Victoria Cross of the First World War, for his action just seven days before the Armistice in November 1918.

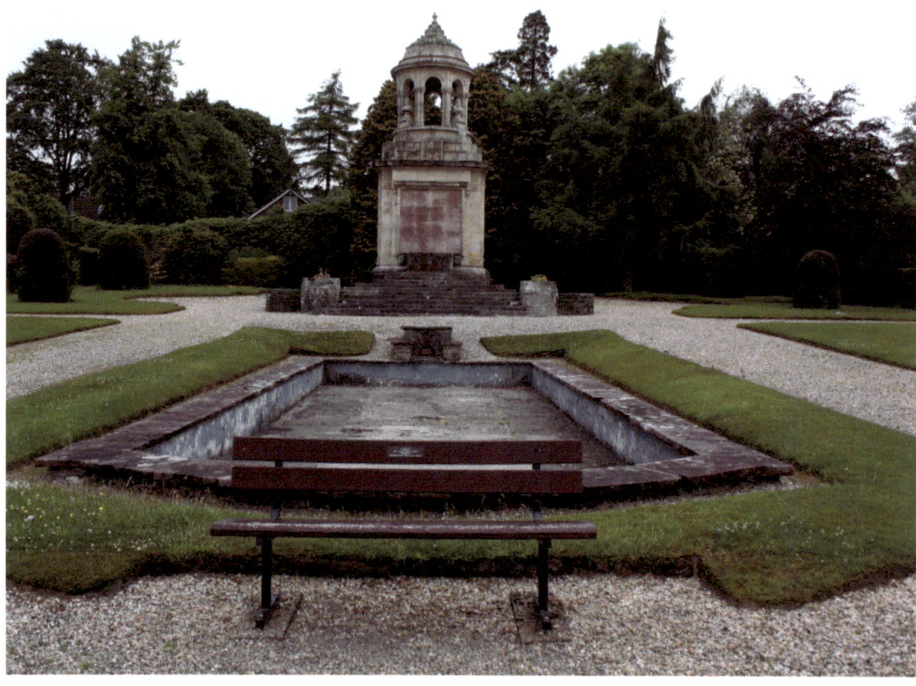

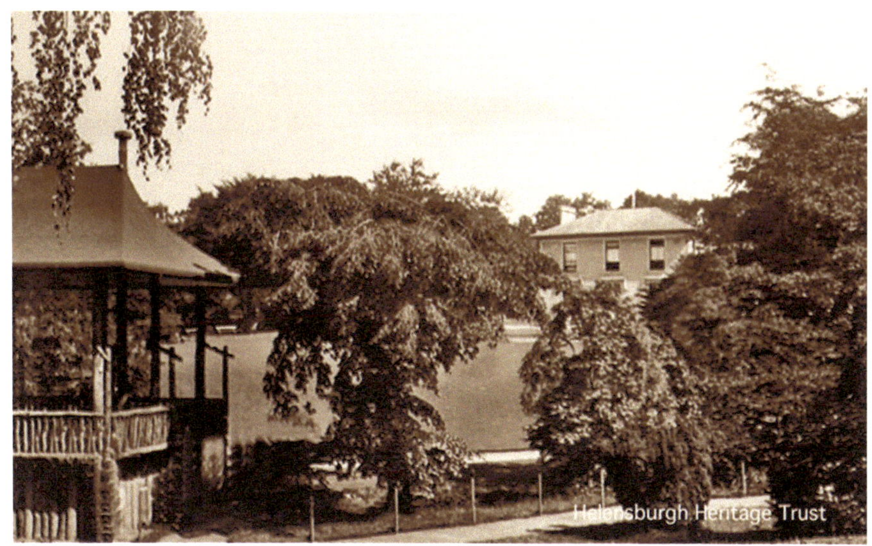

Bandstand

The rustic bandstand in Hermitage Park, with Hermitage House in the distance. The bandstand, which was erected in 1914, matched the style of the bridges over the Millig Burn. Now only the foundations remain, but it is planned to install a performance space as part of the forthcoming renovation of the park.

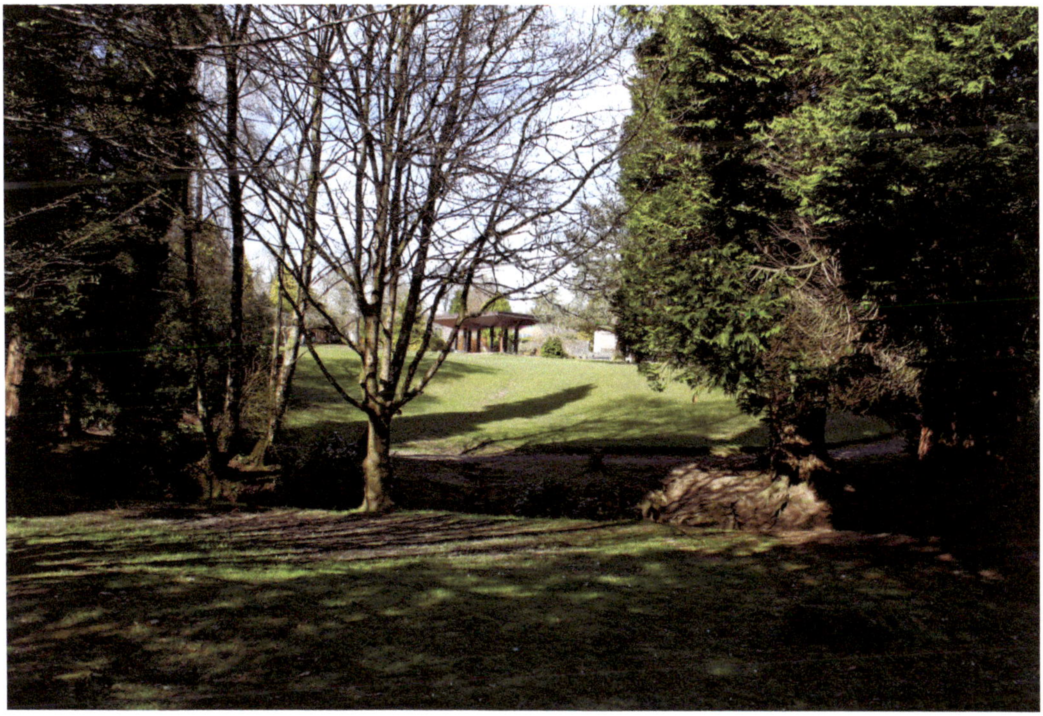

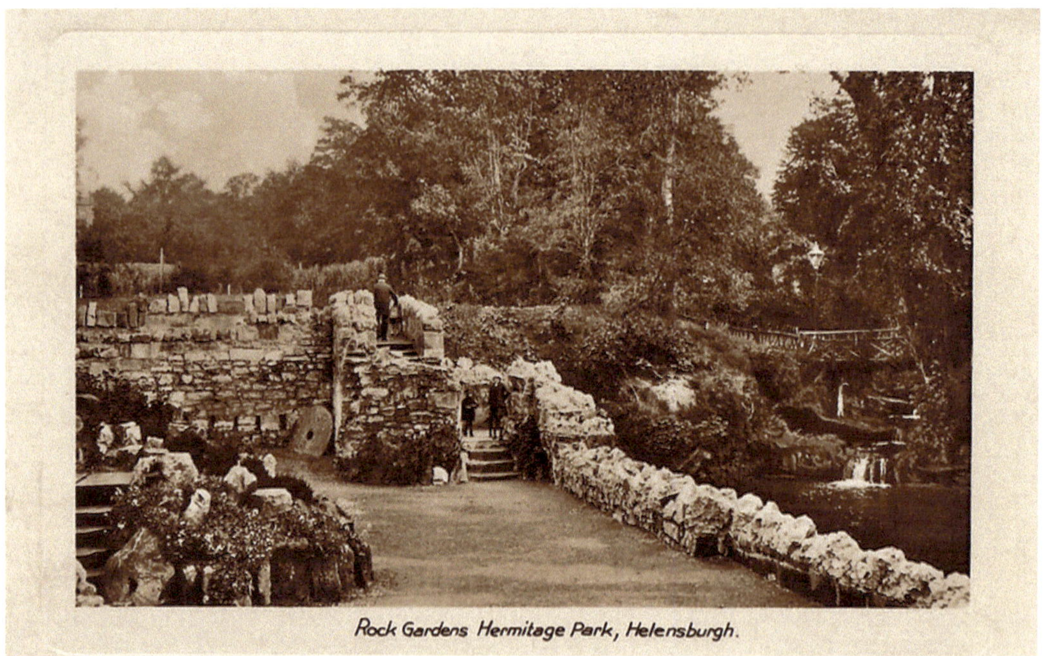

Milligs Mill

There are records of Milligs Mill in the 1350s and it continued as a thriving concern with a large grain-drying plant and associated distillery in the nineteenth century. However, in 1922 it was closed and demolished and the land donated to the town by Sir Iain Colquhoun to form part of Hermitage Park. Now the remaining ruins are hidden in the surrounding vegetation, but it is intended to renovate them as part of the refurbishment of the park.

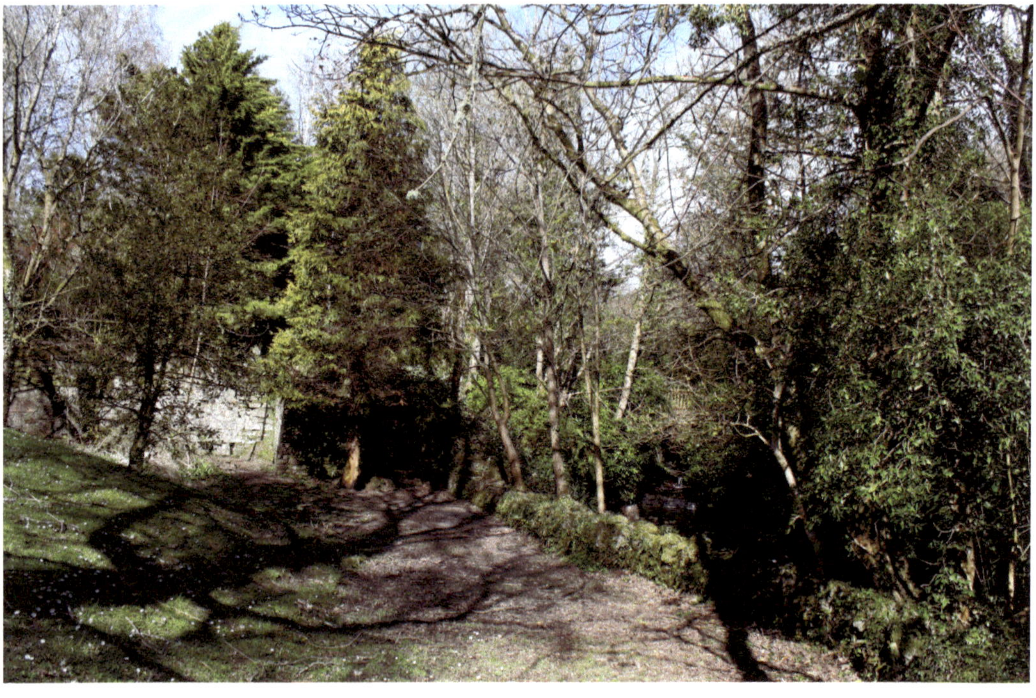

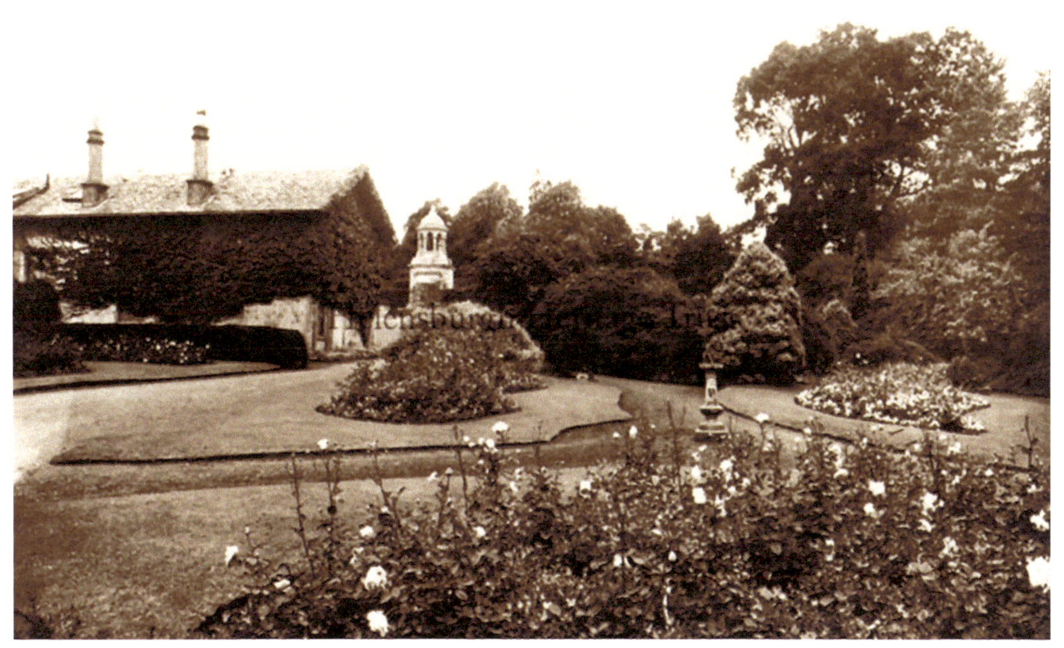

John Muir Way

The rose gardens and Hermitage House in the 1950s. In the spring of 2016, John Muir scholar and actor Lee Stetson planted a Californian sequoia to commemorate the great naturalist, who inspired the US National Park movement. The John Muir Way, from his birthplace in Dunbar to Helensburgh, was opened in 2014.

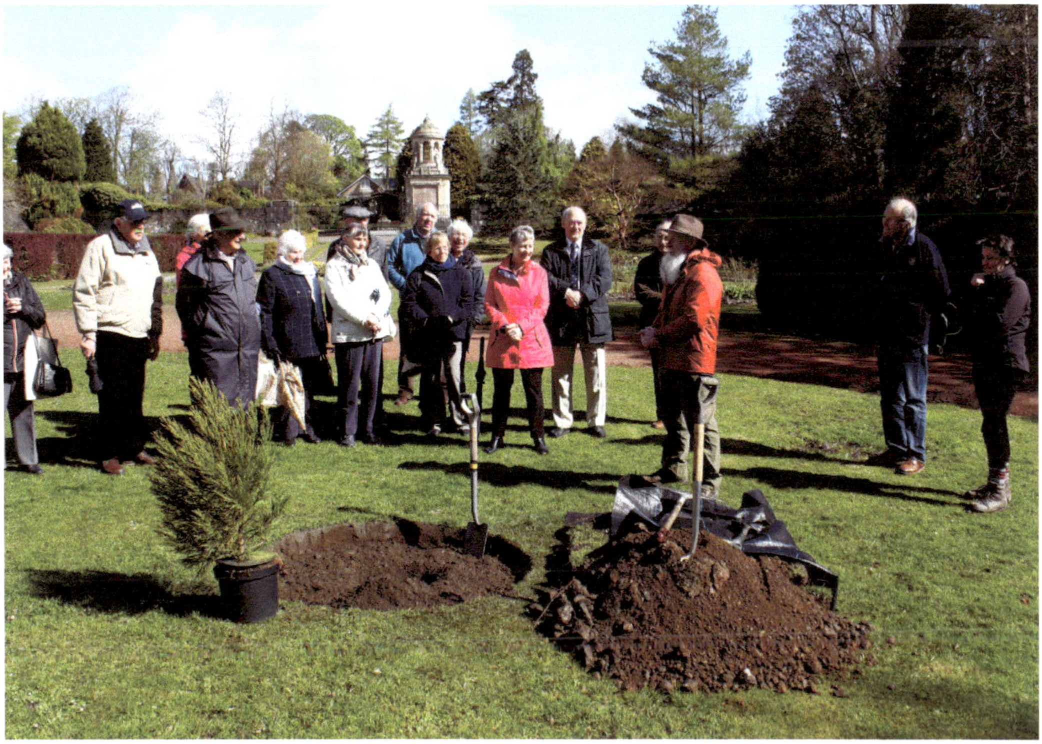

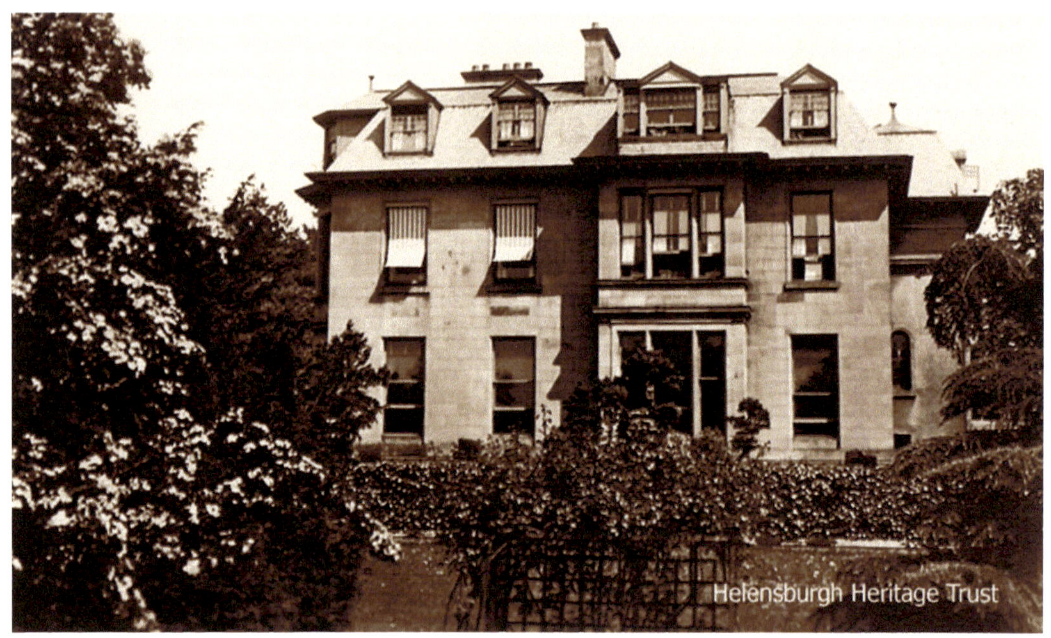

Lansdowne Park

Built in the 1850s with an ornate roof added by architect William Leiper in 1896, Lansdowne Park was at the junction of Victoria Road and Sinclair Street, opposite Prince Albert Terrace. Originally a private house, its last use was as a boarding house for St Bride's School and its successor Lomond School. After it was demolished in 2004, private houses and flats were built on the site.

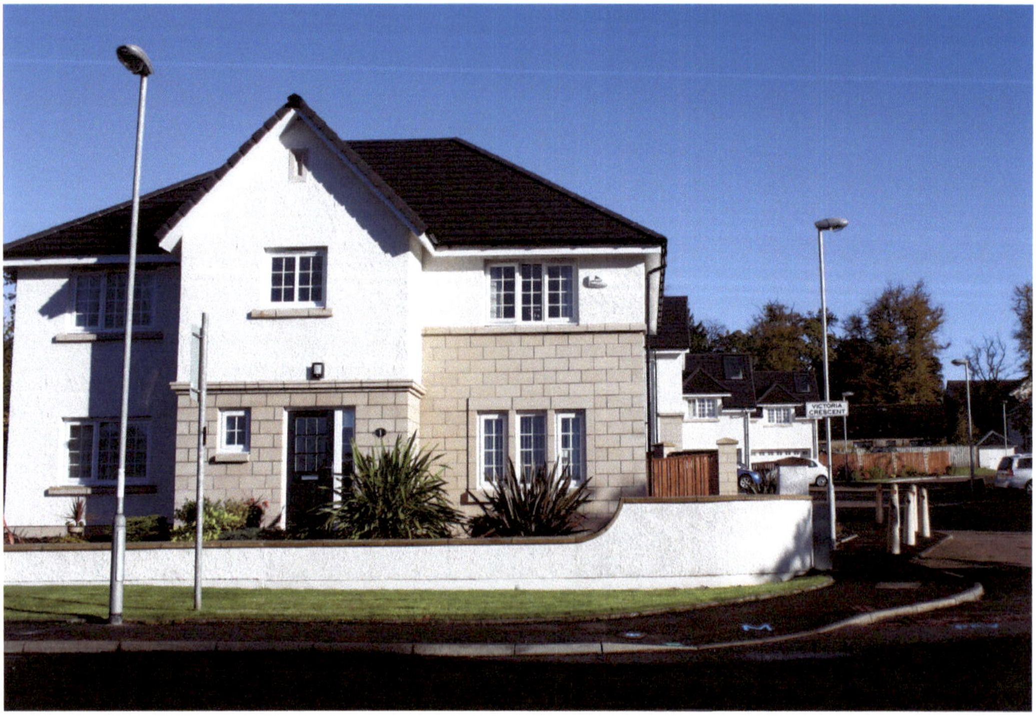

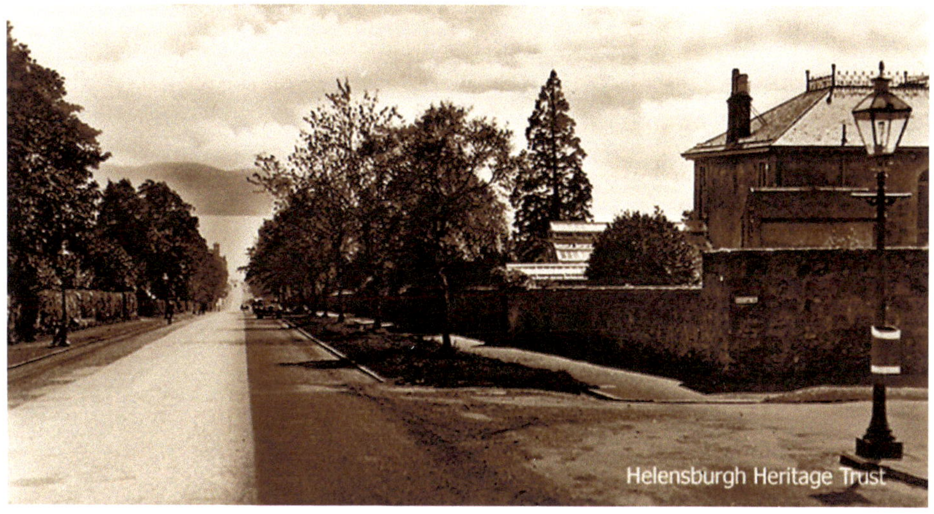

Upper Sinclair Street

A sunlit evening view of Upper Sinclair Street in the 1950s. The street is still lined with trees and has a fine display of daffodils in the spring.

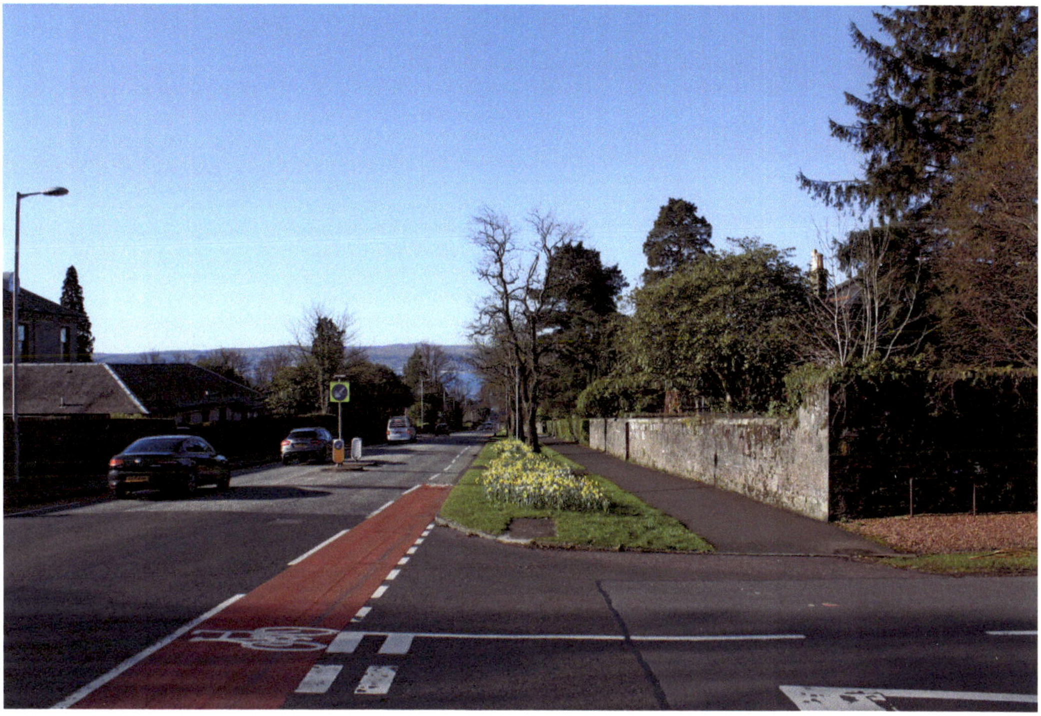

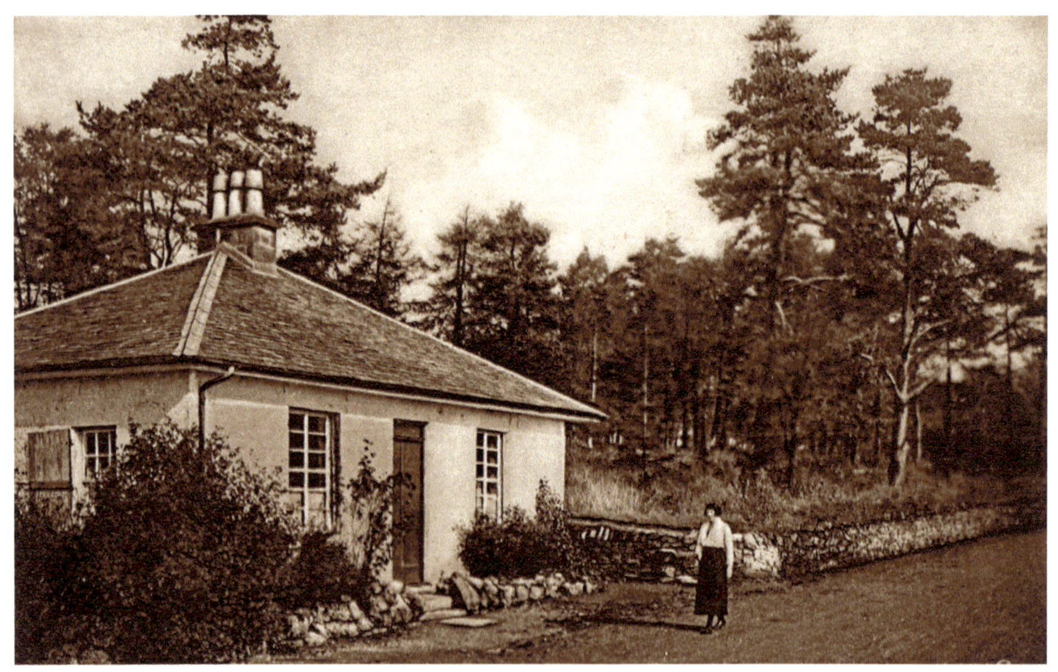

The Toll Cottage

At the top of Sinclair Street, the Toll Cottage looks pristine in this 1911 picture, as a young lady strolls past. The cottage still stands today, but is empty and in need of refurbishment. During the Second World War it was planned to site a roadblock at the cottage, using old tramlines placed in prepared holes, to keep German invaders out.

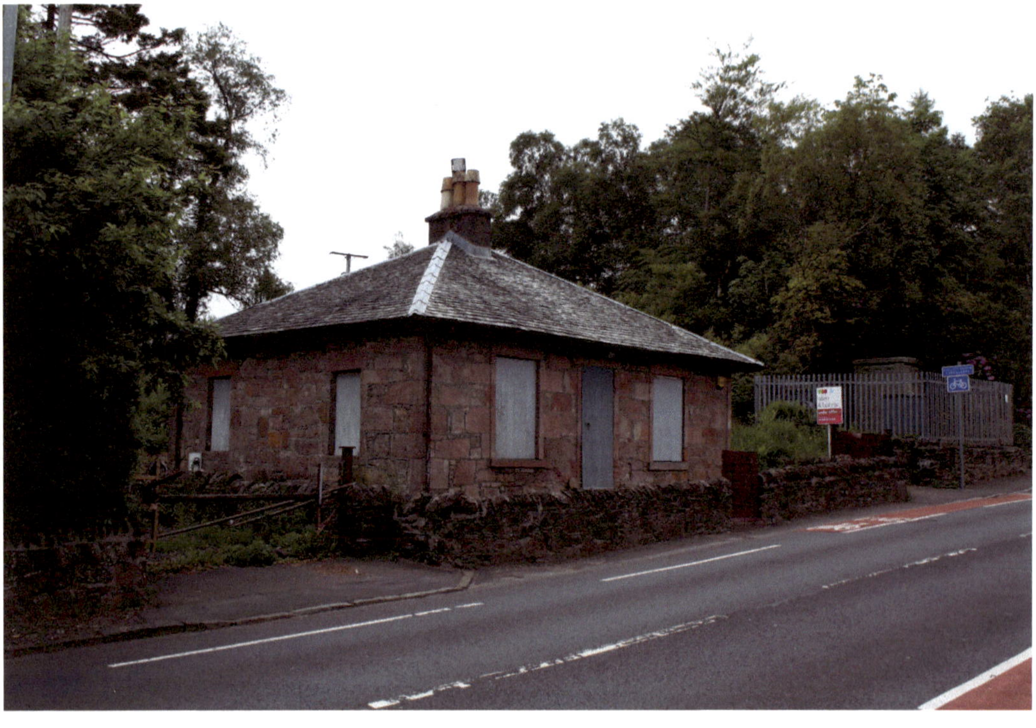

The Hill House

A 1901 image of The Hill House, the Upper Colquhoun Street mansion designed by Charles Rennie Mackintosh for publisher Walter Blackie, under construction. The house, with its magnificent art nouveau interiors, was acquired by the Royal Incorporation of Scottish Architects in 1972 and passed into the care of the National Trust for Scotland in 1982; it is now one of their most important buildings, visited by thousands of people each year.

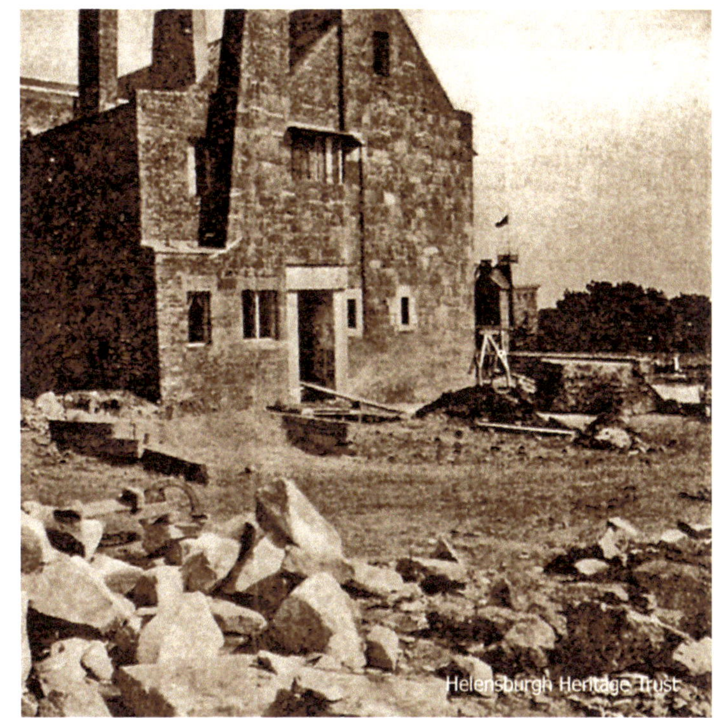

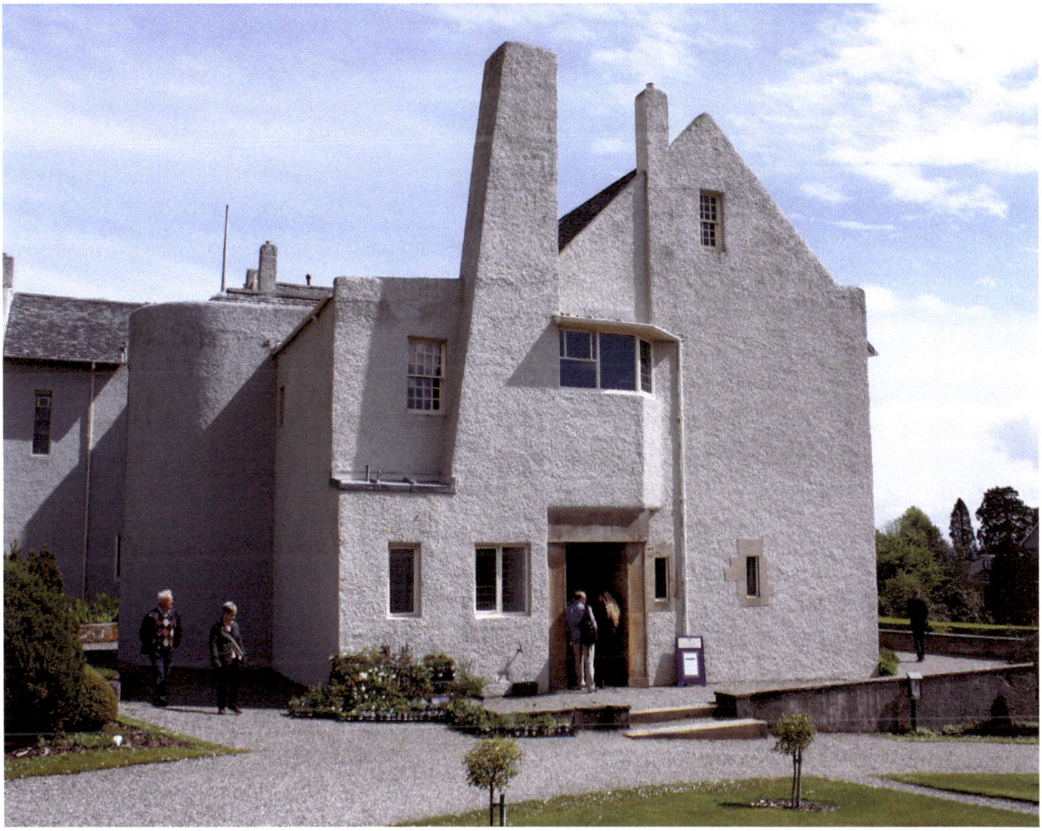

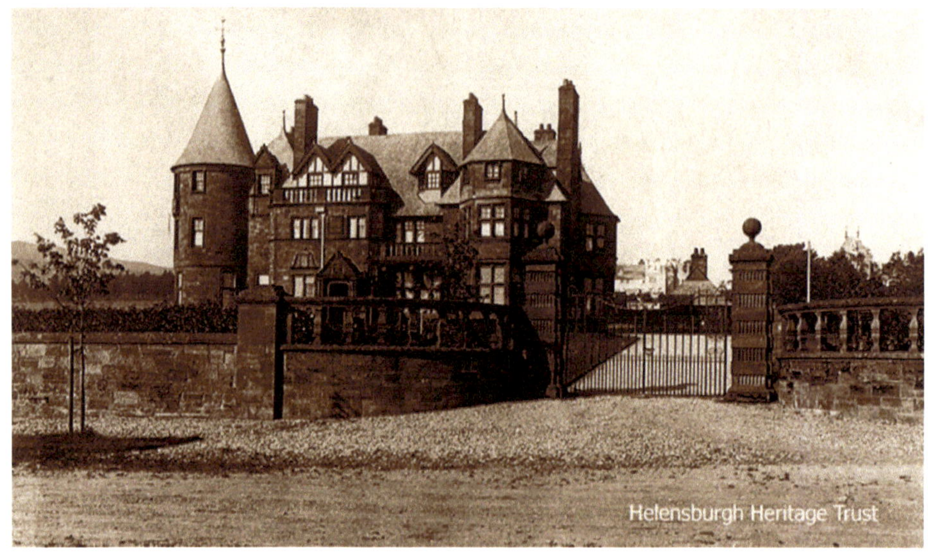

Red Tower

An early image of Red Tower, No. 4 Douglas Drive West, a red sandstone chateau-like mansion built in 1898 by distinguished local architect William Leiper for grocer James Allan. At the end of the twentieth century it was bought by the Roman Catholic diocese of Glasgow and used as a drug rehabilitation centre, but it has since reverted to private use and the name has been changed to Red Towers.

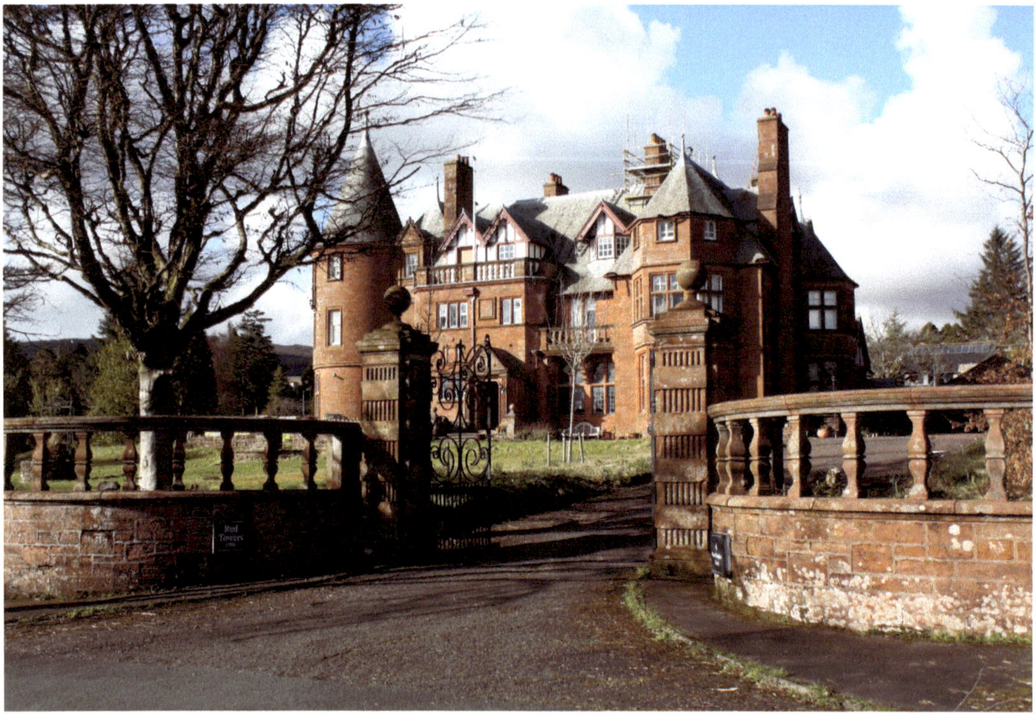

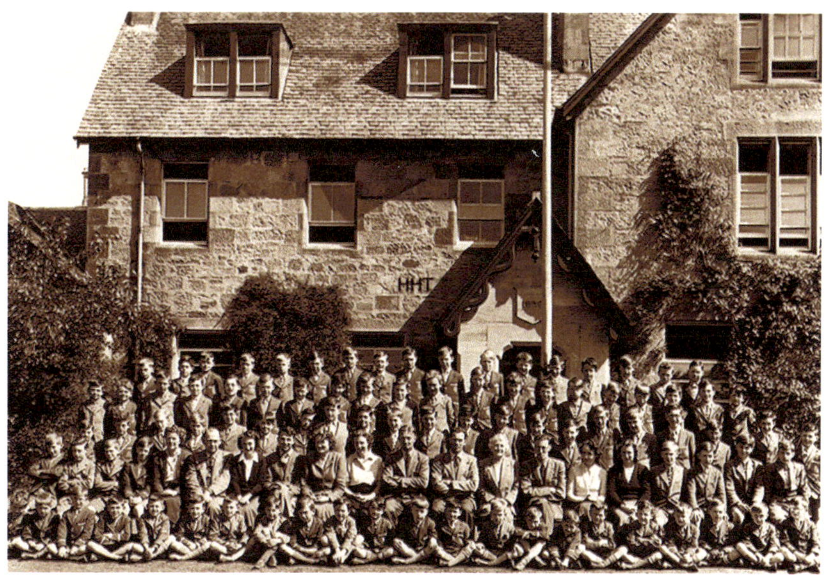

Larchfield School

The staff and pupils of Larchfield School outside the Colquhoun Street building in 1951. Notable pupils included John Logie Baird, and W. H. Auden was a member of staff for a year. Larchfield later became part of Lomond School, but when that was consolidated on the St Bride's site it was sold to be redeveloped as flats.

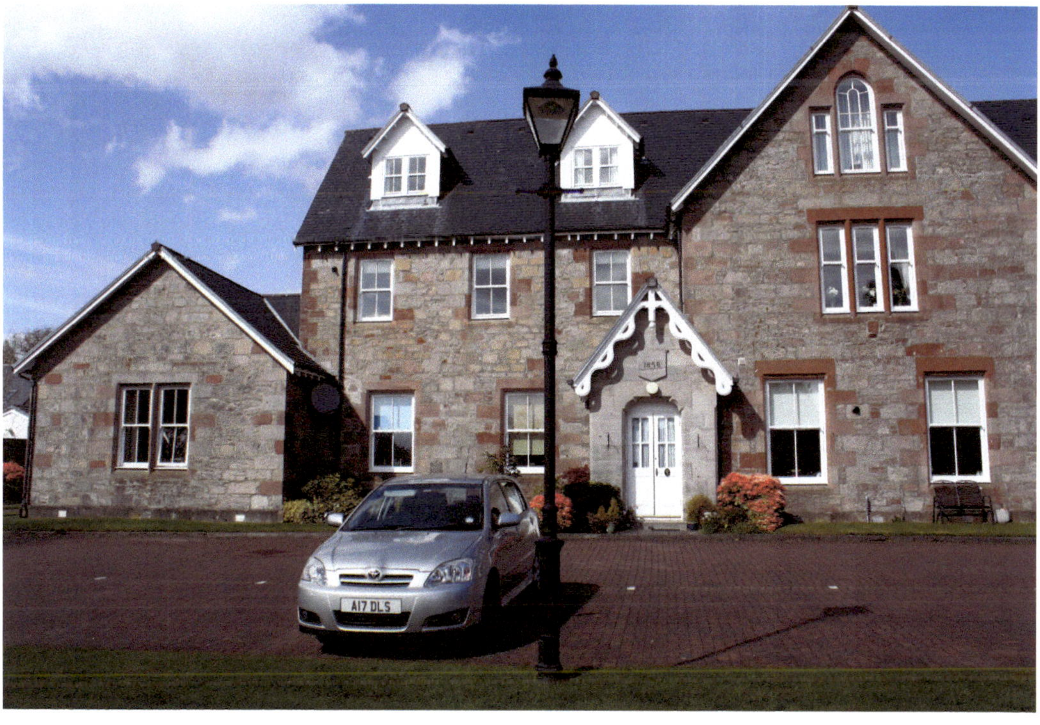

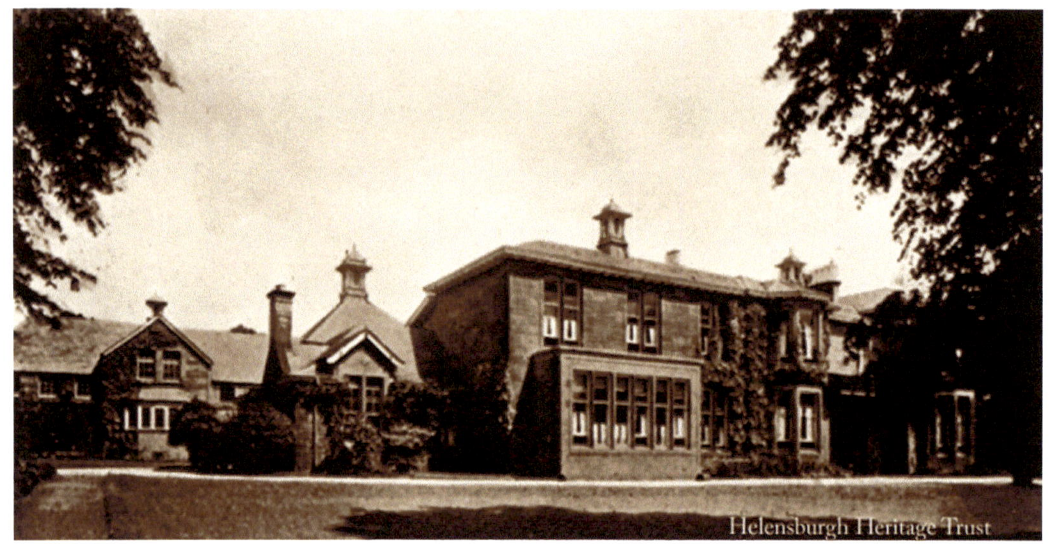

St Bride's School

The school for girls at No. 10 Stafford Street was founded in 1895. In 1977 it merged with Larchfield School for boys to become Lomond School. The St Bride's building was largely destroyed in an overnight fire in 1997, but was rebuilt to a design by Ian McKellar, a local architect and a member of staff.

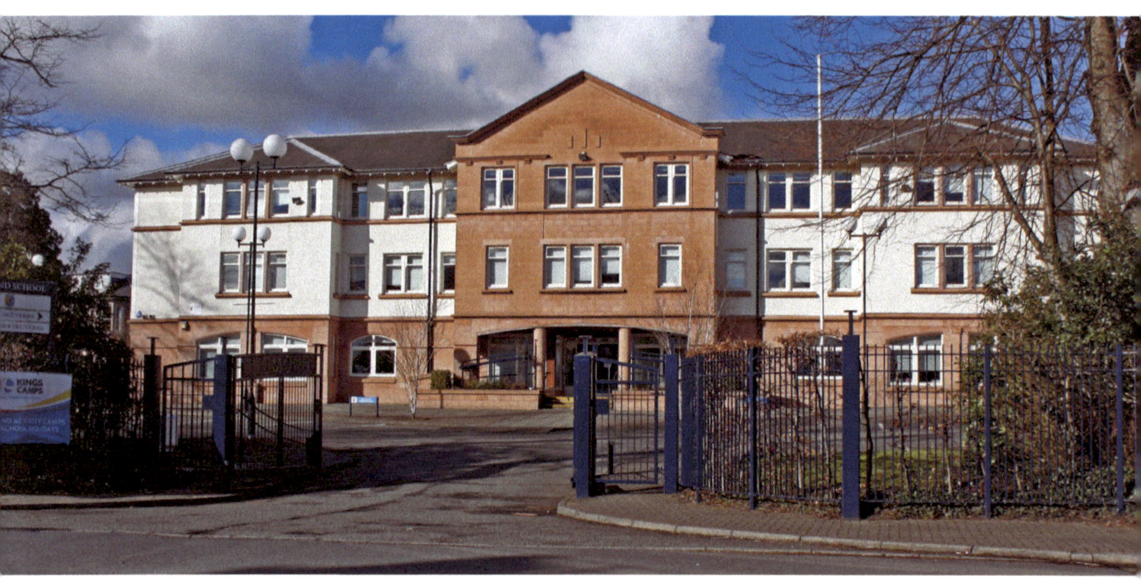

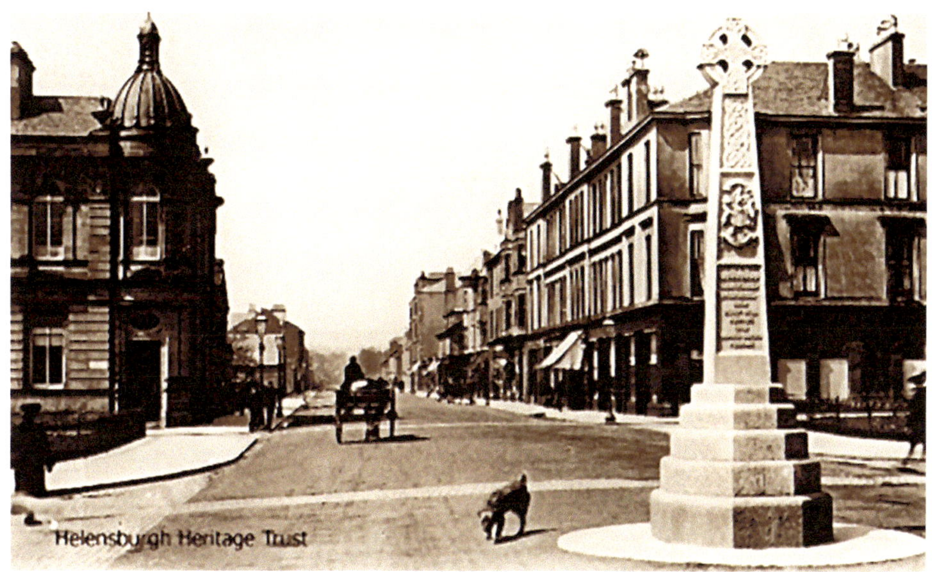

Centenary Monument

The pink-granite centenary cross in 1905 in the centre of Colquhoun Square was donated in 1903, by Sir James Colquhoun of Luss, to mark the centenary of the granting of the Burgh Charter in 1902. Later it was moved to the north-west quadrant of the square for road safety reasons. The post office building on the left remains, but is not in use.

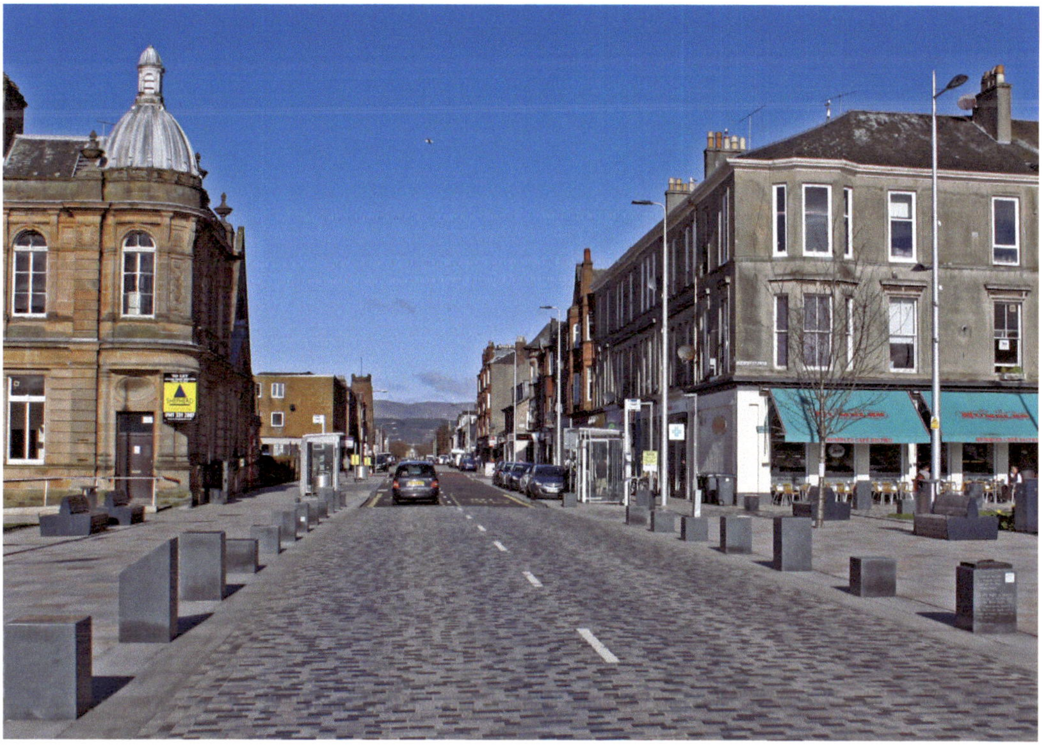

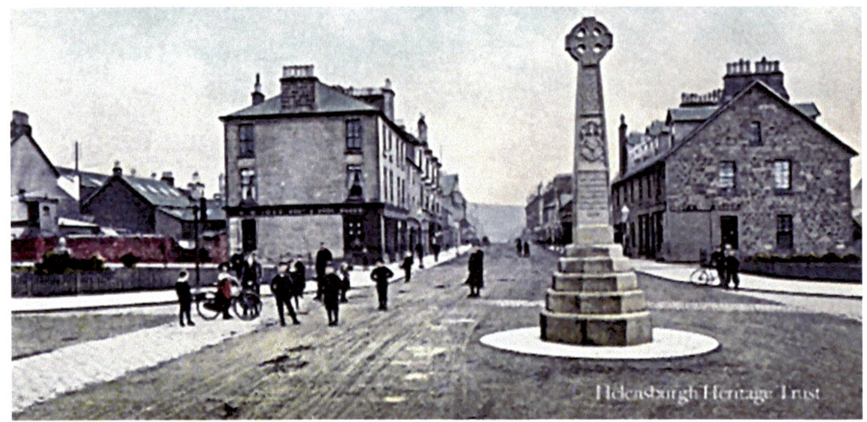

Colquhoun Square

The centenary cross in its original place in Colquhoun Square, looking east. The terrace on the left of West Princes Street is unchanged but the buildings on the right were replaced with flats and a bank in 1982. The square was remodelled with a new road layout on either side and granite paving in 2014.

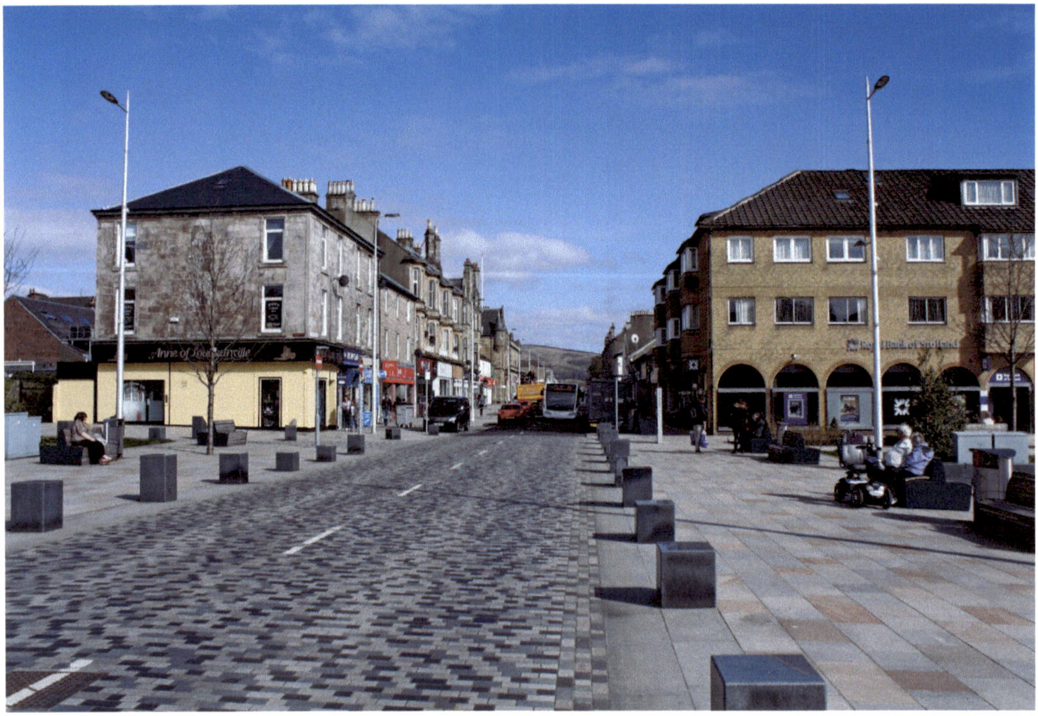

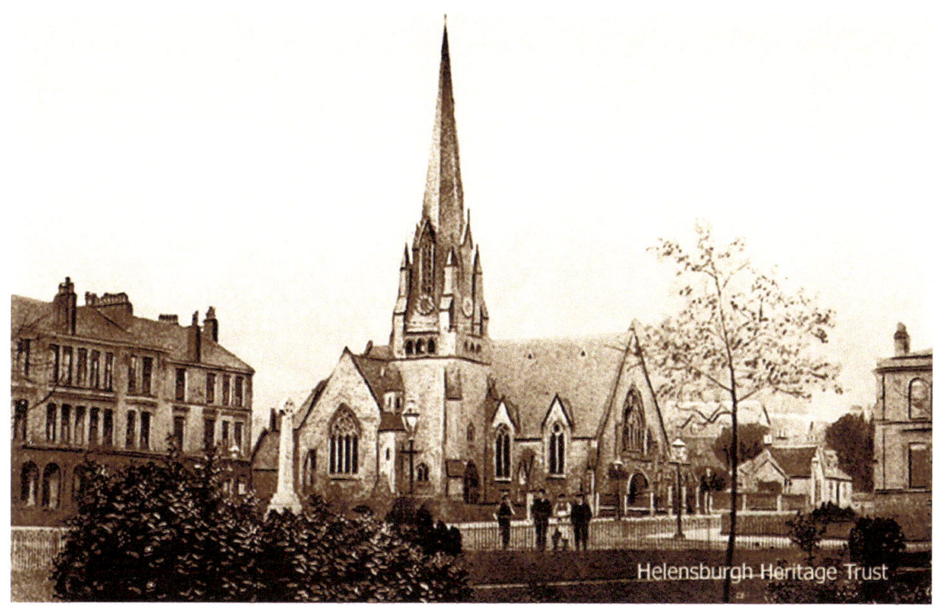

Market Place

Colquhoun Square is pictured in 1905 when the centenary monument was in the centre, the quadrants had metal fences, and what is now the parish church did not have a porch. The square was remodelled in 2014 and is now the site of regular open markets and other events.

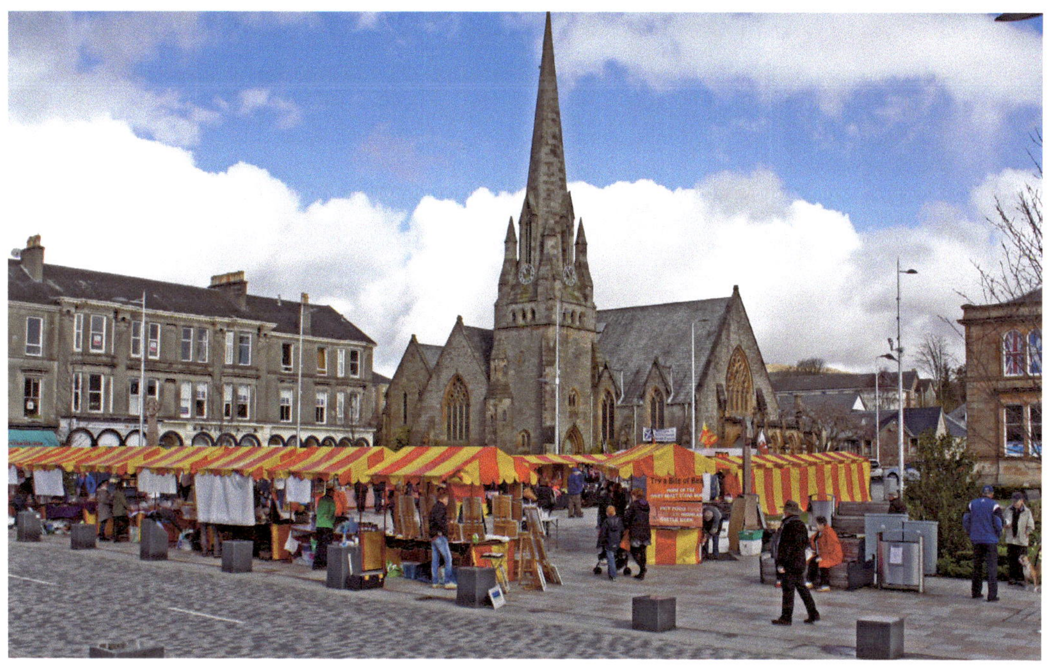

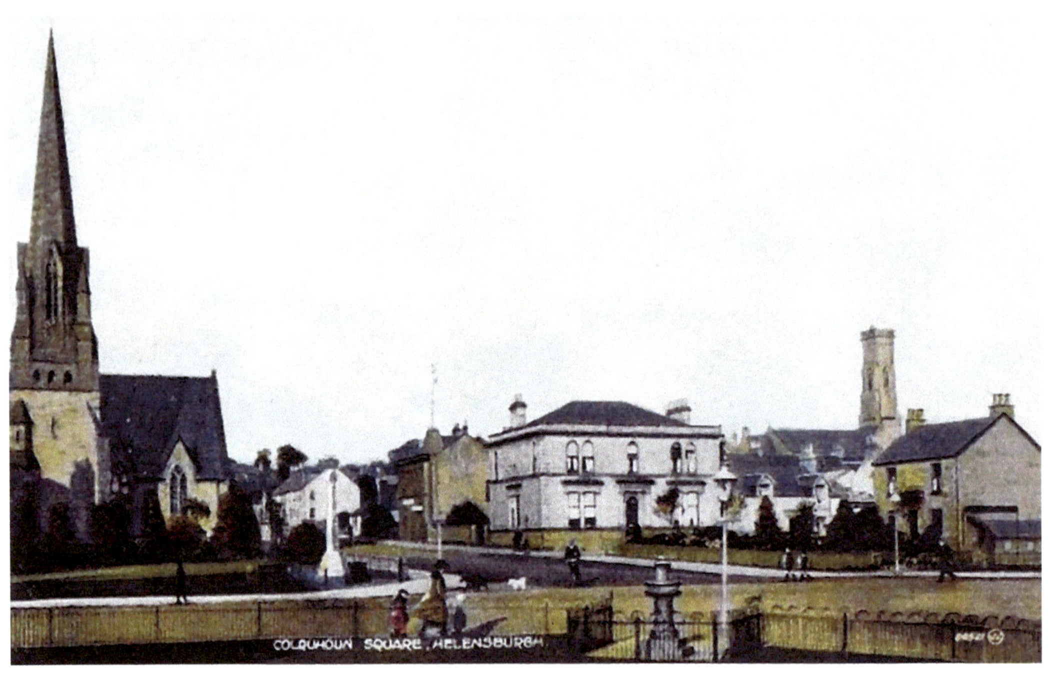

Parish Church

This colour-tinted picture from the 1920s shows the Free Church, now the parish church, combining the congregations from two other churches, a prominent bank building, now used as temporary offices and the tower of St Columba Church, now converted into a digital arts centre, The Tower.

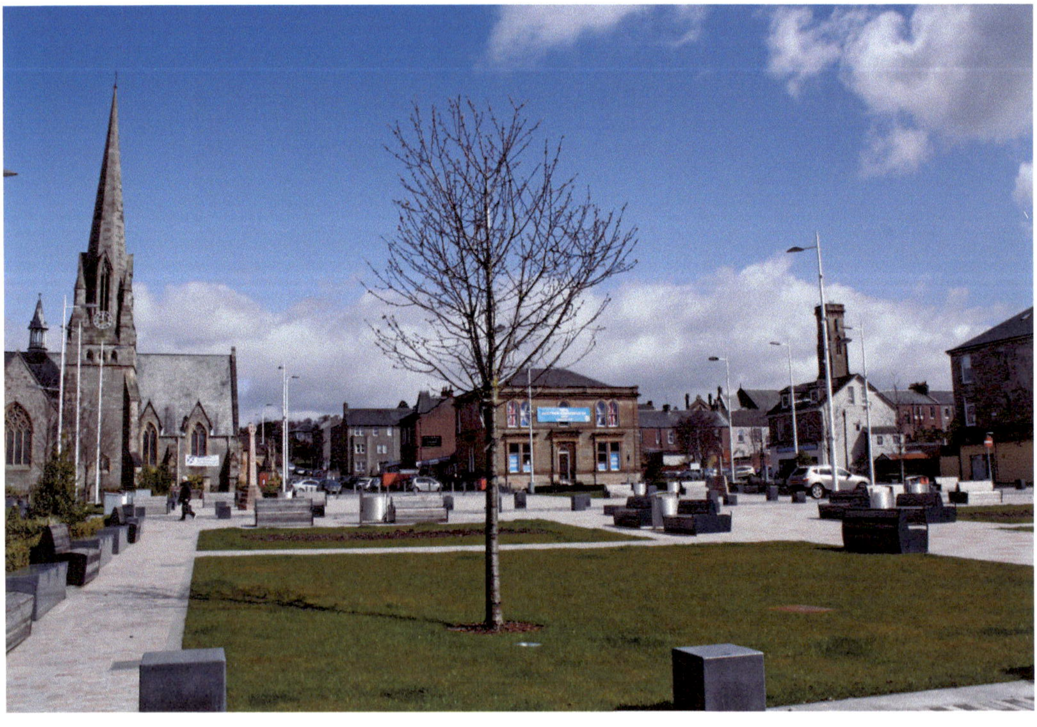

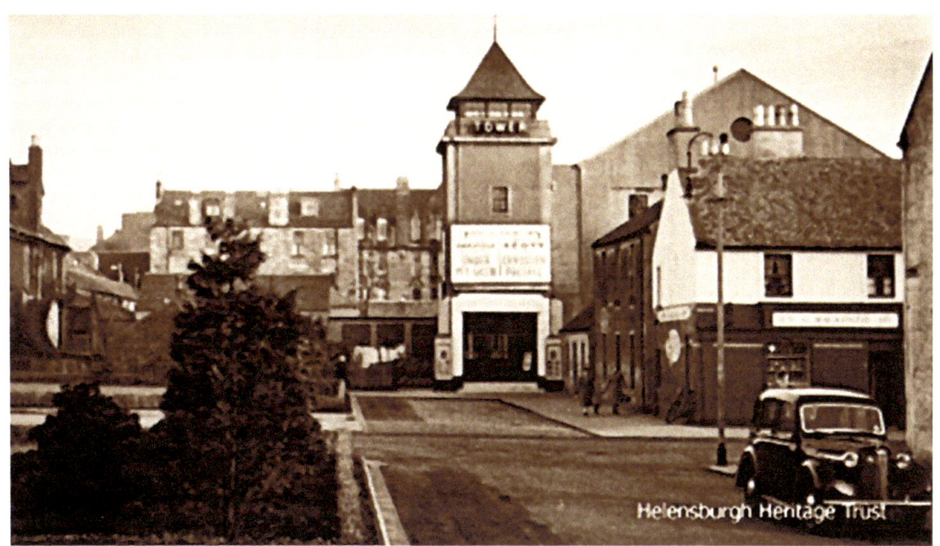

Built in the south-east corner of Colquhoun Square, the Tower Cinema competed for patrons with La Scala in James Street. Forced to close because of storm damage in January 1968, it was demolished in 1973 and that side of the Square redeveloped in 1982, although the shop on the corner of Colquhoun Street has survived.

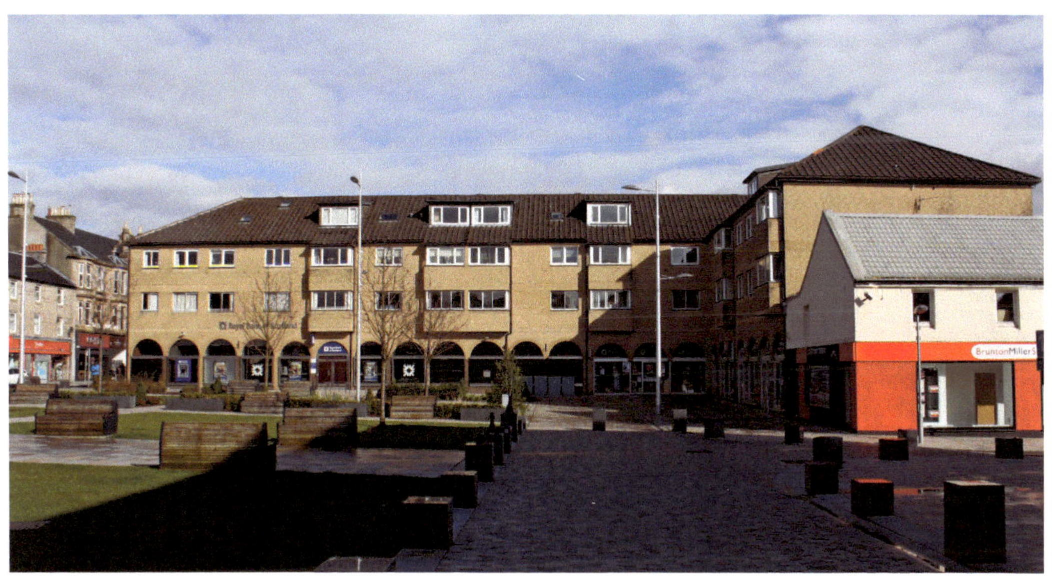

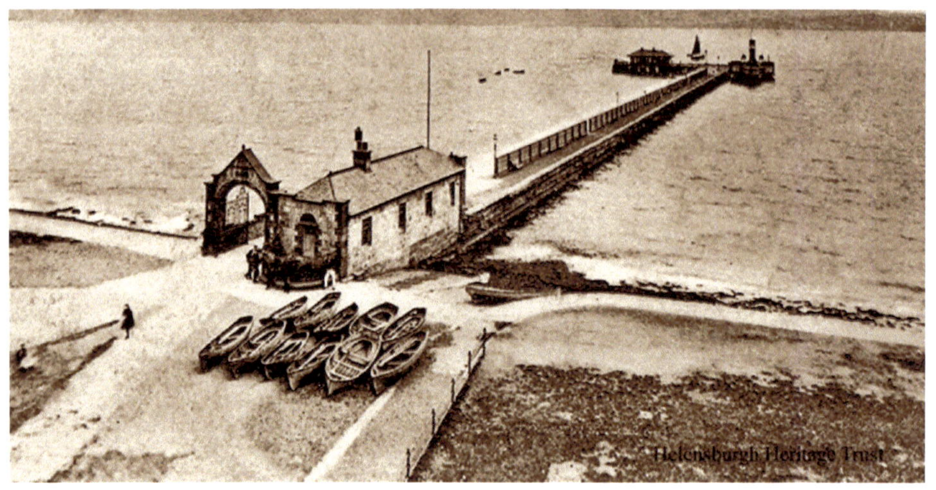

Helensburgh Pier

An unusual picture of Helensburgh Pier before the outdoor swimming pool was built in 1928 on the left of the entrance arch; this was demolished in the 1970s. Men and children can be seen standing around, while the fishing boats are ready to be launched. The present-day photograph, taken from a slightly different angle, shows the indoor swimming pool and skateboard park, built on the site of the outdoor pool.

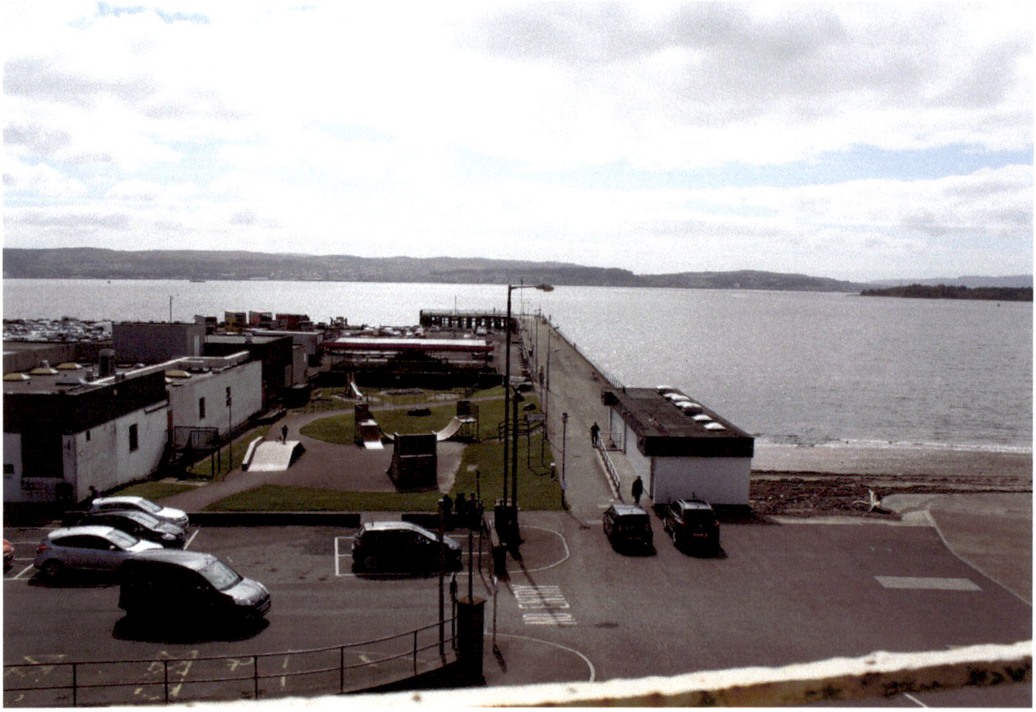

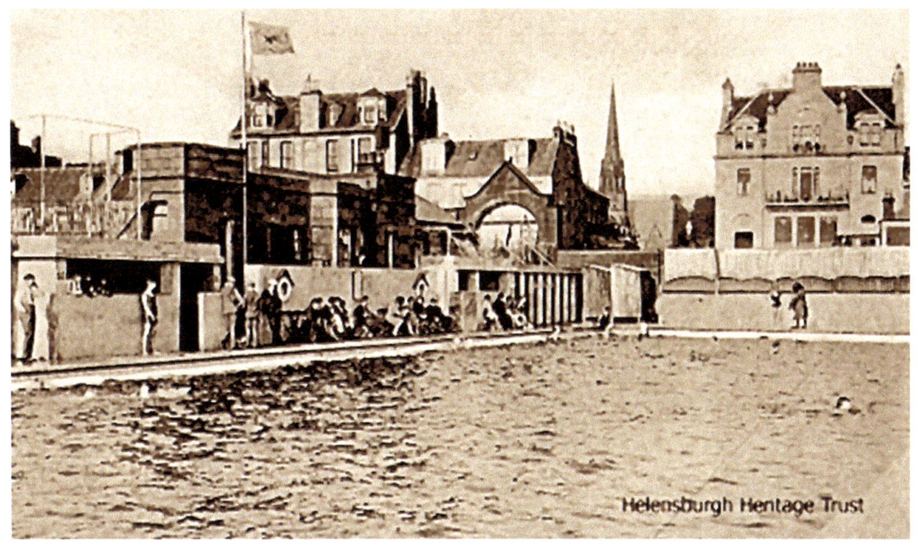

The Outdoor Swimming Pool

Built in 1928 as a gift from Provost Andrew Buchanan, beside the pier, the Helensburgh outdoor swimming pool was replaced in 1976 by an indoor pool on an adjacent site, and a year later the outdoor pool was closed. It was demolished in 1996 and replaced by a children's play area and skateboard park.

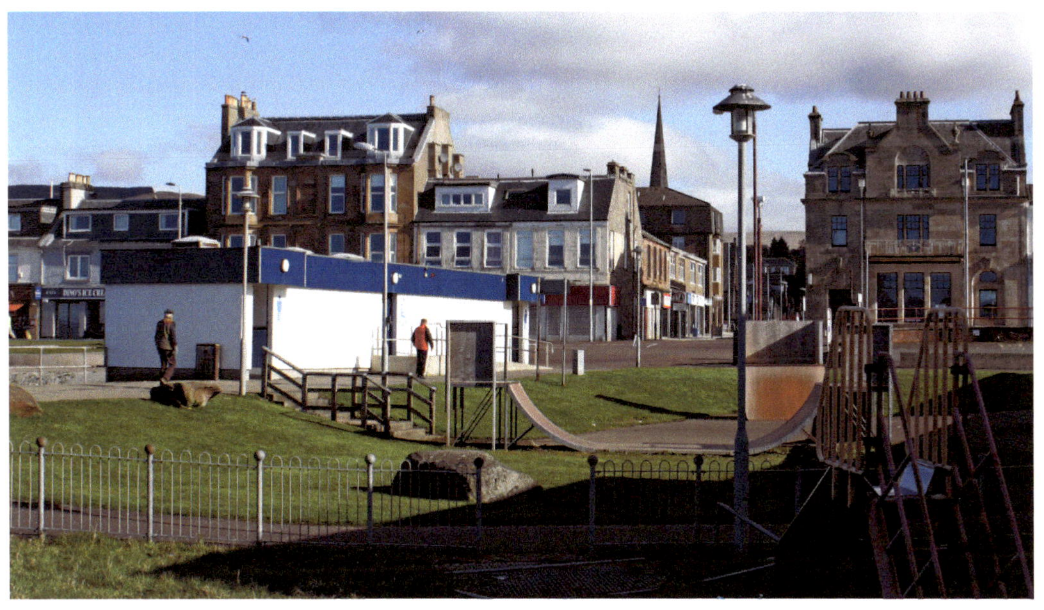

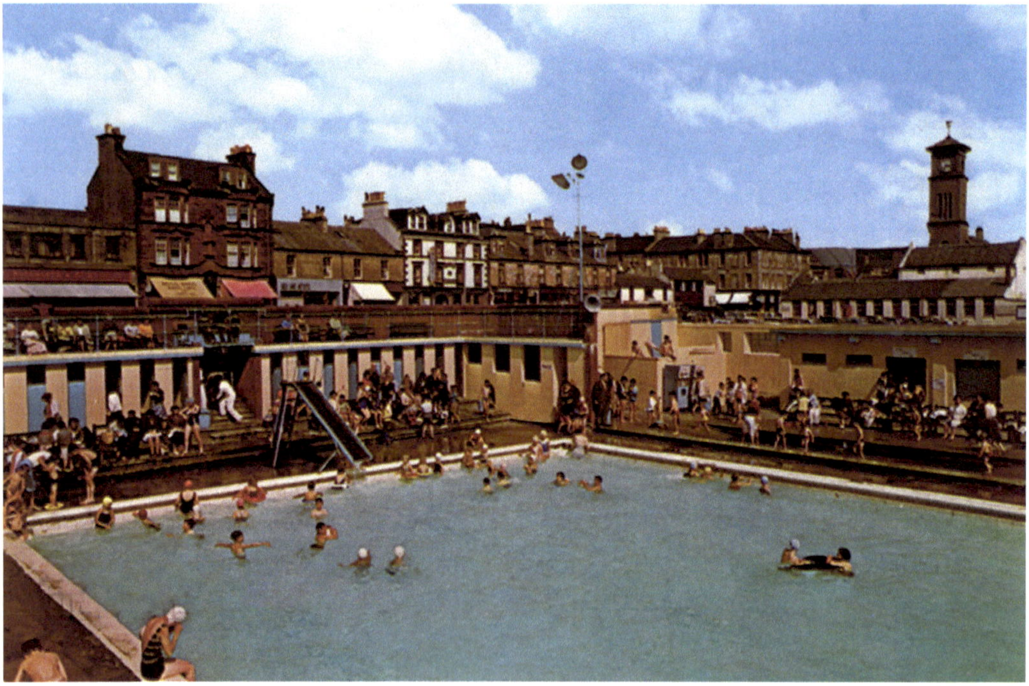

Summer Swimming Pool

The outdoor swimming pool on a fine summer's day in the 1960s. There are currently plans to build a major new leisure centre, including a large indoor pool on this site.

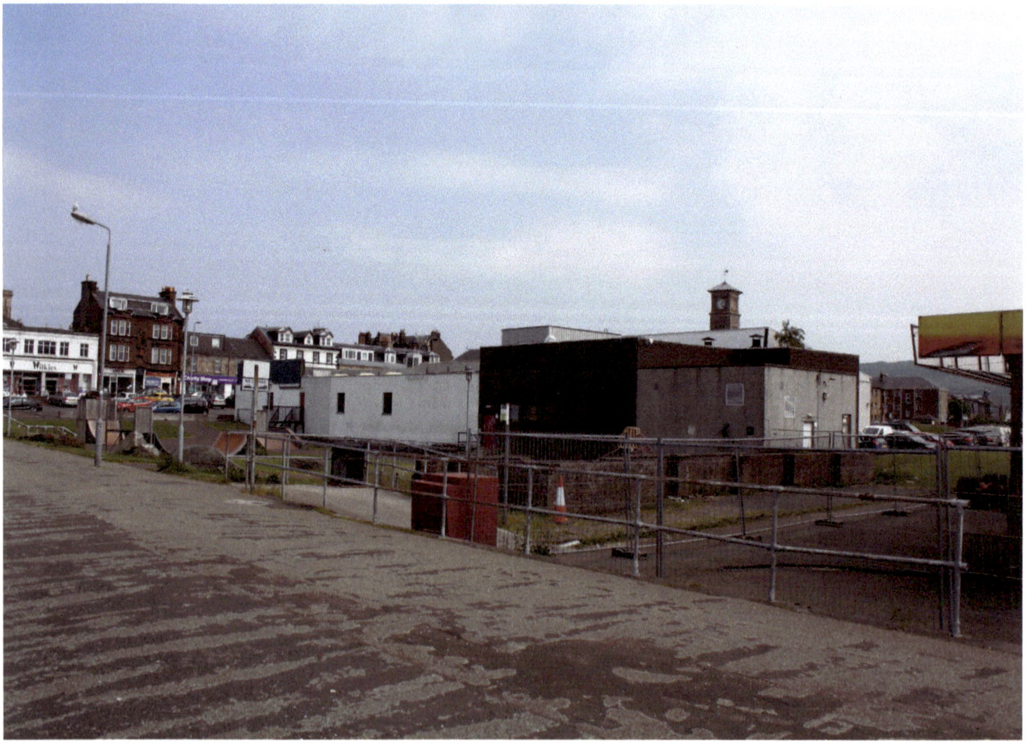

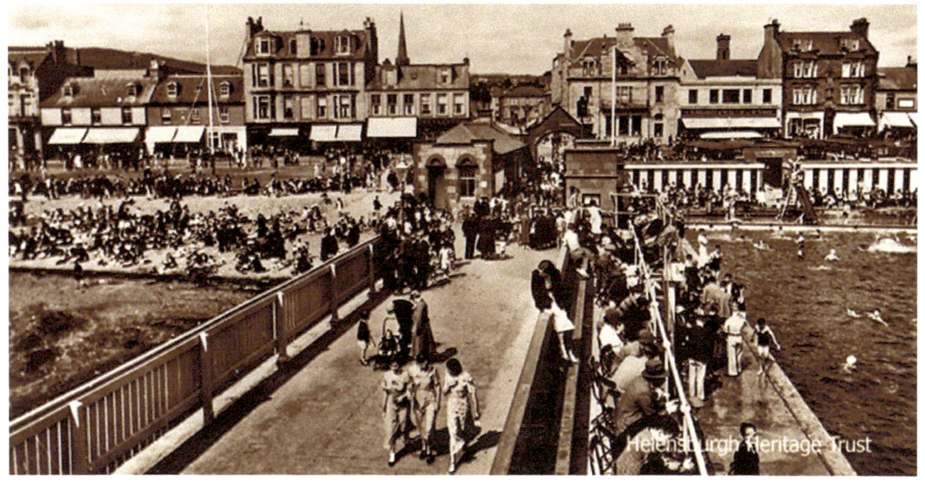

Packed Pier

The pier, swimming pool and adjacent beach and seafront are packed on this fine day in the 1930s. The area is much quieter now, but the buildings behind are little changed, apart from missing sun awnings.

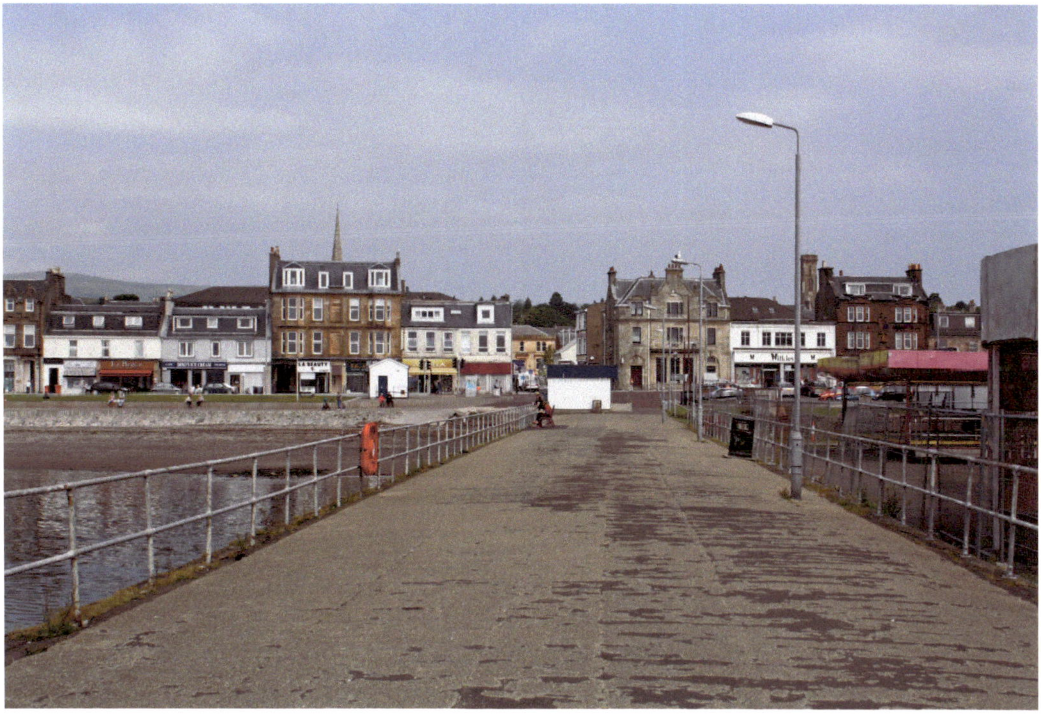

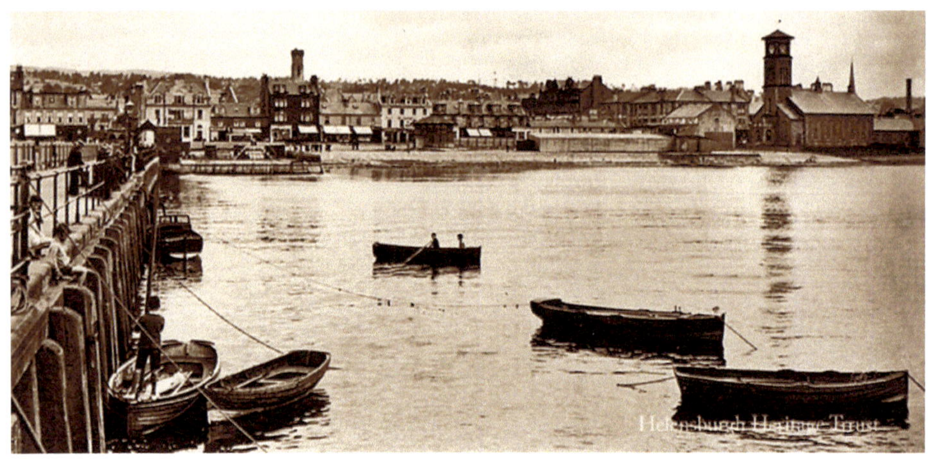

The Seafront from the Pier

While there was never any large-scale fishing from Helensburgh, the number of small boats moored off the pier show the importance of the sea to the local community. The present-day picture shows the car park on reclaimed land, which extends out over around half the length of the pier and contains an indoor swimming pool.

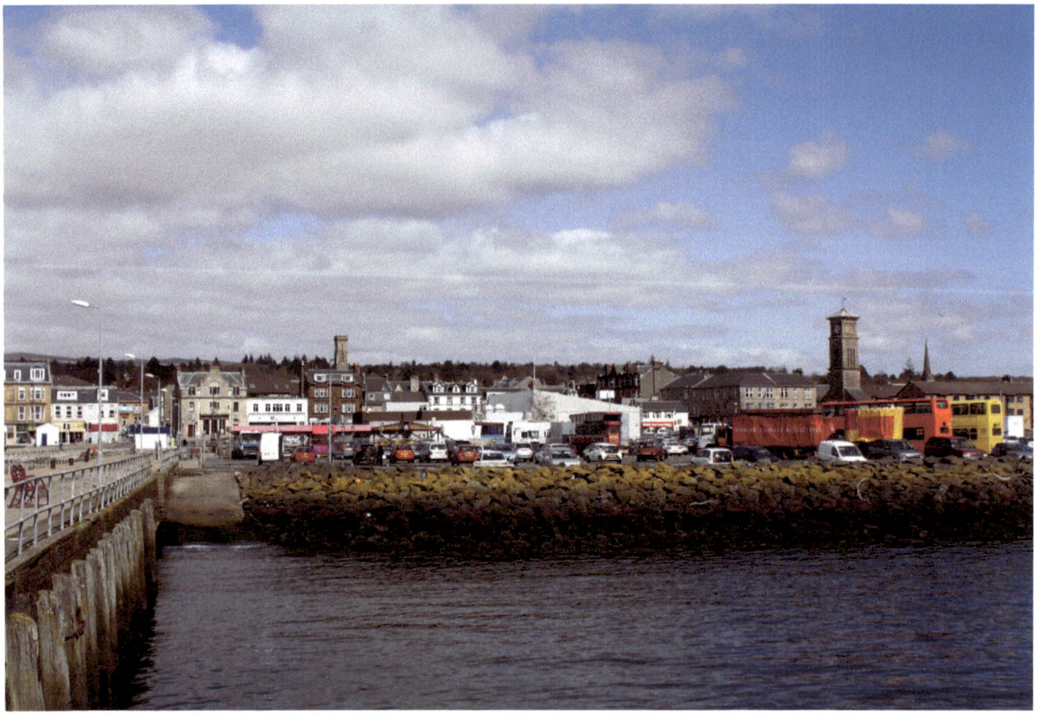

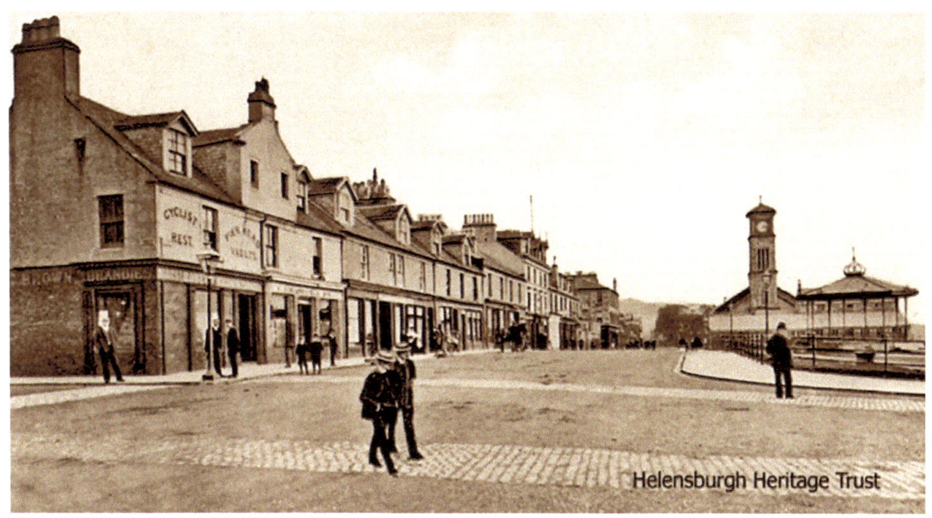

Helensburgh Heritage Trust

Colquhoun Street and West Clyde Street

The junction of West Clyde Street and Colquhoun Street in 1907, with a cobbled walkway across the road to the pier. On the corner, where there is now a three-storey shop and office block, is Robert Brown's 'Cyclist's Rest Pierhead Vaults' public house.

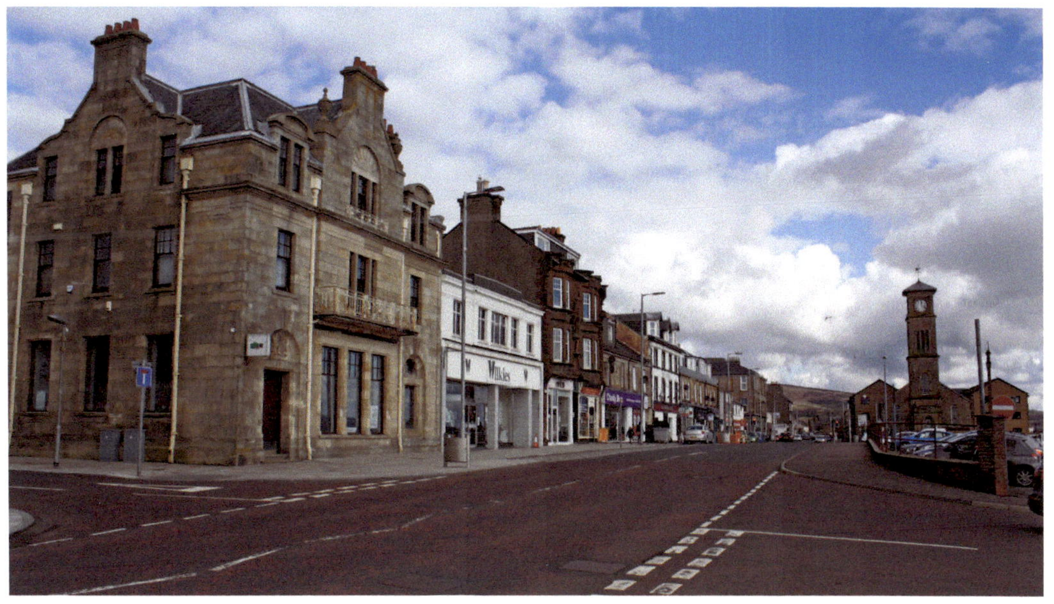

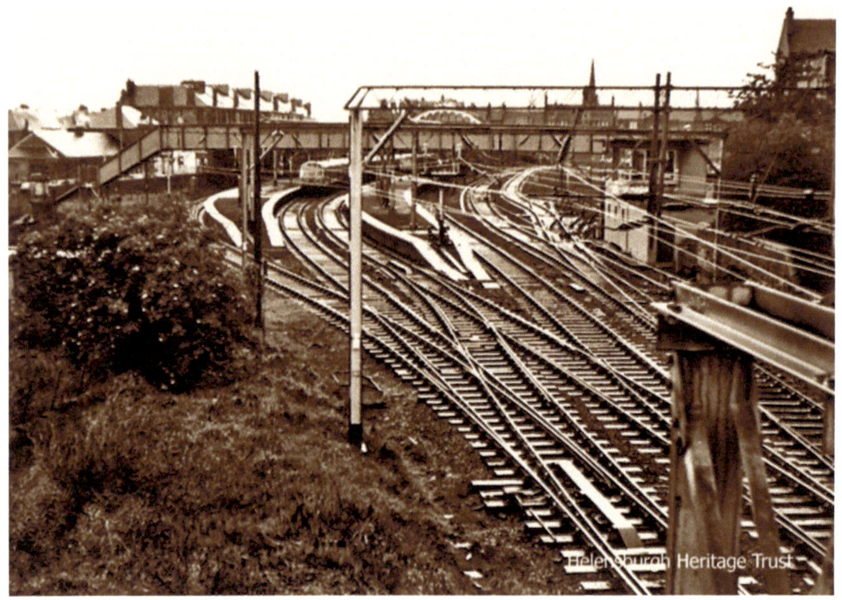

Helensburgh Central

The Glasgow Dumbarton and Helensburgh Railway came to Helensburgh in 1857, and Central Station was built in its present location in 1862; the line was the first in Scotland to be electrified in 1959. When this picture was taken in 1971, there were still marshalling yards and sidings to the right of the station on land now occupied by the Co-op and its car park.

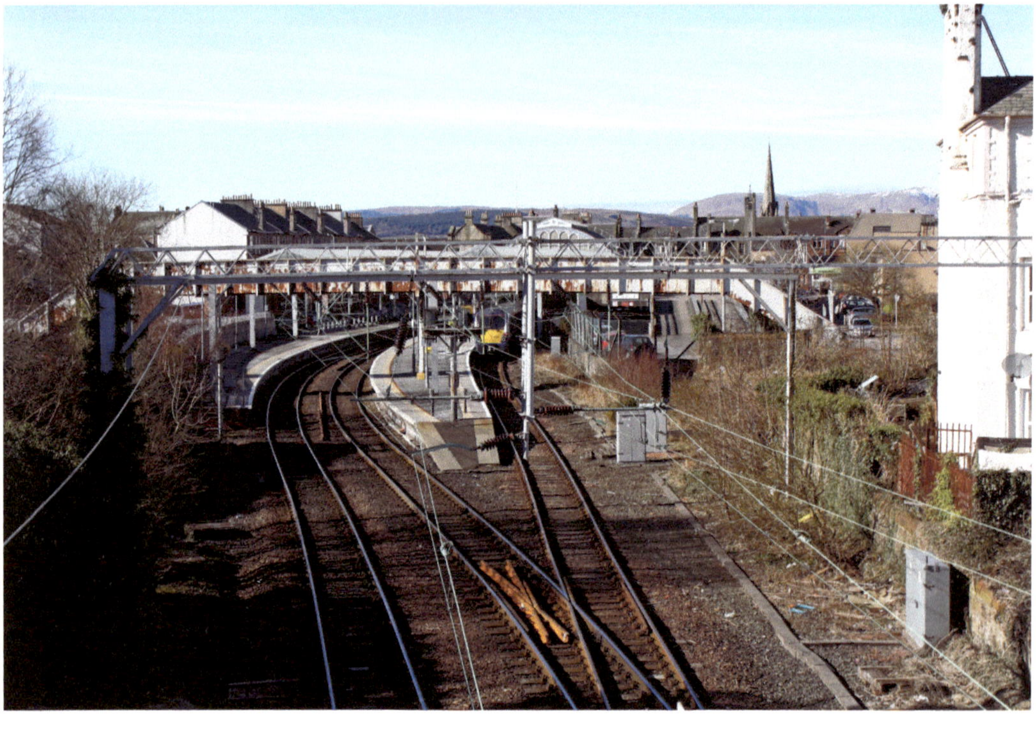

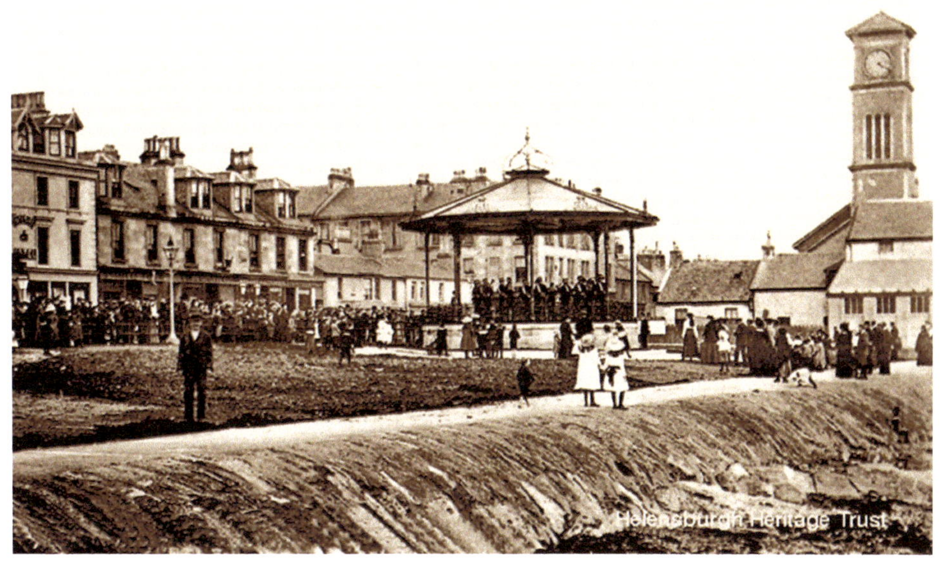

Seafront Bandstand

A Boys Brigade band gives a concert on the seafront bandstand, opposite West Clyde Street and the Eagle (now the Imperial) Hotel in 1912. The Granary, associated with Millig Mill and the Old Parish Church are on the right. The area has been absorbed into the present-day car parks.

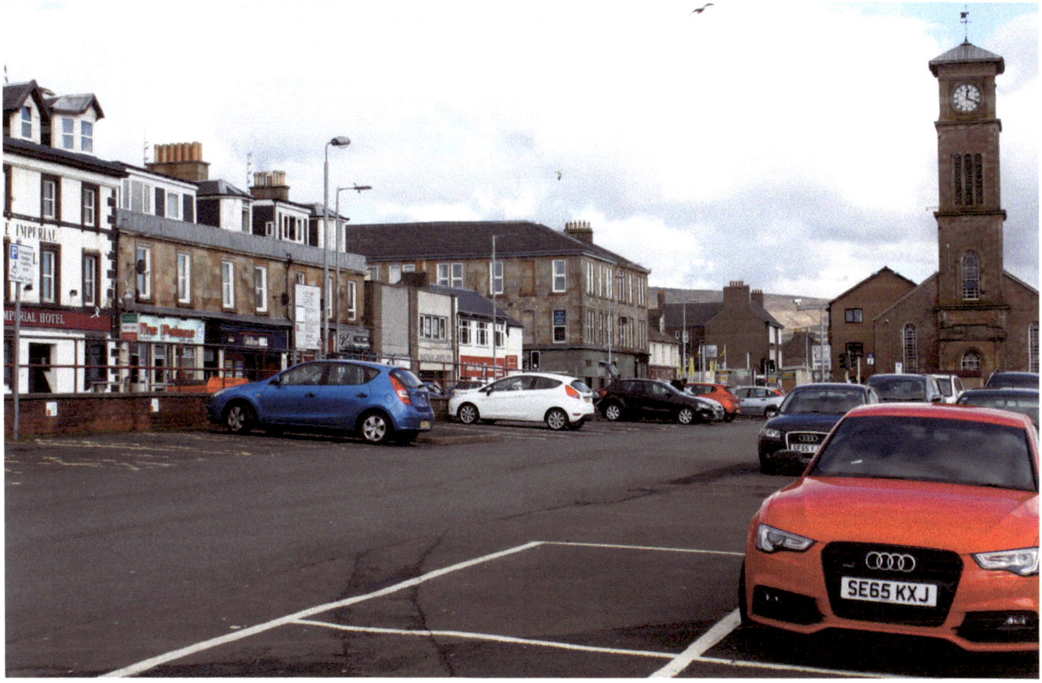

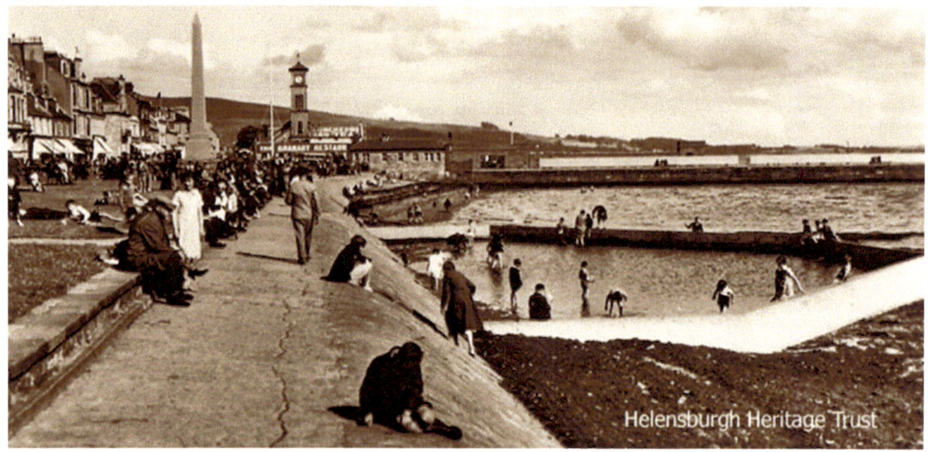

Paddling Pool

Provost Andrew Buchanan, whose family ran a large confectionary business, was a major benefactor of the town in the 1930s and donated the paddling pool at the foot of James Street in 1935 – it fell into disuse and was removed in the 1970s.

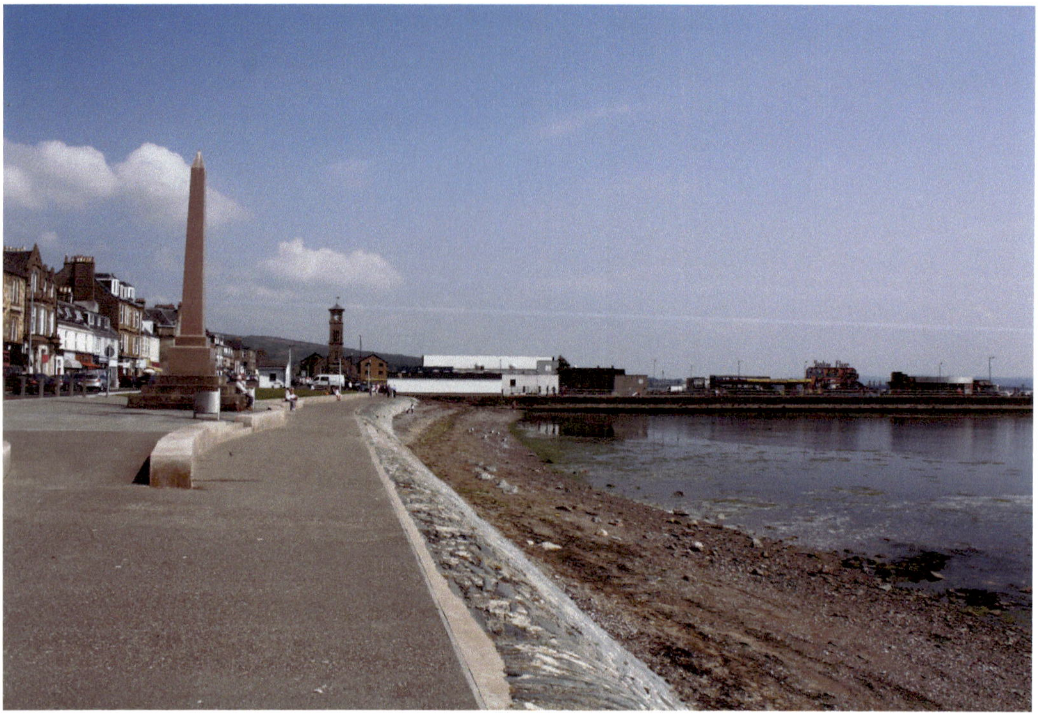

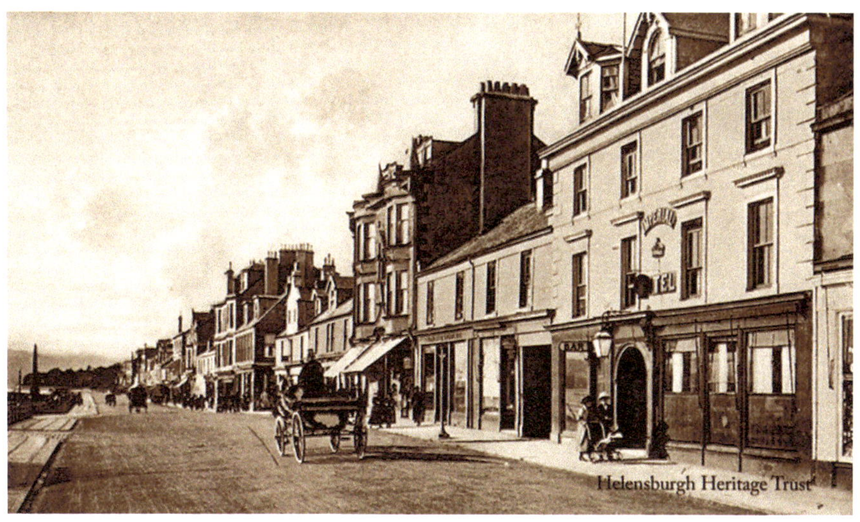

The Imperial Hotel

Originally called the Tontine Hotel and first recorded in 1833, 'The Imps' opposite the pier has long been a centre of Helensburgh life. After periods being called the George and the Eagle, it became the Imperial Hotel in 1875. To the regret of many, it closed in February 2014 and is now being refurbished.

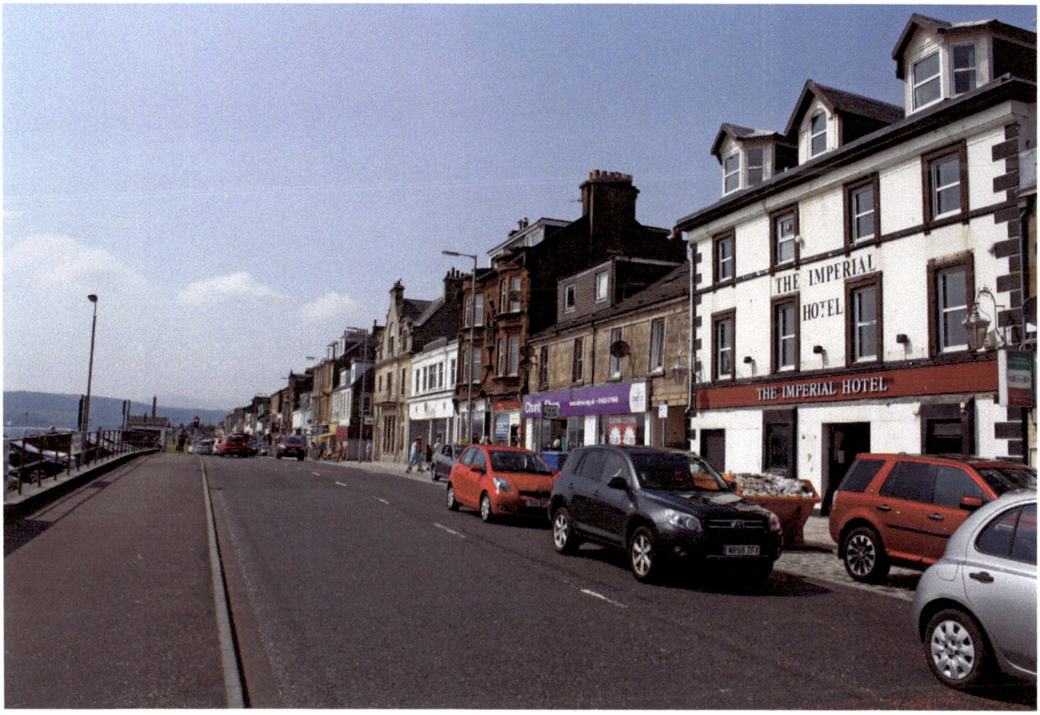

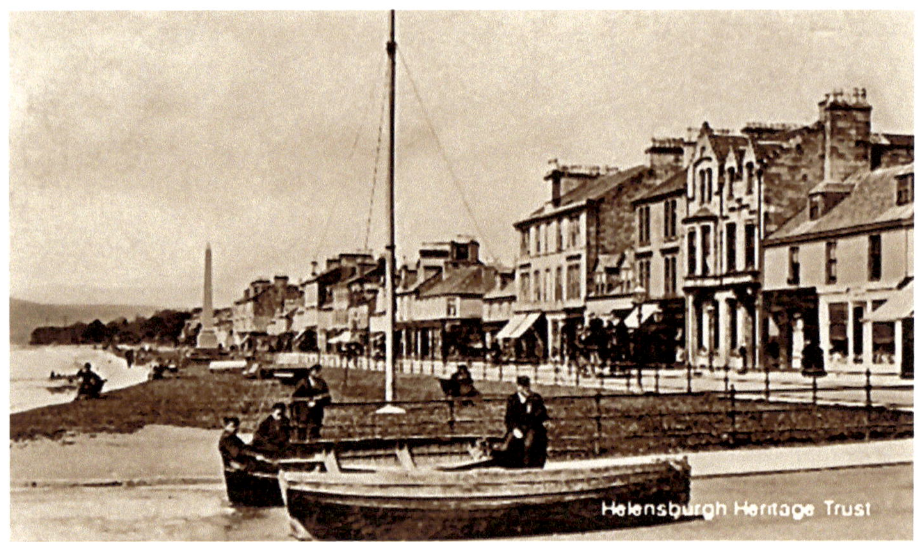

Boatmen

The boats for hire are waiting in this 1909 view of the West Esplanade from the pier head. The disc in the foreground of the present-day picture is at the end of the John Muir Way, commemorating the great naturalist who inspired the National Park movement in the USA.

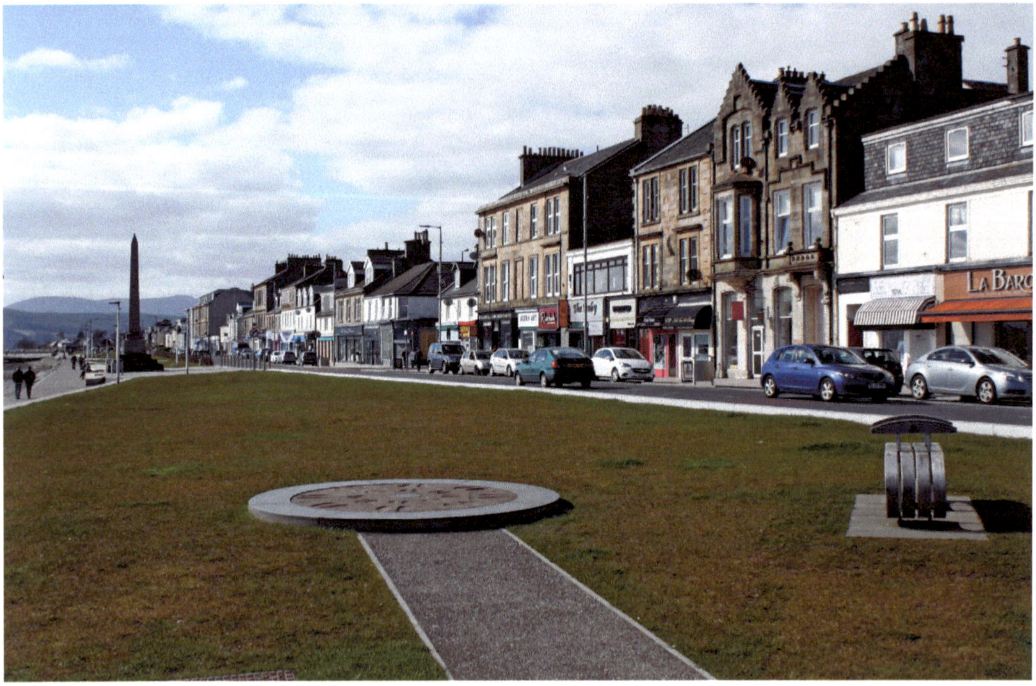

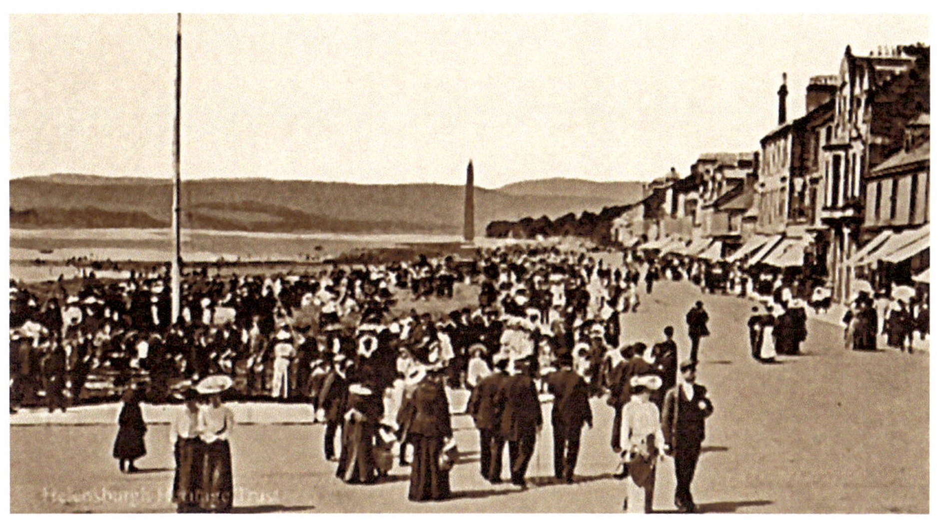

Packed Seafront

A sunny and busy day on the West Esplanade in Edwardian times. The large flagpole which was at the base of the pier has gone but the Henry Bell obelisk is still in the background.

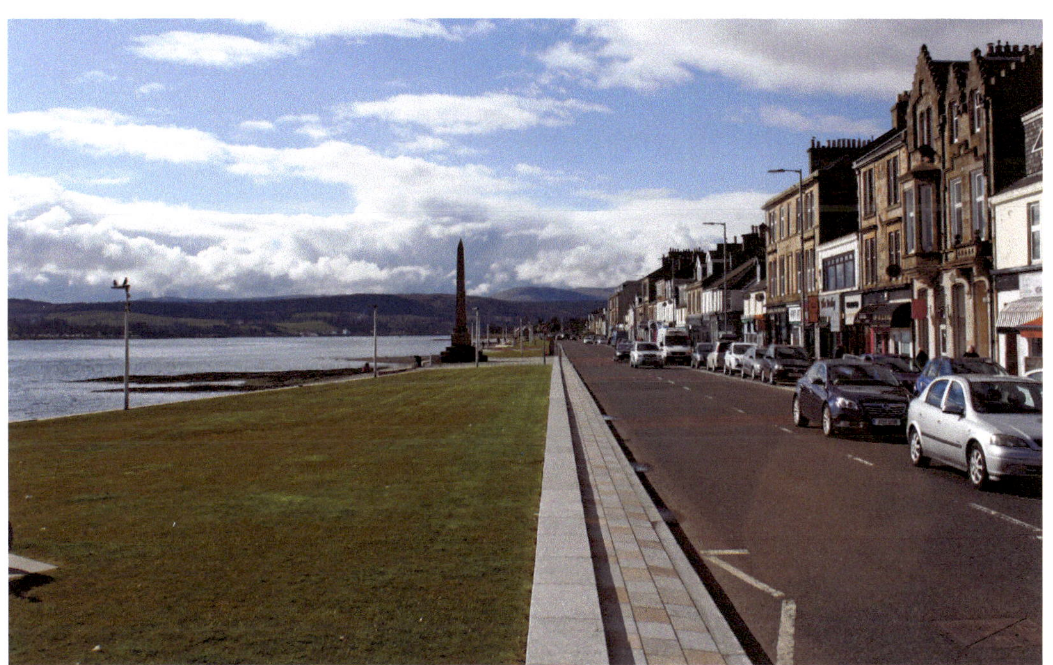

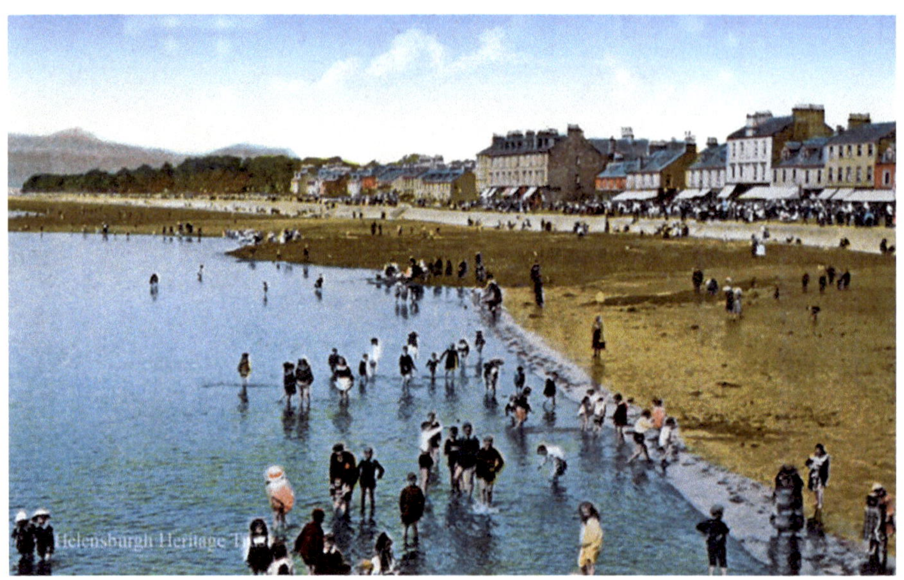

Crowded Beach

Crowds enjoy the seafront at the West Esplanade, when Helensburgh was one of the Firth of Clyde resorts frequented by visitors going 'doon the watter' from Glasgow by steamer and train. The seafront has recently been renovated, but the beach is little used as the sand has been washed away.

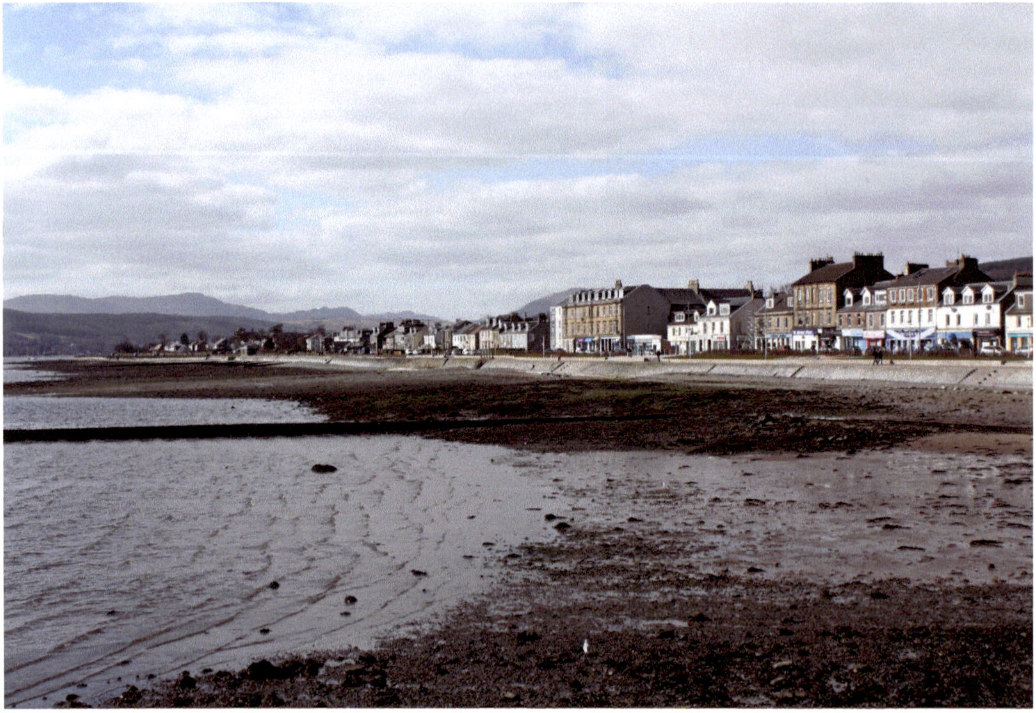

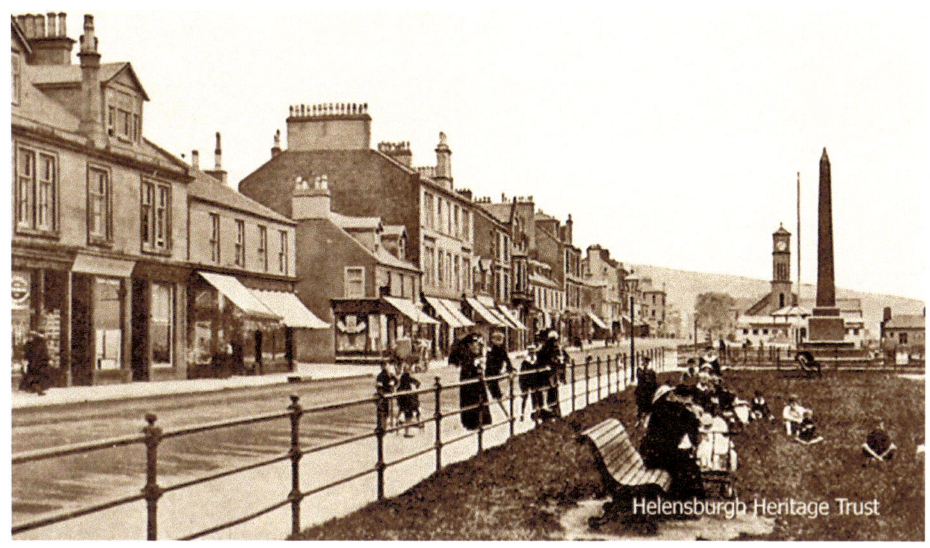

West Esplanade

A pre-First World War view of the West Esplanade looking towards the east from near the foot of James Street. The seating has now been replaced with sculptural play areas.

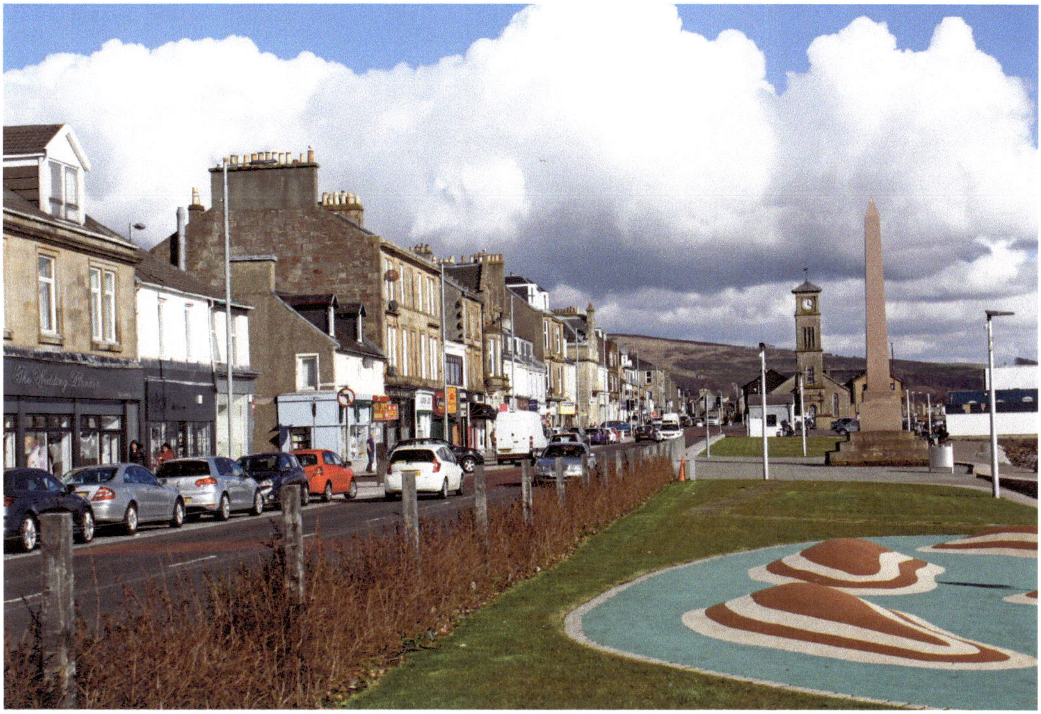

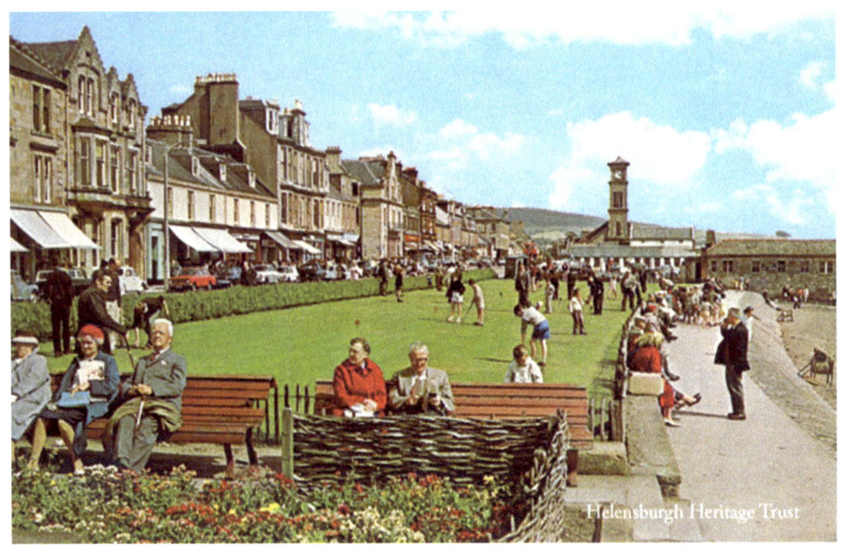

Putting Green

Looking east along West Clyde Street to the putting green on a sunny day in the 1960s. The putting green opened in 1922 but has not been replaced since the redevelopment of the seafront.

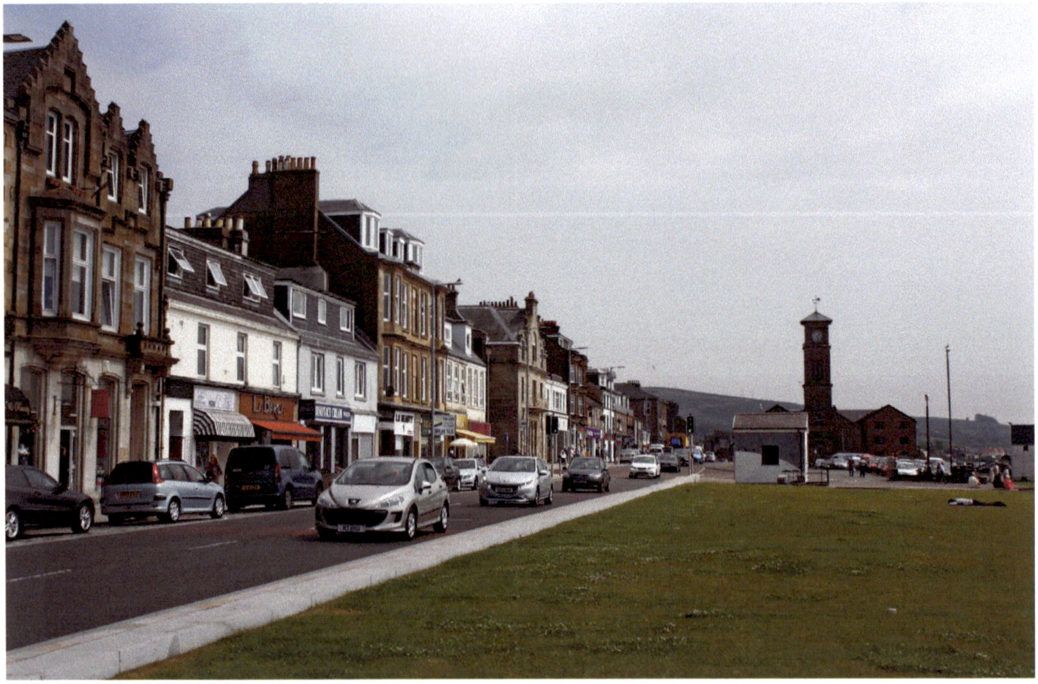

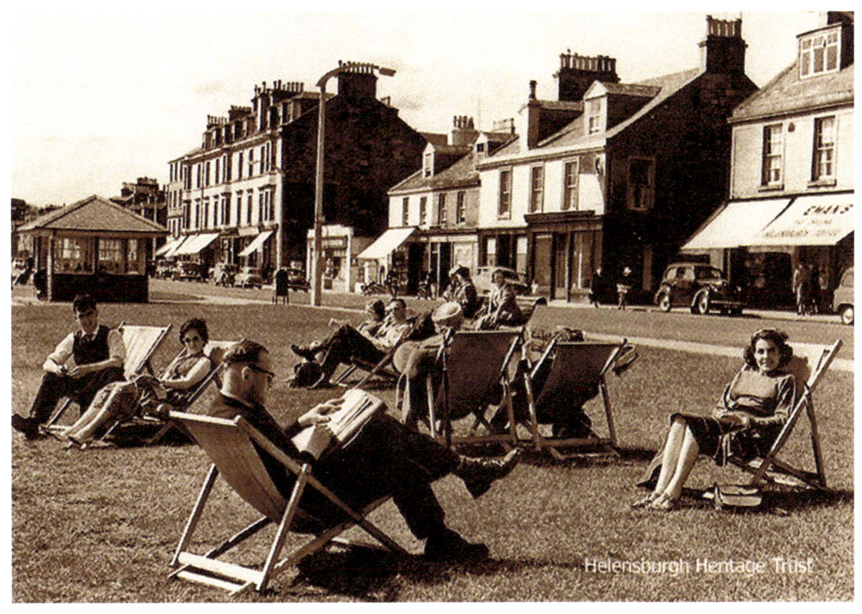

Relaxing on the Seafront

Deckchairs on the seafront provide relaxation near the foot of John Street in the 1950s; Eman's shop on the right was the home of Helensburgh Toffee. The amount of traffic along West Clyde Street now makes this area less relaxing.

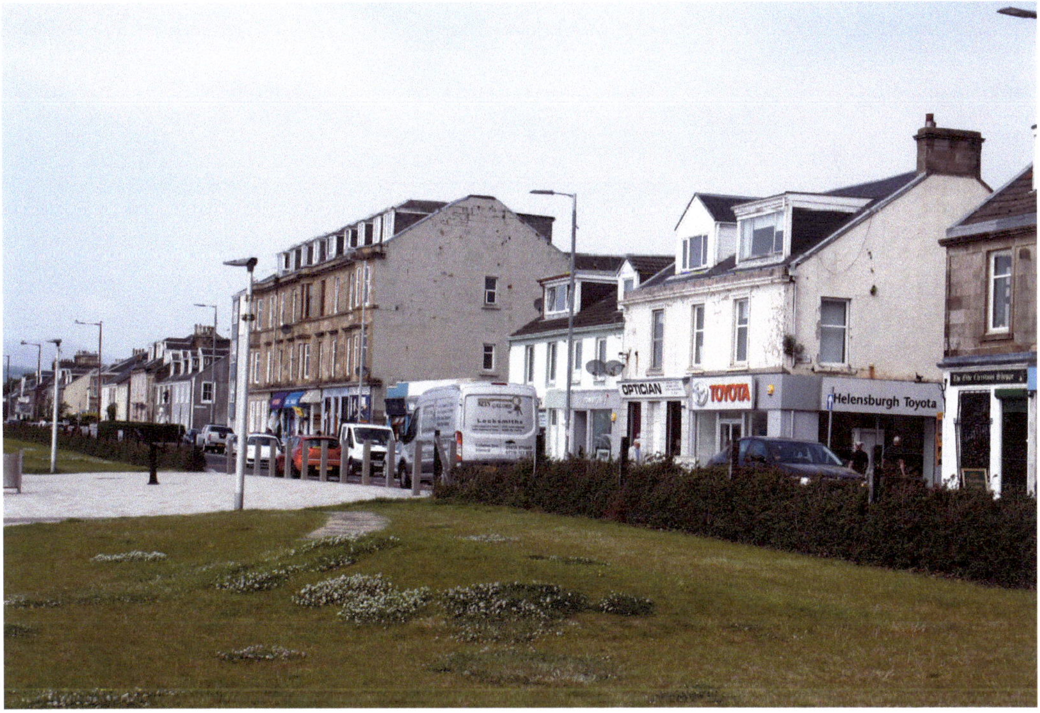

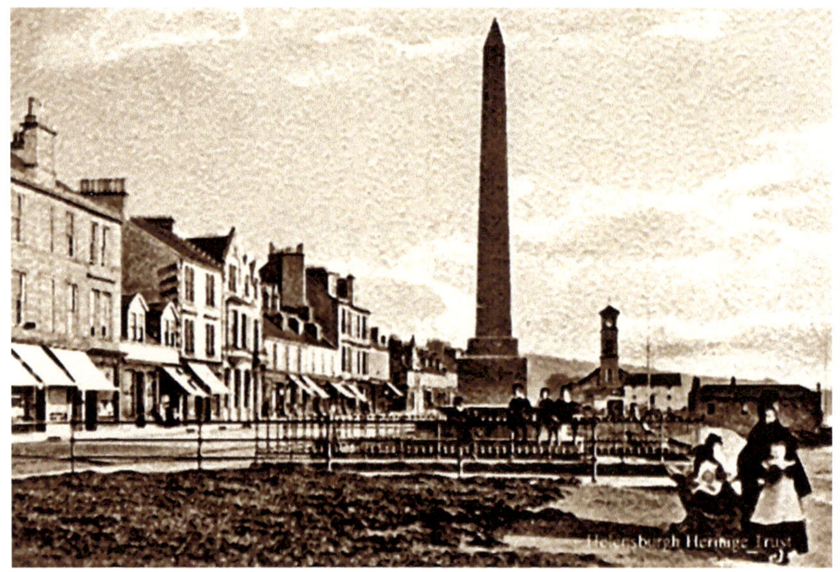

Henry Bell Obelisk

The obelisk commemorates Henry Bell, the first Provost of Helensburgh, who developed the Baths Inn, later the Queen's Hotel on the East Seafront and who introduced regular sailings to Glasgow on the *Comet*, the first seagoing steam ship in the world.

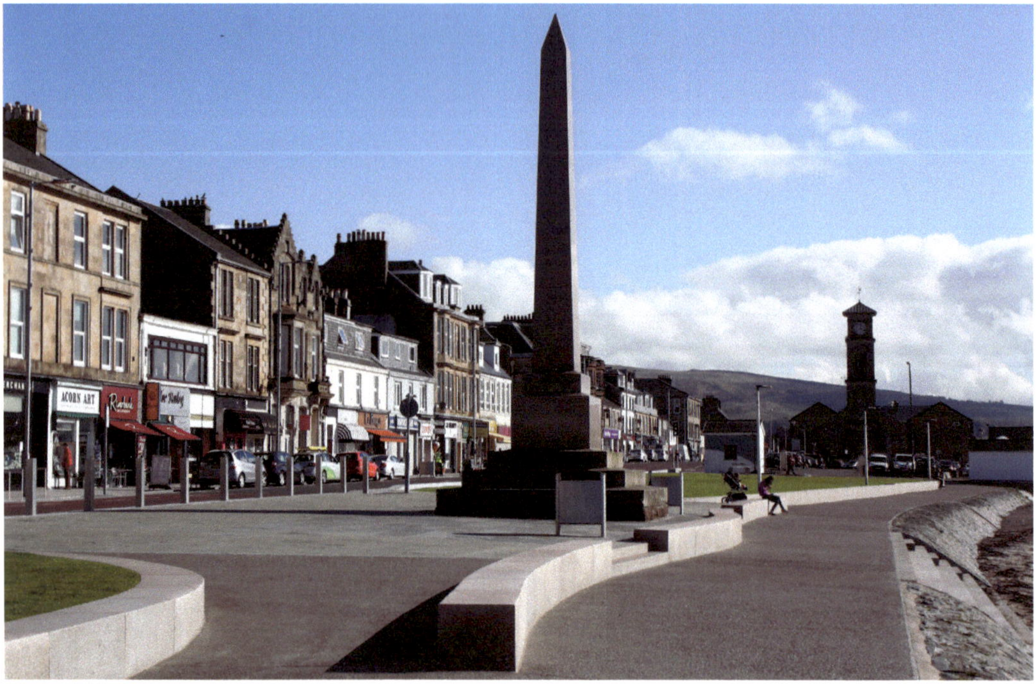

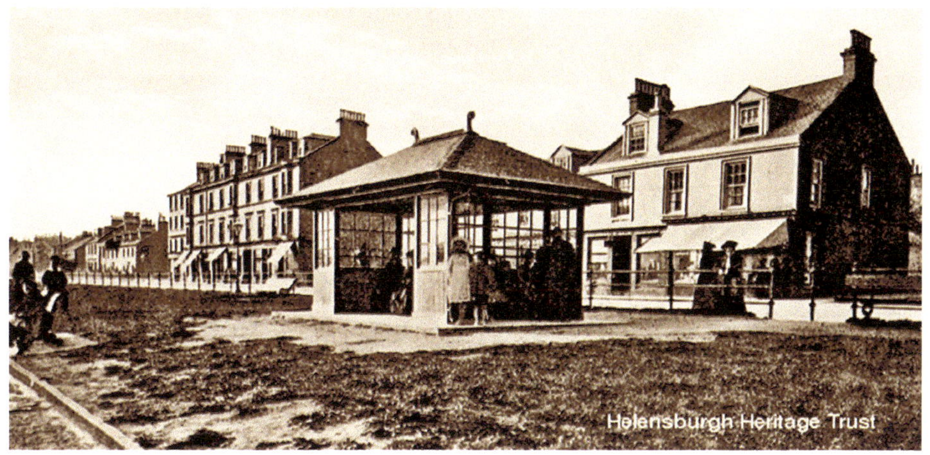

Shelter

The John Street shelter on the West Esplanade in around 1912 was one of several shelters that fell into disrepair and was demolished towards the end of the twentieth century. The seafront has recently been paved as part of an overall renovation, but the buildings behind are generally unchanged, except for the removal of chimneys.

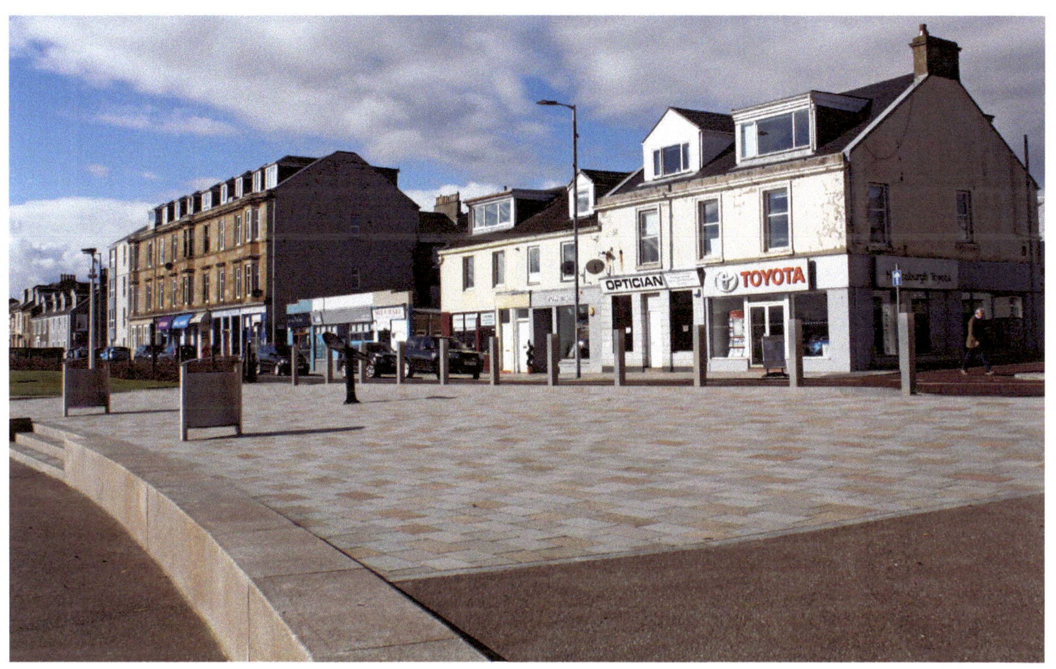

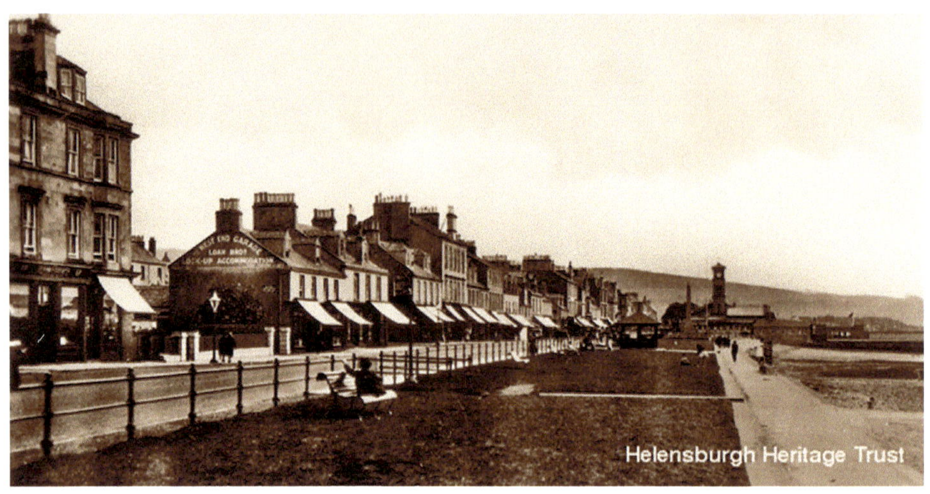

Augusta Lodge Entrance

The west-bay seafront, with railings along the prom, a shelter in the distance and an advertisement for the West End Garage on a gable wall on the far side of the road. Beside it, where the Wee Kelpie chip shop now stands, is the entrance to the former home of Lady Augusta Clavering, eldest daughter of the 5th Duke of Argyll. It was a plain, substantial house, built around 1804, with a grass plot in front and an iron railing next to the street.

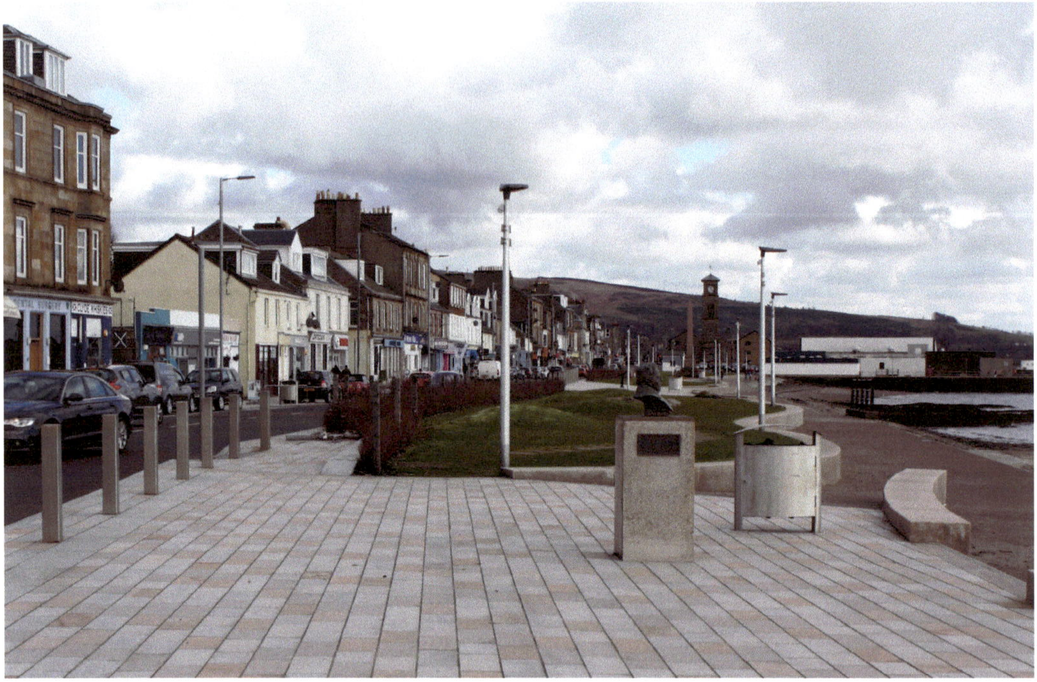

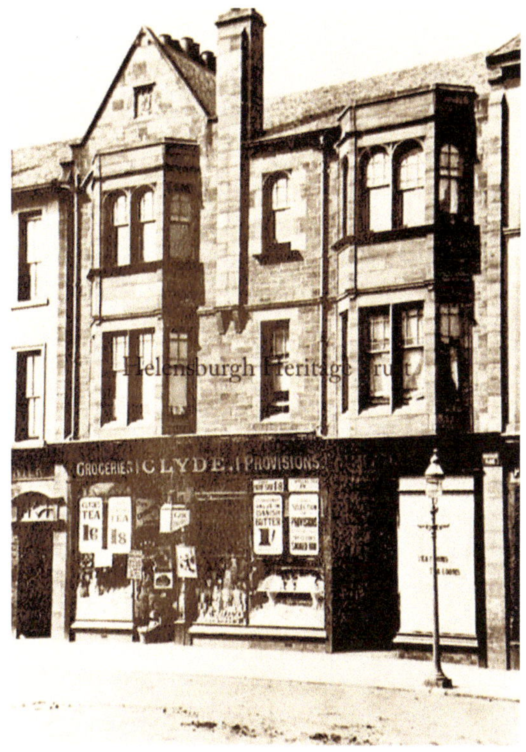

Grocers

The R. M. Clyde grocery at Nos 64 and 66 West Princes Street. The red-sandstone building was called Waverley Place, designed by Robert Wemyss and built in 1897, opposite the post office. Next door to the shop is the tearoom of McAdam the baker, now a hardware shop and a hairdressers.

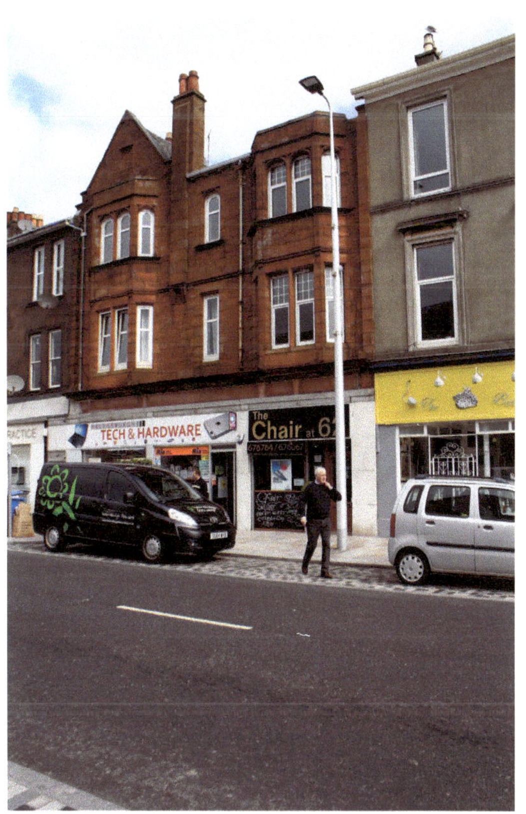

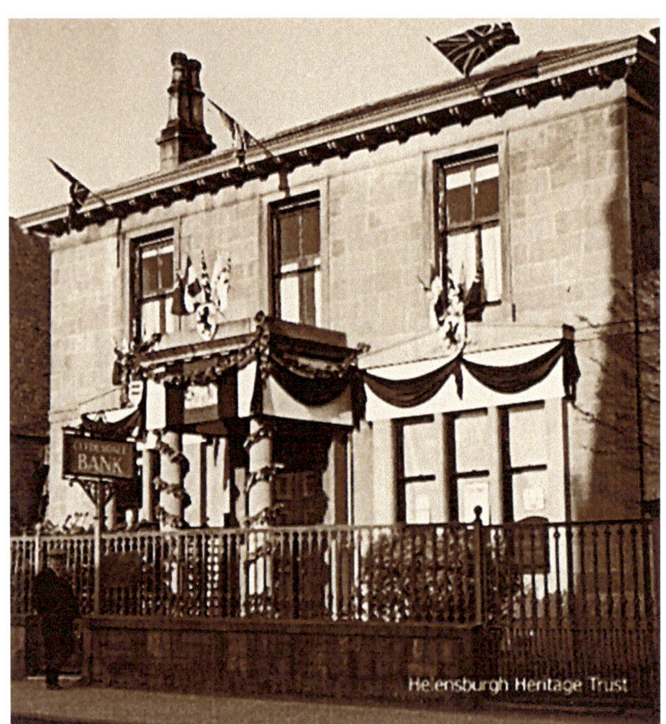

Clydesdale Bank

In 1857, the Clydesdale Banking Co. built these handsome offices in James Street. The presence of the metal railings outside the bank show that the photo was taken before the Second World War, as metal railings were removed during the war as part of the war effort. The bank is covered in flags, probably to commemorate either the Silver Jubilee of George V in 1935 or the coronation of George VI two years later. The branch is now closed and the building for sale.

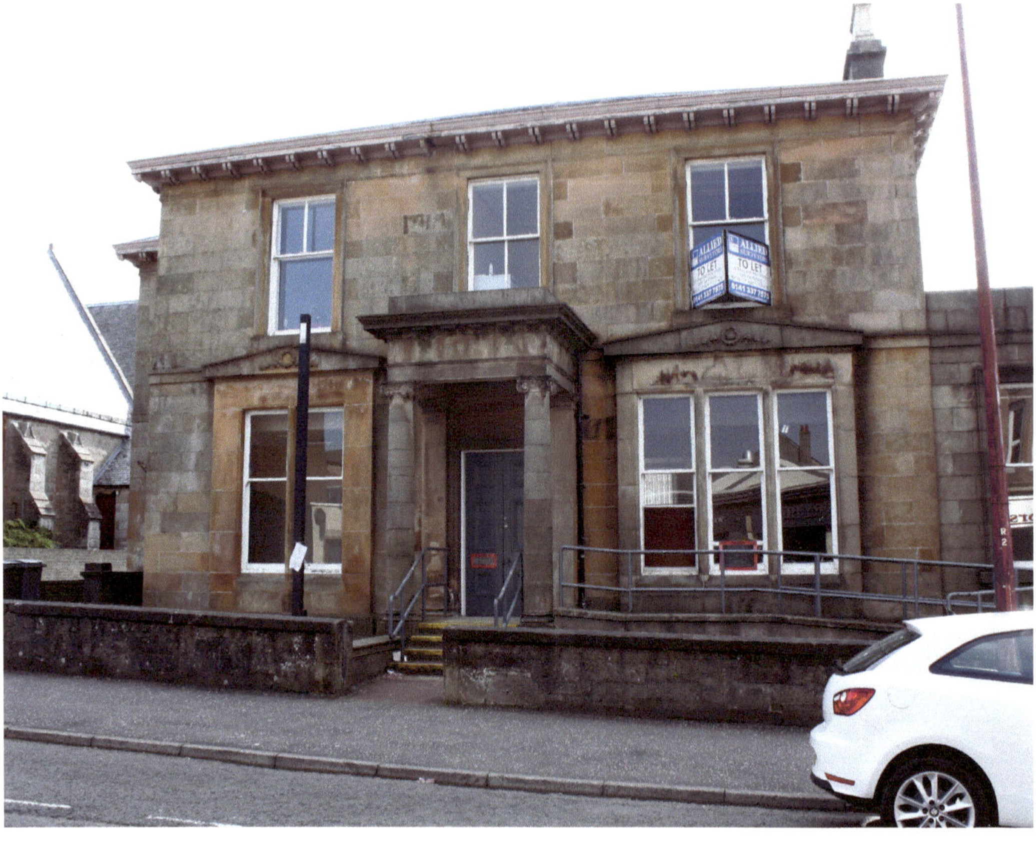

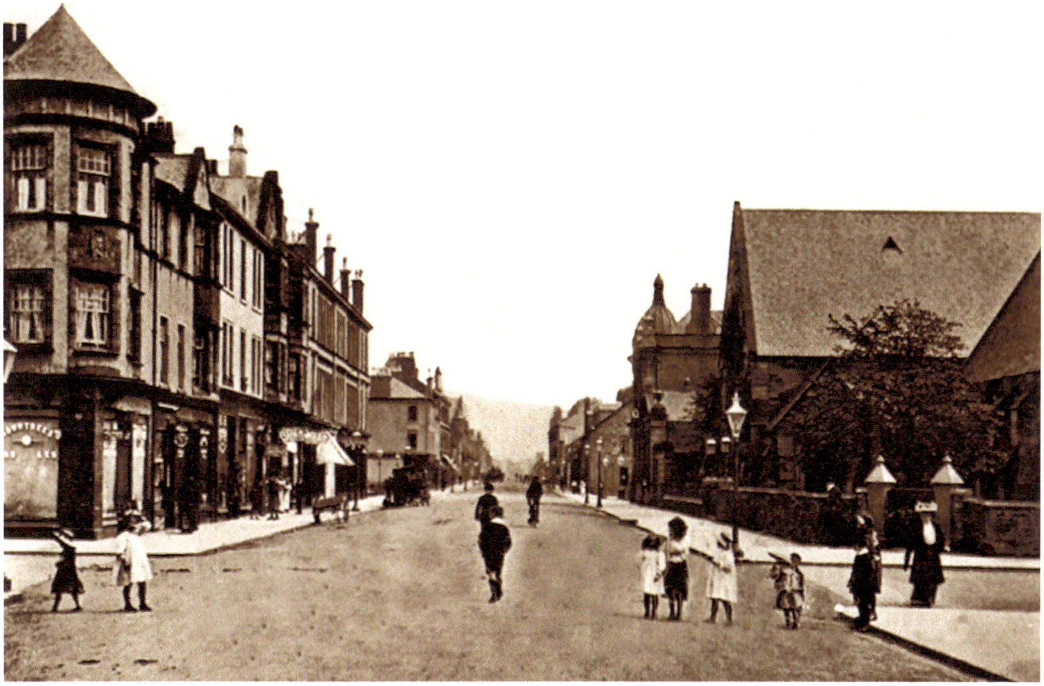

West Princes Street

Children played in the street at the junction between West Princes Street and James Street, with the United Reformed Church on the left and the Post Office beyond. Provision for car parking has reduced the present width of the carriageway.

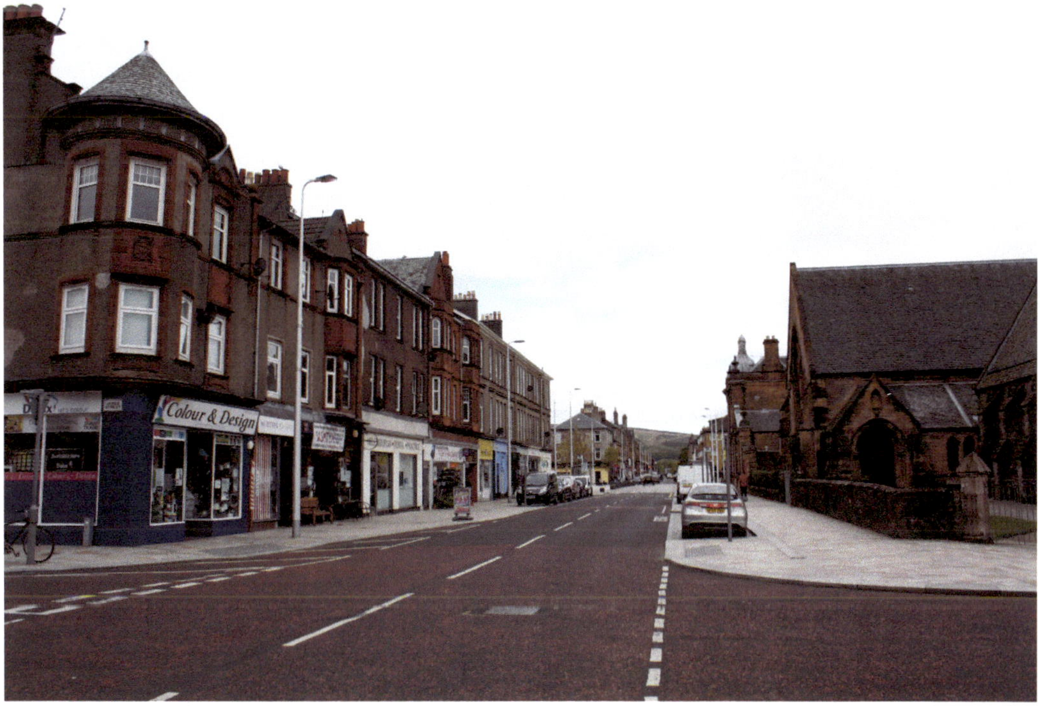

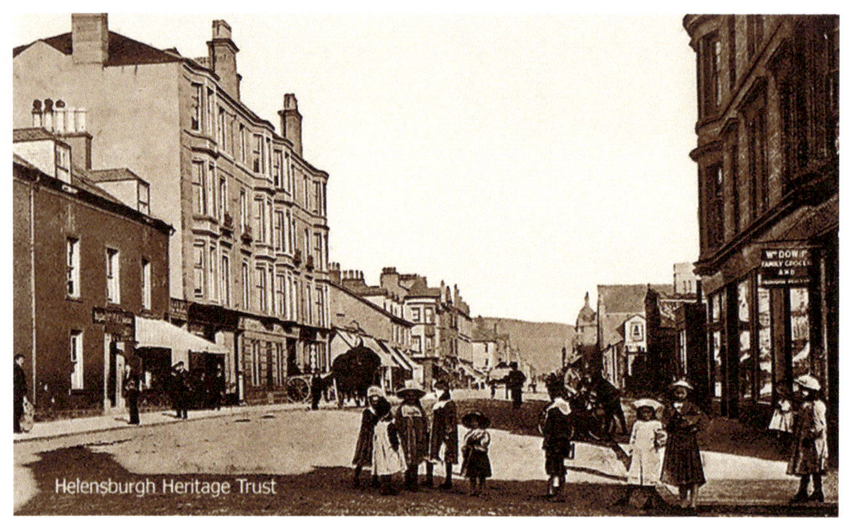

Children Crossing

Children prepare to cross West Princes Street at the junction with John Street in 1916. The post office dome is still visible in the distance on the right, but new flats over council offices obscure the United Reformed Church.

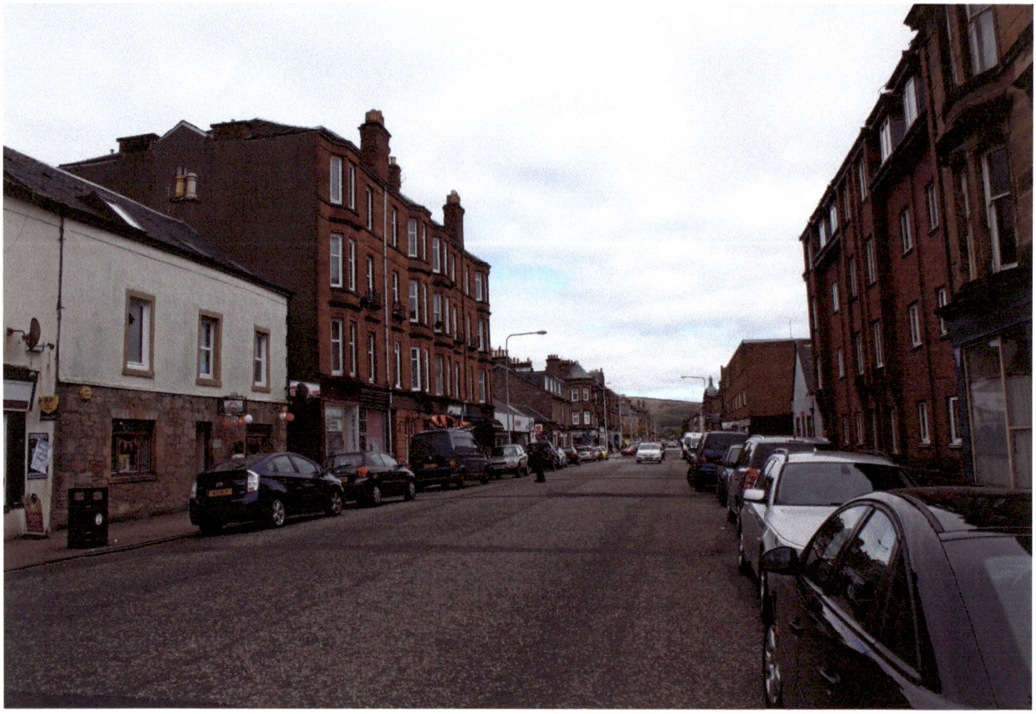

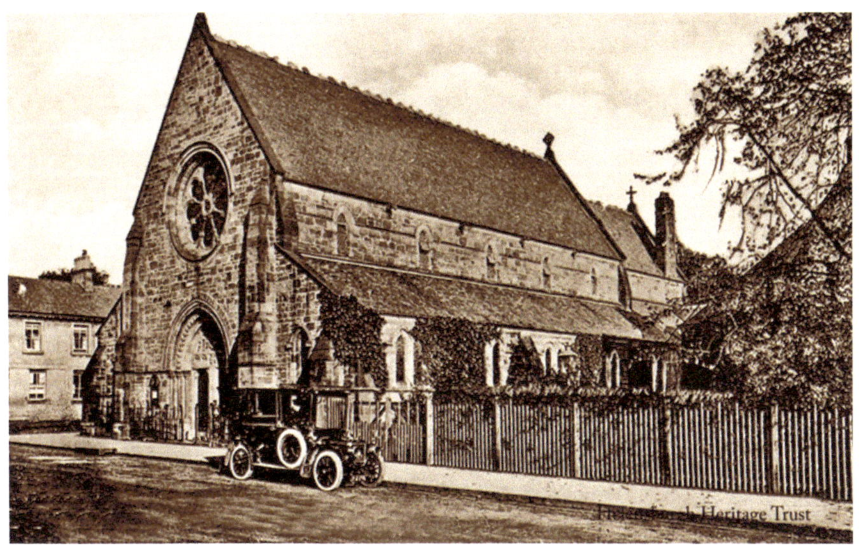

St Michael and All Angels

Sir Robert Rowand Anderson, a pupil of George Gilbert Scott, designed St Michael and All Angels Scottish Episcopal Church, at the corner of William Street and West Princes Street. Among the important contributors to the cost of its erection in 1867 was William Gladstone. The tower was added in 1930 and the church was extensively refurbished with the aid of the Heritage Lottery Fund from 2007 to 2012.

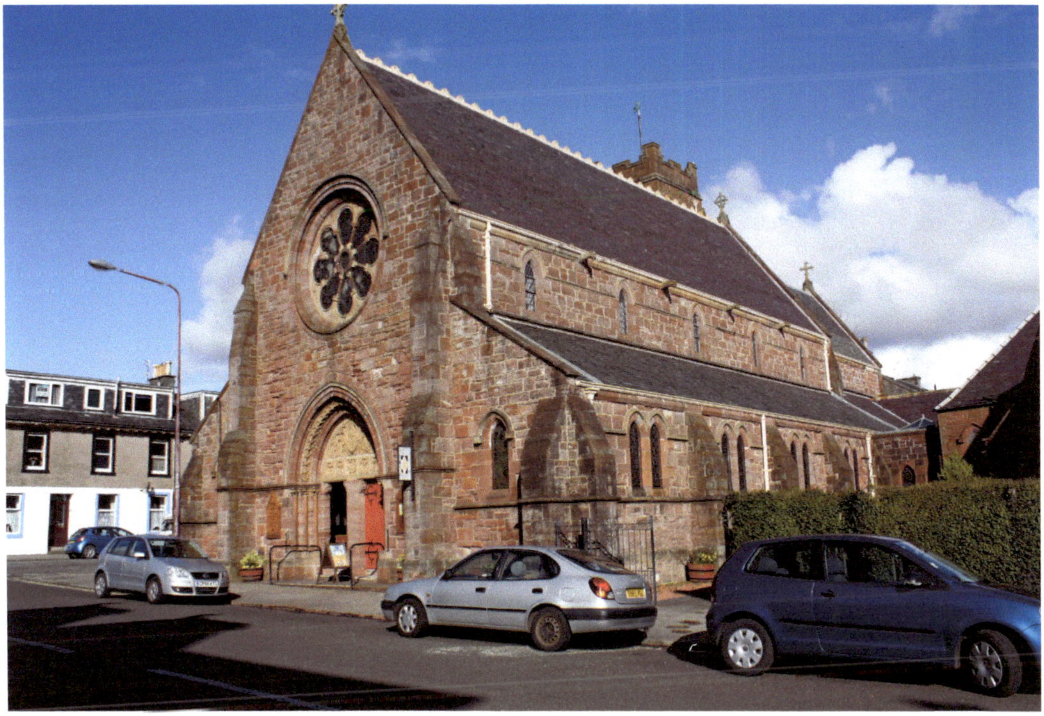

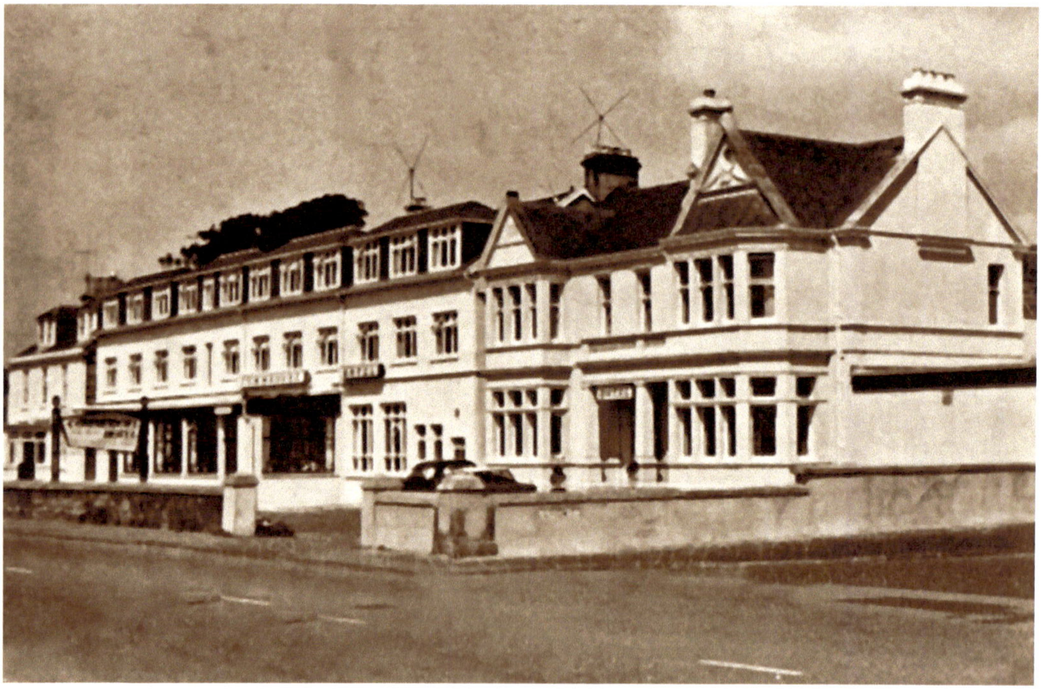

The Commodore

Formerly the Kingsclere Hotel, the Commodore Hotel on the west seafront in 1968. It was burnt down during the firemen's strike in December 1978 when soldiers in Green Goddesses attended the middle-of-the-night blaze which was fanned by strong winds. Most of the hotel was destroyed, but it was rebuilt and has since been altered and extended several times.

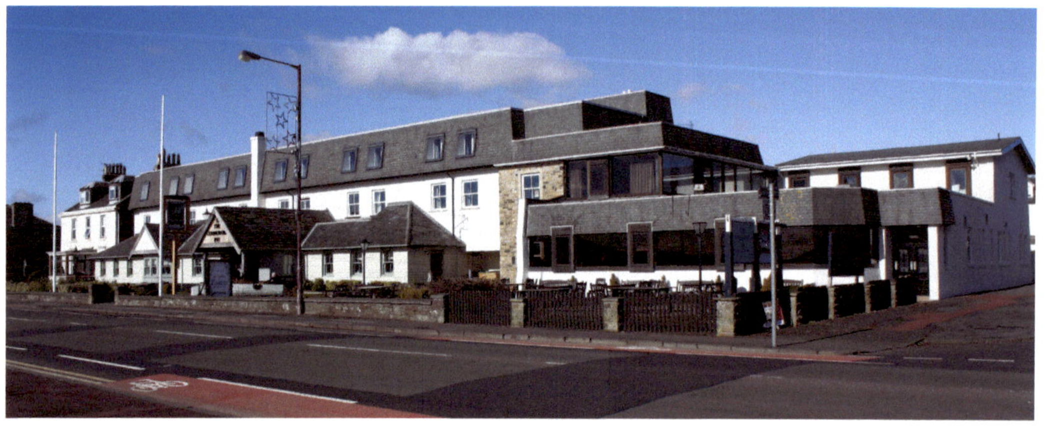

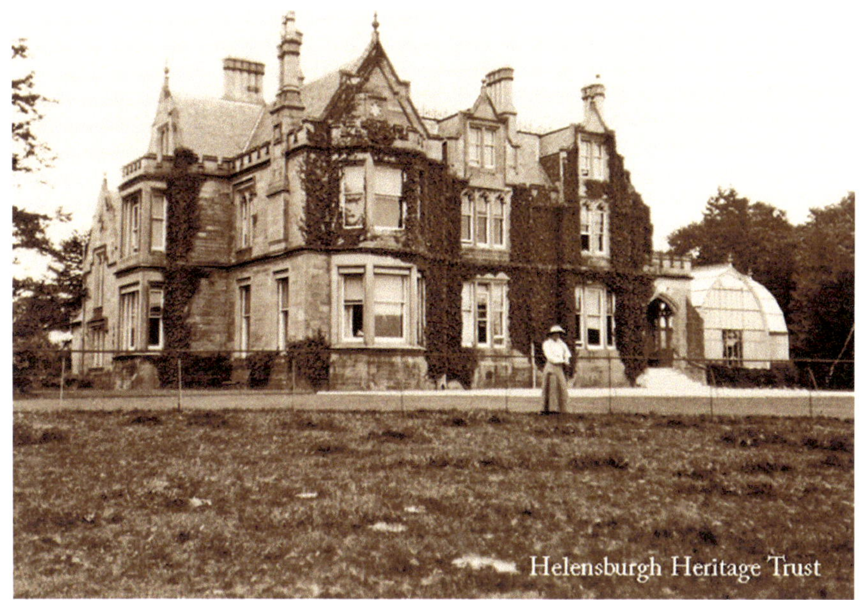

Ferniegair

Ferniegair on West Clyde Street, immediately east of Cairndhu, was built in 1869 by architect John Honeyman for the Kidston family who were closely involved in shipping, potteries and other businesses; they donated the land to form Kidston Park. The house was demolished in the 1960s and replaced with housing, which retains the name of the house in one of the streets.

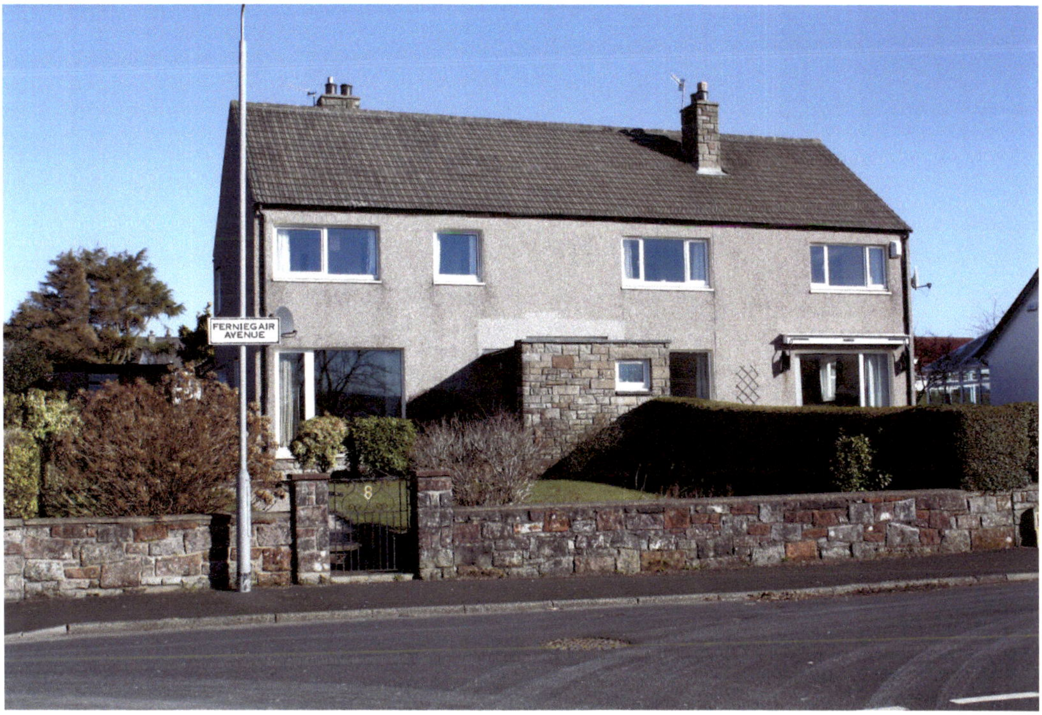

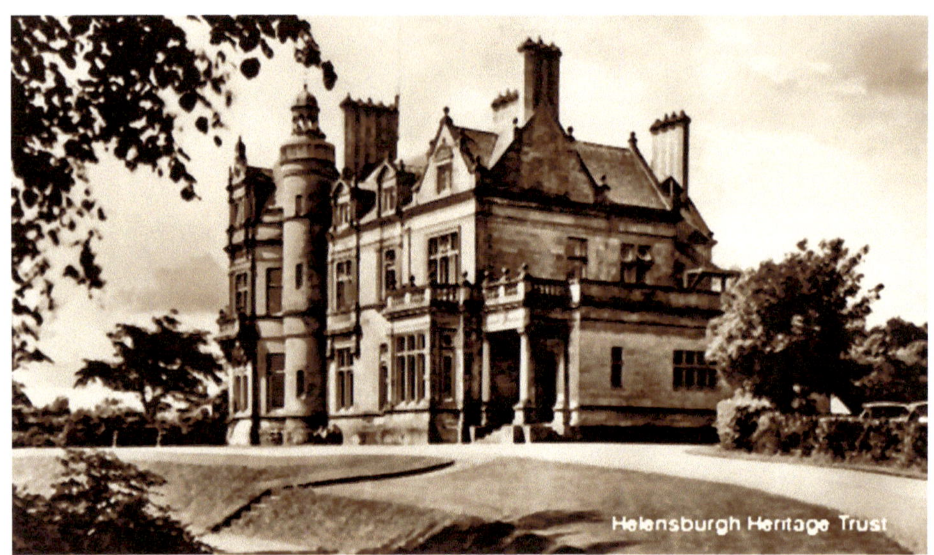

Cairndhu

Cairndhu House was built in 1871 to a William Leiper design in the style of a grand chateau with black-and-gold Japanese-style interiors for John Ure, Provost of Glasgow, whose son became Lord Strathclyde and lived in the mansion. It became the Cairndhu Hotel and later a nursing home but is currently disused.

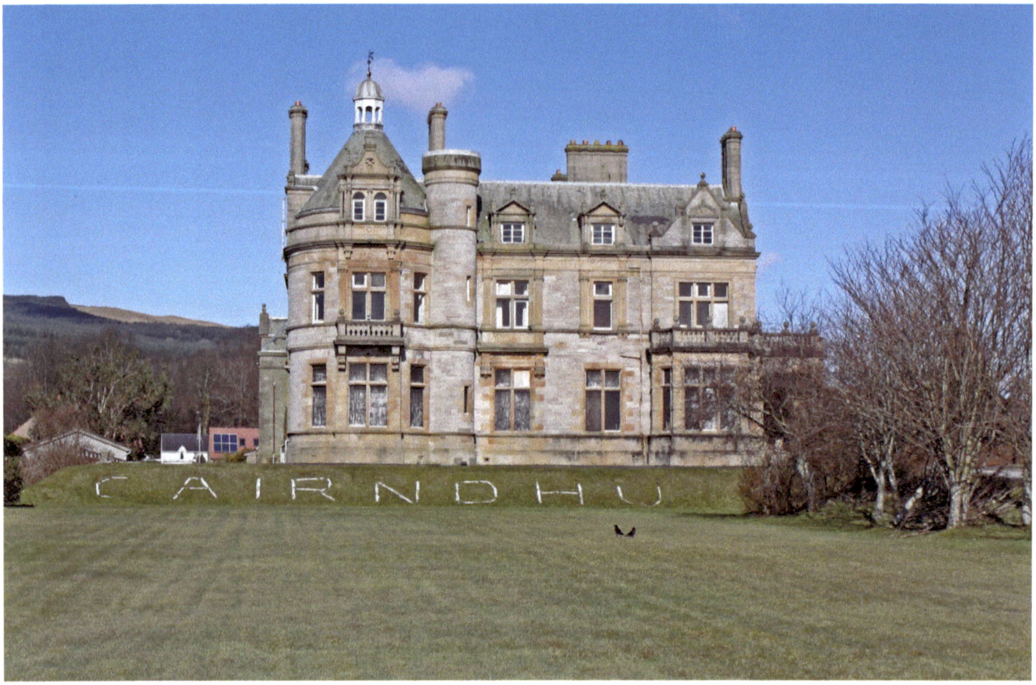

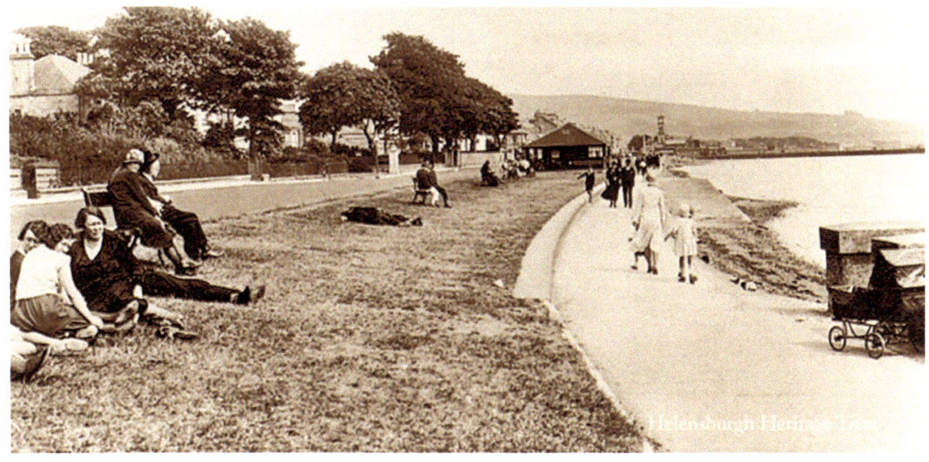

West Esplanade

Relaxing on the grass of the West Esplanade in 1935, with mature trees in the gardens of the villas and one of the now-demolished shelters in the distance.

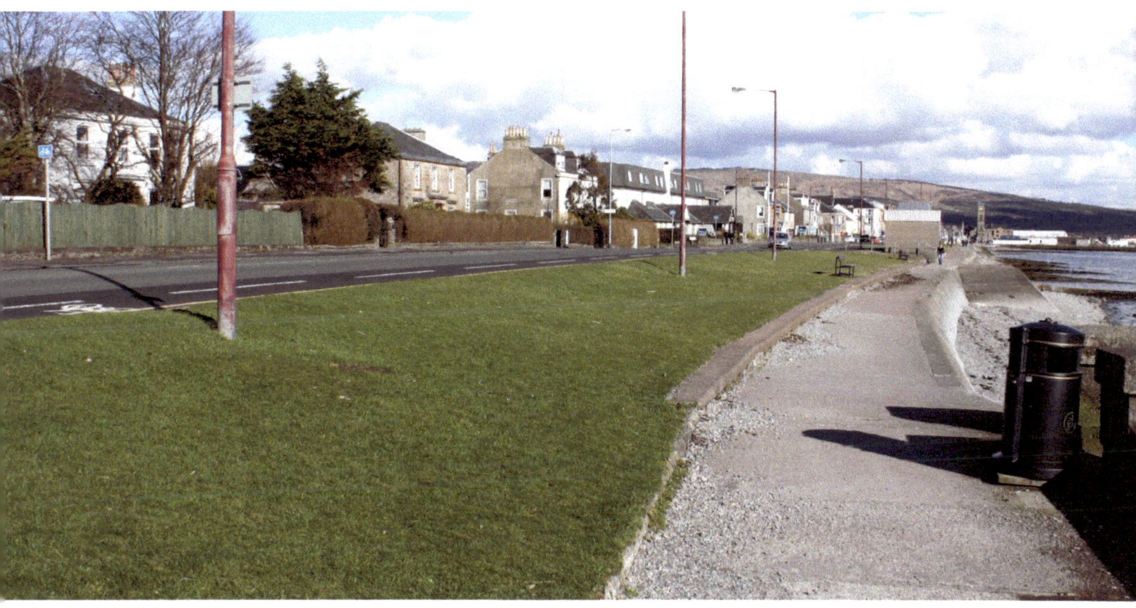

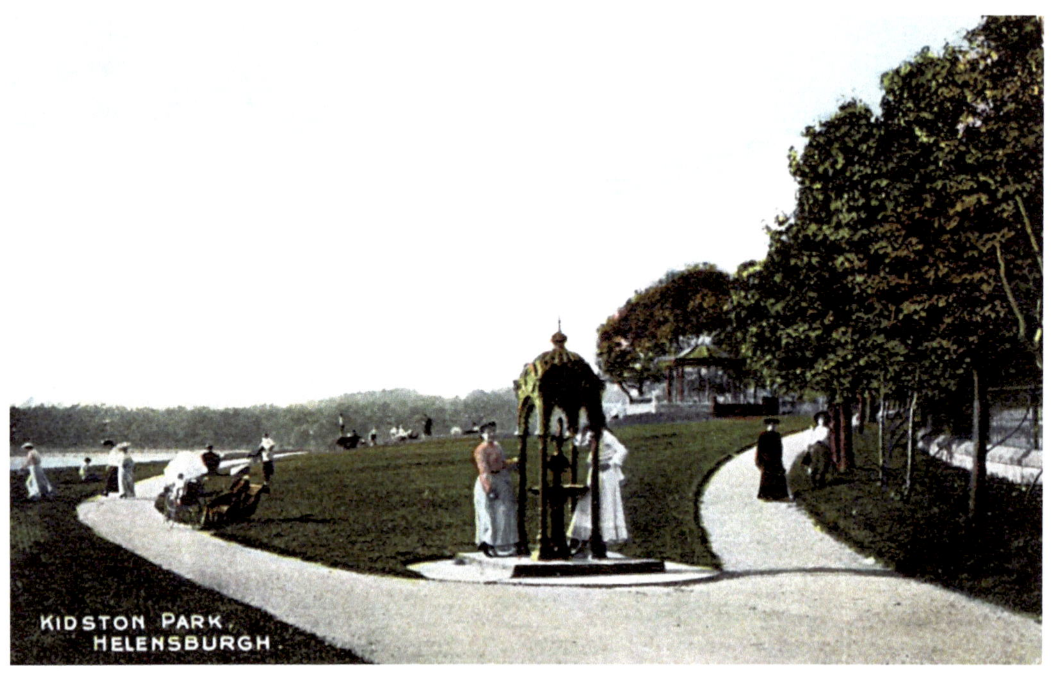

Kidston Park

Originally Cairndhu Point but known locally as Neddy's Point after a well-known fisherman and ferryman who lived nearby, Kidston Park at the end of West Clyde Street was bought from the Duke of Argyll in 1877 for £650 by William Kidston and was renamed from 1889 when he left money to support its maintenance and requested the name change. There is now a very popular café on the point.

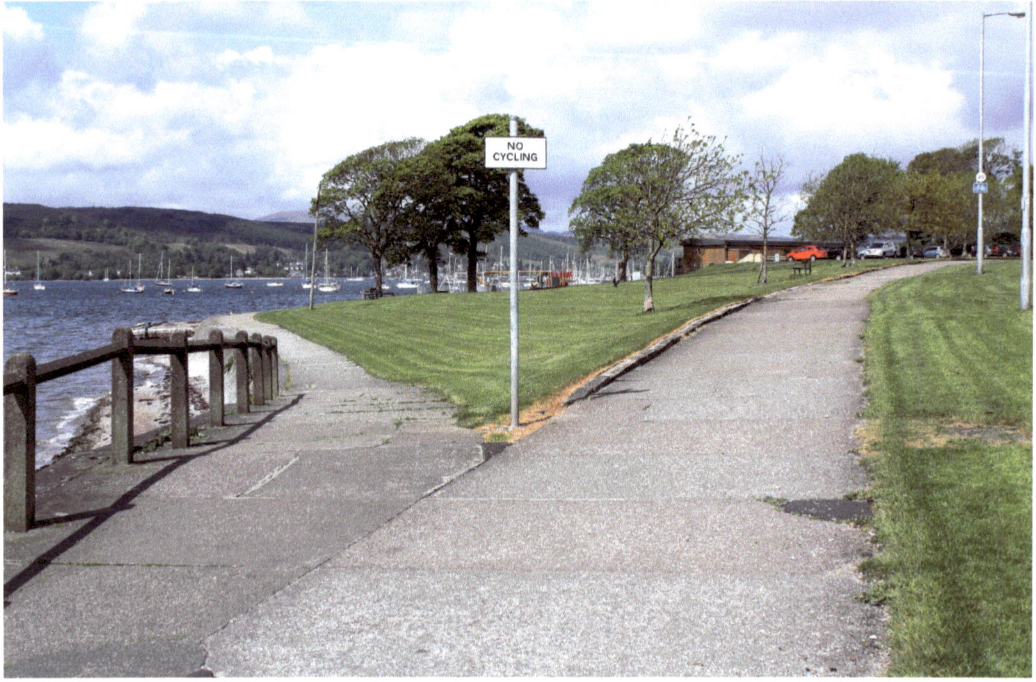

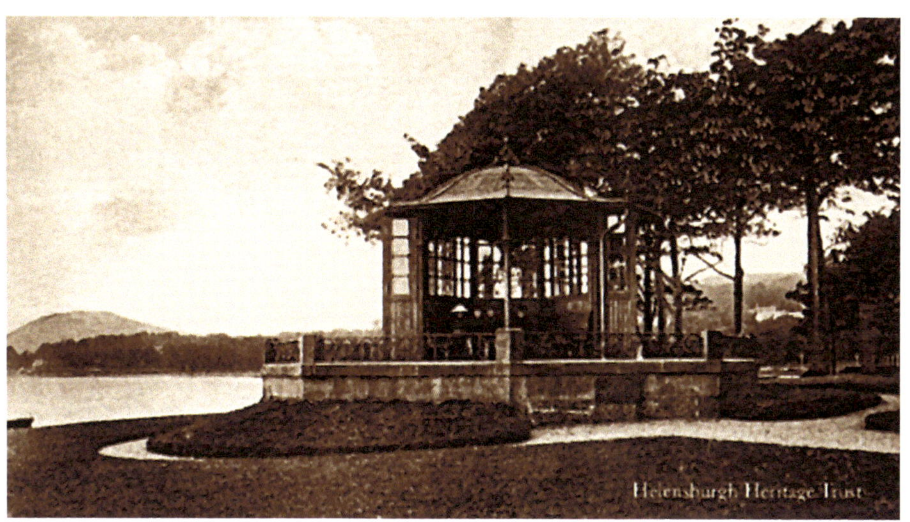

Kidston Bandstand

Only the foundations of the bandstand, where the boy bands from the training ships *Empress* and *Cumberland* used to perform, remain at Kidston Park. There is now a well-used children's play area in the park.

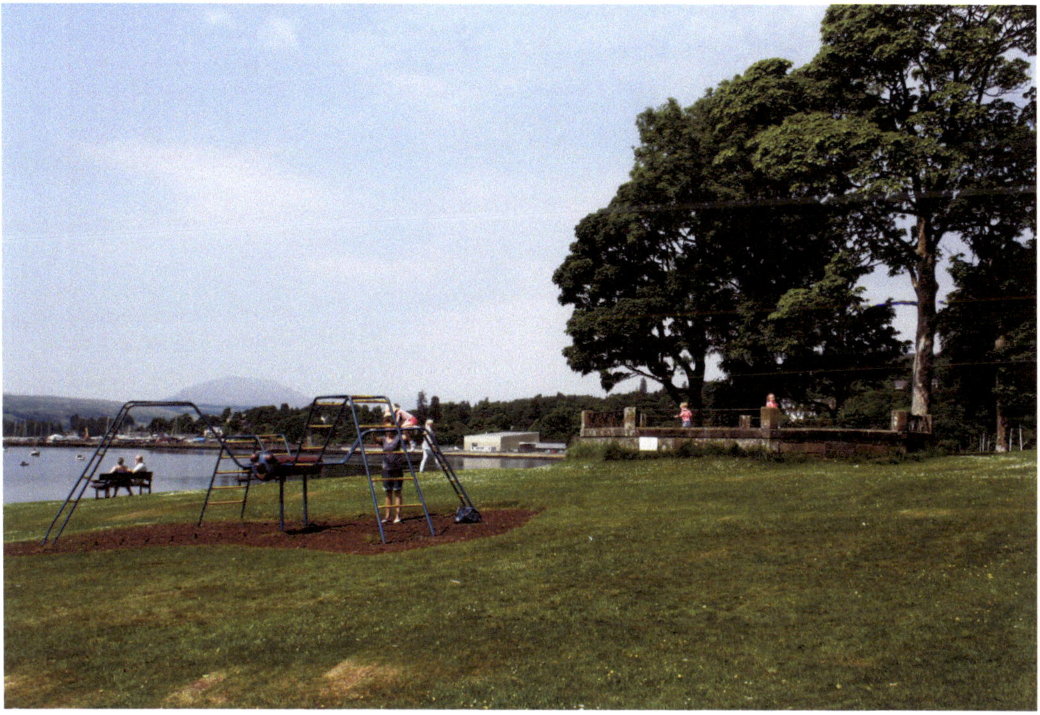

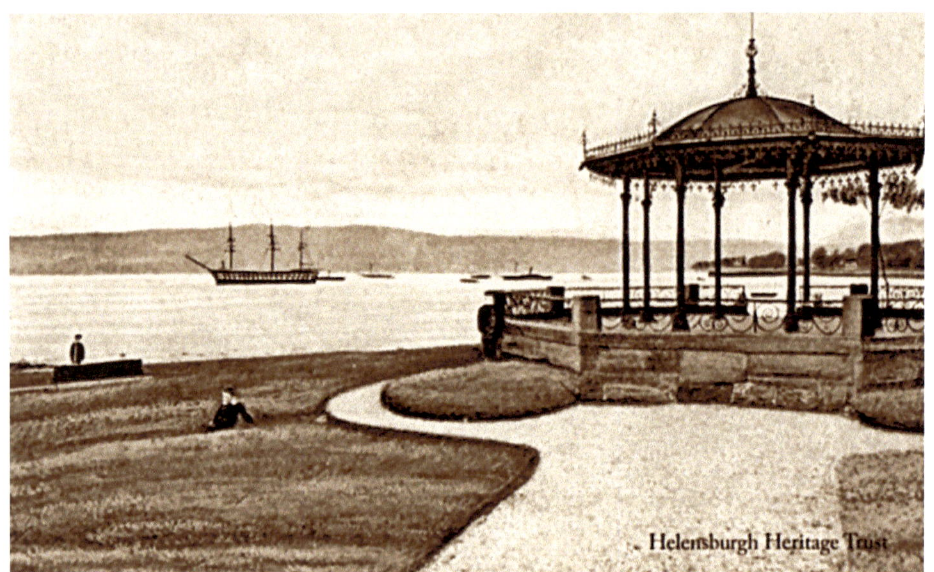

The Empress

Kidston Park bandstand in 1905, with the training ship *Empress*. Formerly the warship *Revenge*, the Clyde Training Ship Association vessel was the second of two charitable training ships for boys, and was in the Gareloch from 1889 until the 1920s, with staff giving a tough training to the 300 boys on board. In the present day only the base of the bandstand is left, however, the naval tradition of the area remains, with a submarine heading for the base at Faslane.

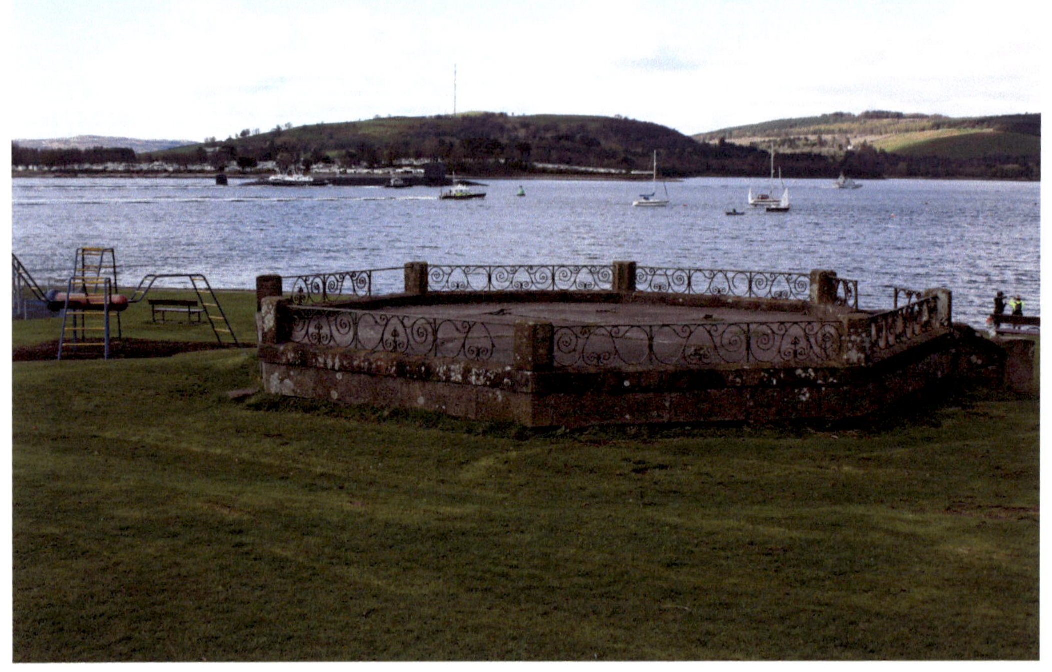

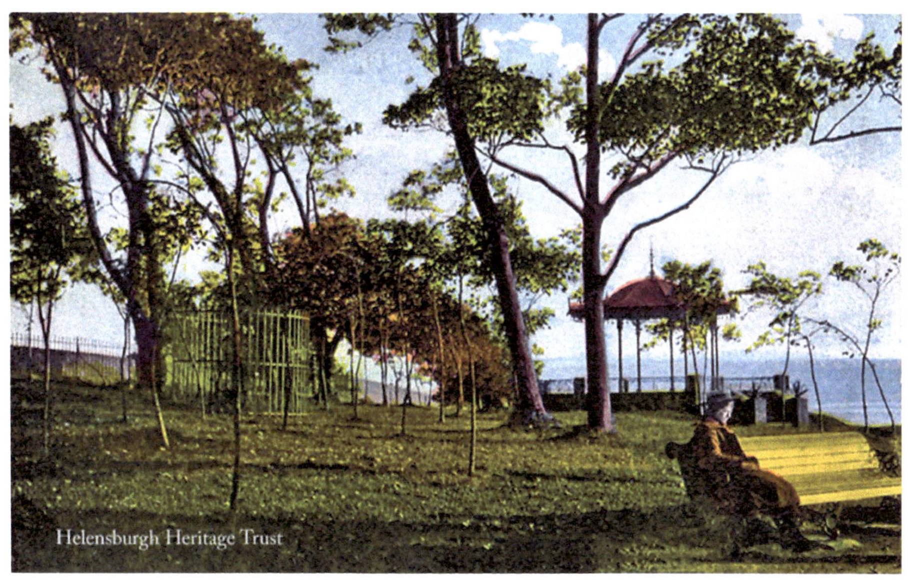

Evening Sun

A lady sits on a bench in the evening sun in Kidston Park. The trees have since matured and the park is still a haven of peace overlooking the Firth of Clyde.

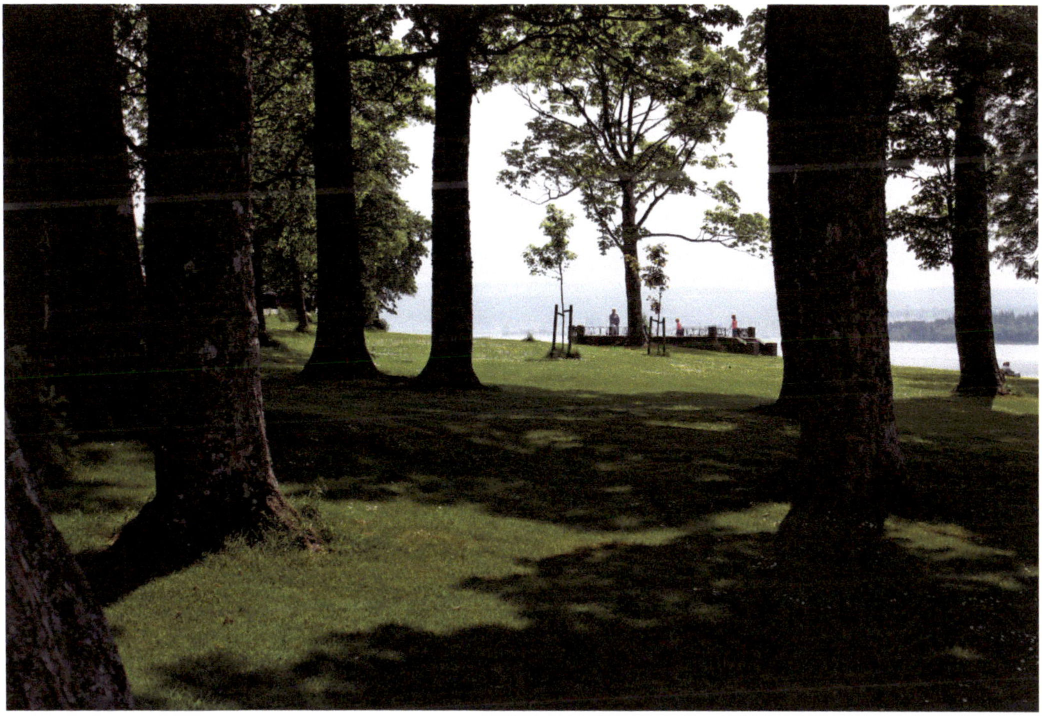

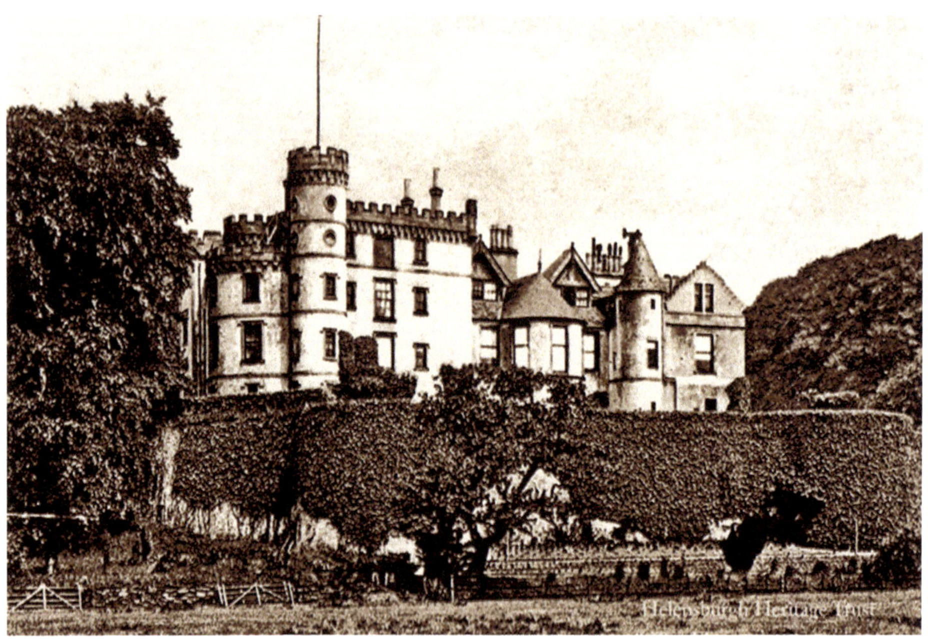

Ardencaple Castle

First recorded in 1296, Ardencaple Castle was the stronghold of the MacAulay clan until it was bought by the Duchy of Argyll in 1752. Robert Adam converted the castle into a mansion which was again remodelled in 1877. The last private resident, Mrs H. MacAulay-Stromberg, bought the castle from Sir Iain Colquhoun in 1923 and the castle finally returned to MacAulay ownership. During the Second World War it was used by the Admiralty as naval married quarters, and it was demolished in 1957, leaving a solitary tower displaying navigation lights.

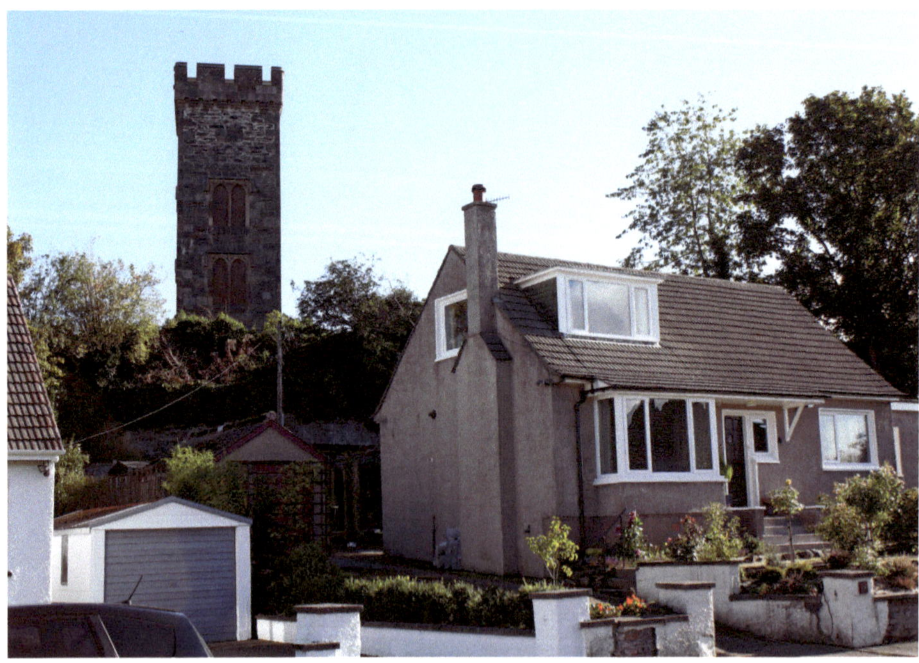

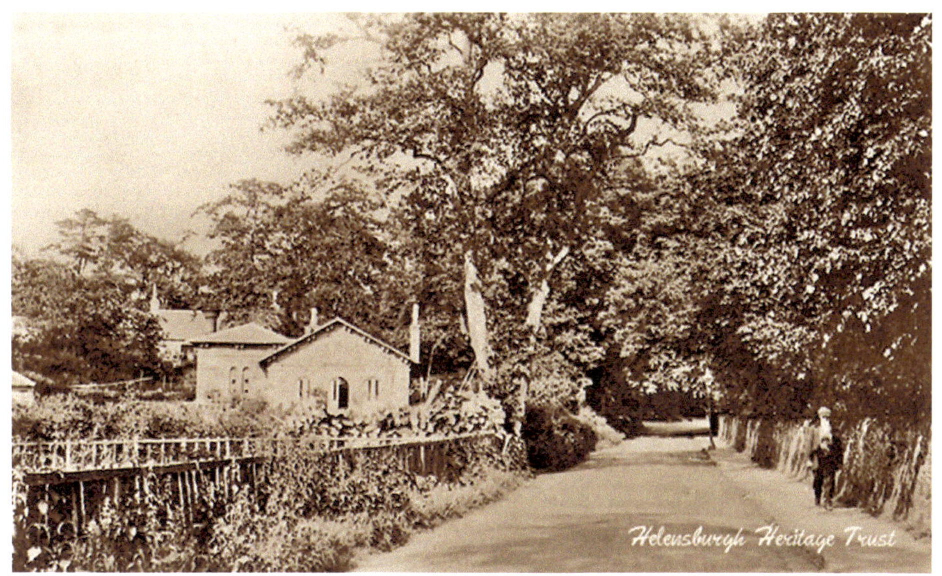

Ardencaple Mill

On the left beside Rhu Road Higher in 1917, Ardencaple Mill was part of the estates of Ardencaple Castle and in the nineteenth century was the site of a very profitable toll gate on the road from Helensburgh to Rhu. The mill was demolished in the 1960s and Dalmore Crescent built on the land.

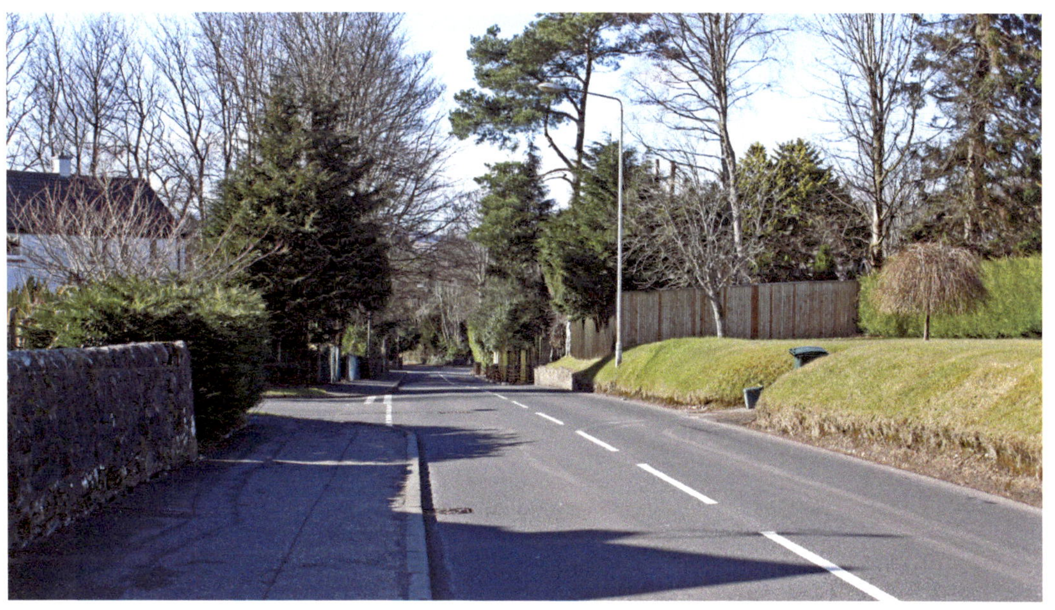

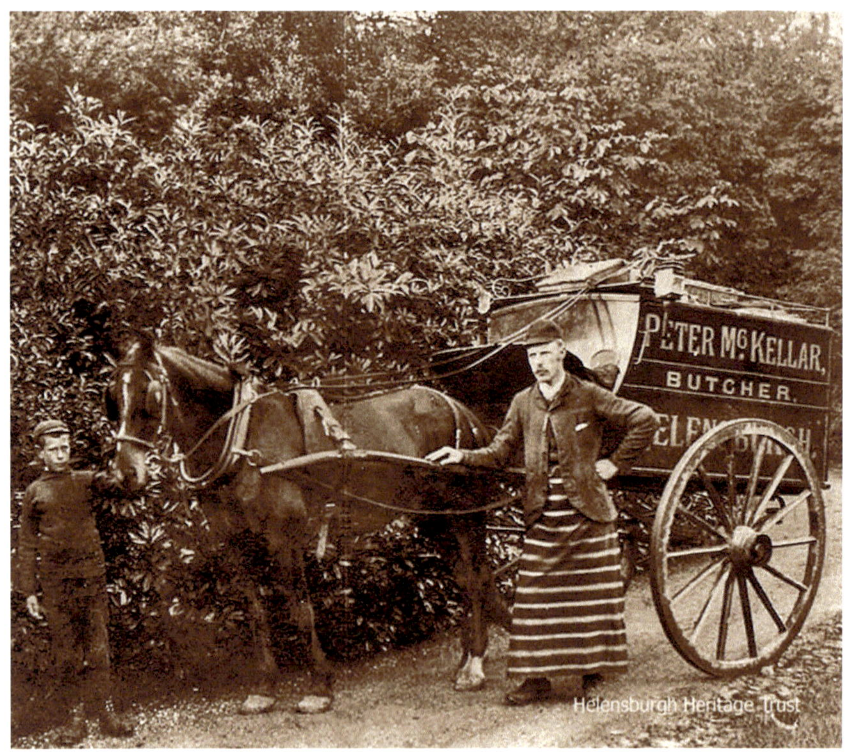

Deliveries

Helensburgh butcher Peter McKellar, assisted by a young boy, delivers meat to one of the local mansions with a rhododendron-ringed drive. Deliveries continue, with more up-to-date transport.

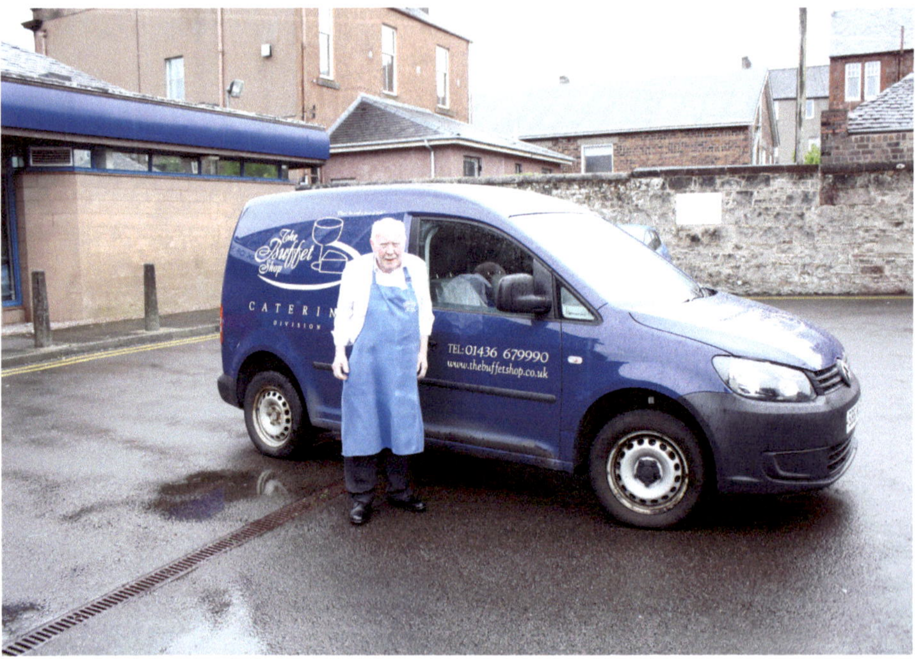

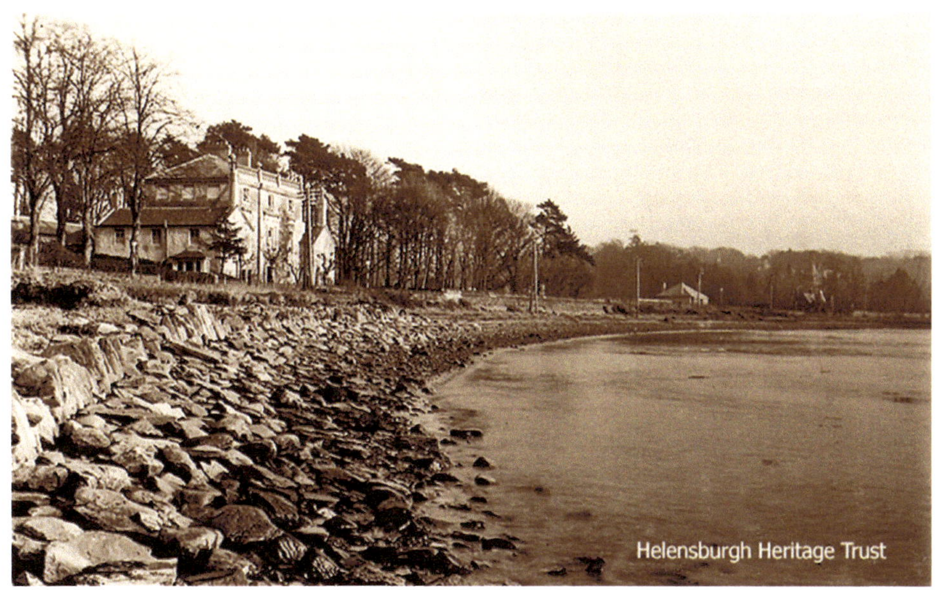

Ardencaple Hotel

Beside the main road between Helensburgh and Rhu, the Ardencaple Hotel was a former coaching inn named the Ardencaple Inn. It was built in the early 1800s by the Duke of Argyll and had its own stables to cater for travellers between Glasgow and Argyll. Around 1860 it became a private mansion owned by Mrs Rosina Drew and her husband Peter, but by 1912 it had reverted to a hotel.

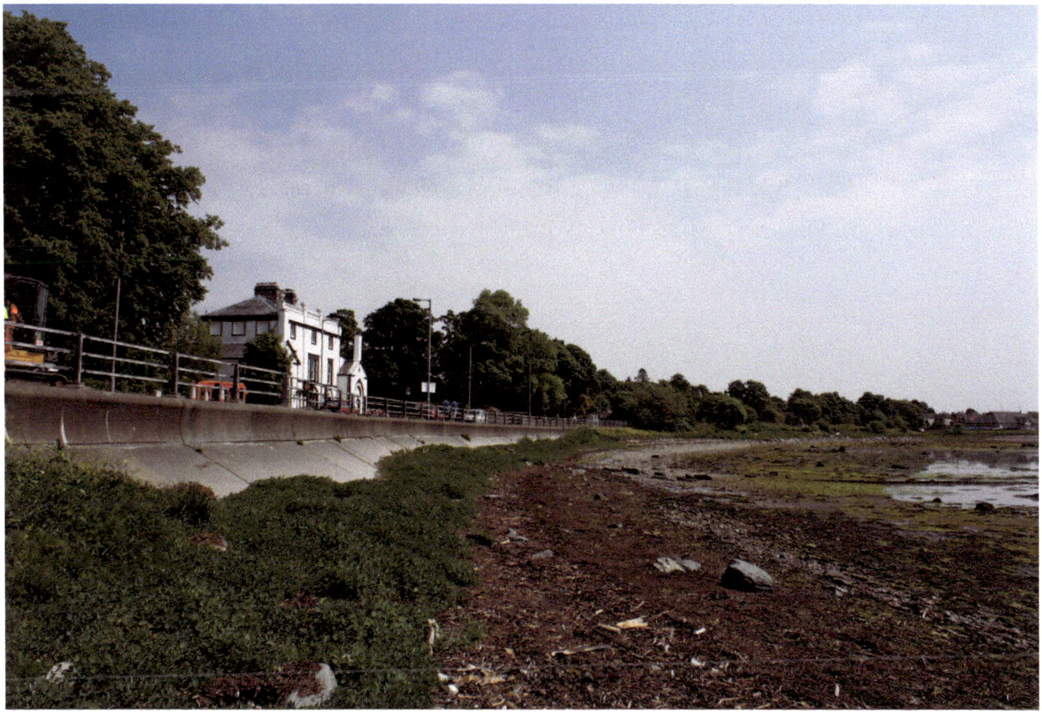

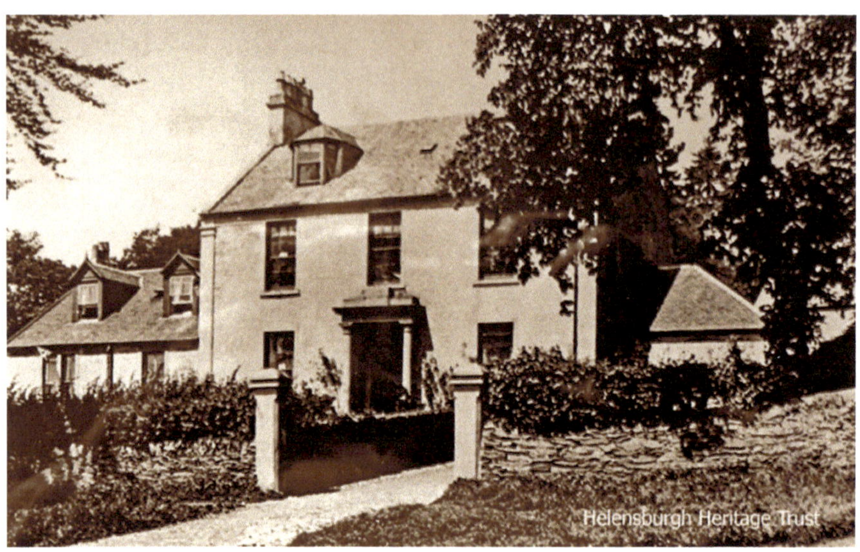

Dunmore House

The last owner of Dunmore House, which stood beside Pier Road, Rhu, opposite the pier, was a recluse who allowed the building to deteriorate to such an extent that latterly he was living in a tent inside one room because the roof was leaking so badly. It was demolished in the 1970s and replaced by two matching modern houses – Dunmore East and Dunmore West.

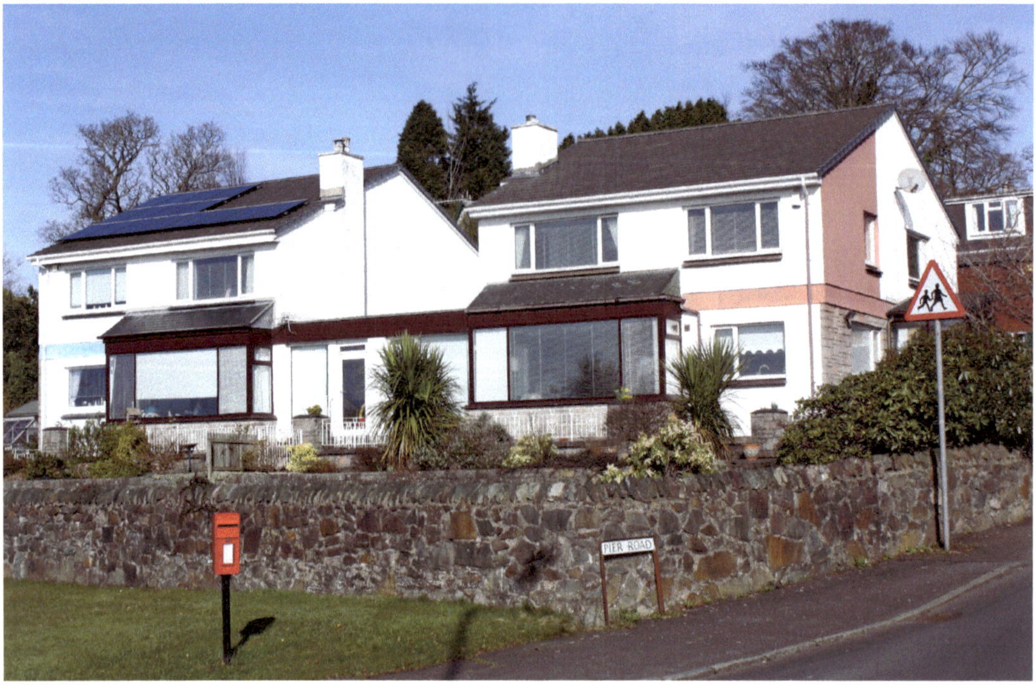

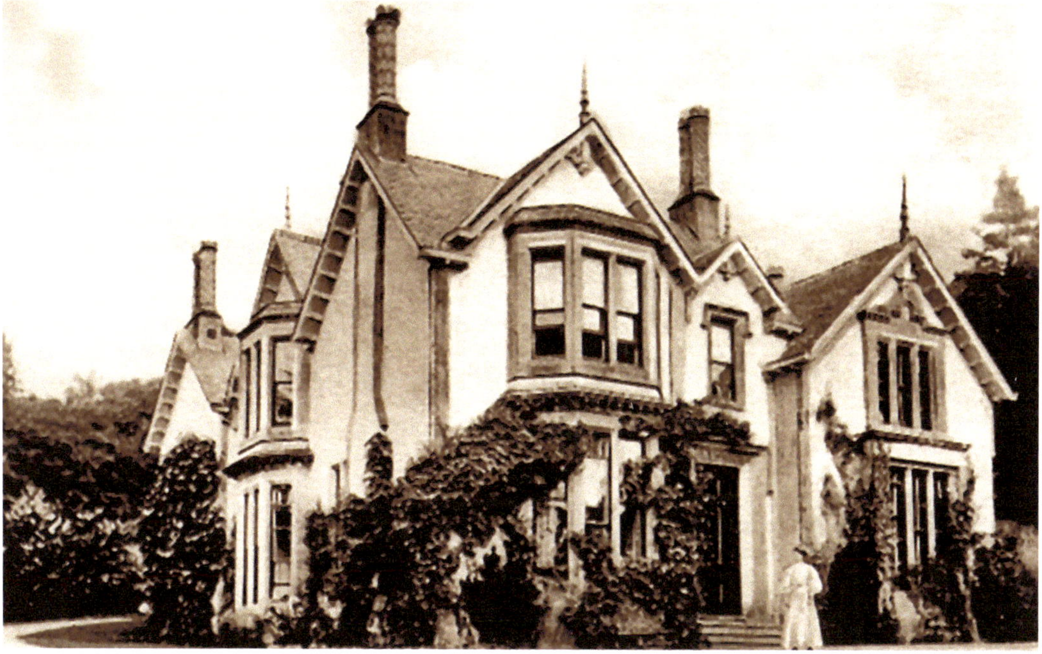

Glenarn

Initially built in 1847, Glenarn was subsequently expanded later in the century. The garden received plants from Joseph Hooker's 1849–50 expedition to Sikkim, notably the rhododendron falconeri at the side of the house. After the Gibson family acquired the property in 1927, they developed the garden over the following fifty years. The Thornley family arrived at Glenarn in 1983 to find much to be done to restore the garden to its former glory, and to extend its scope still further – work which is continuing today.

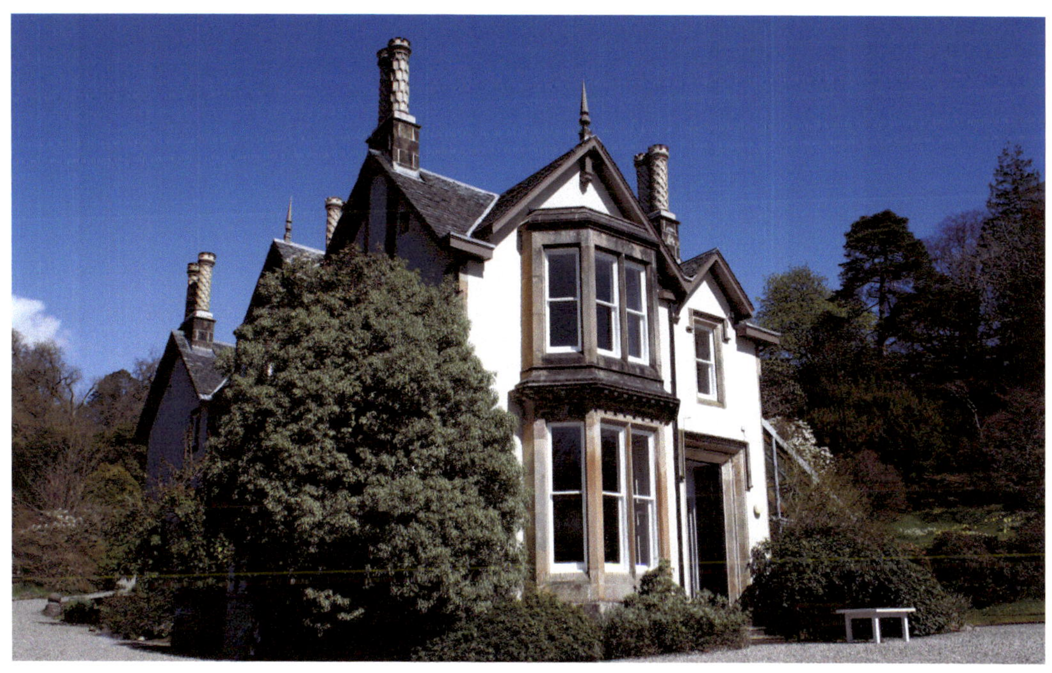

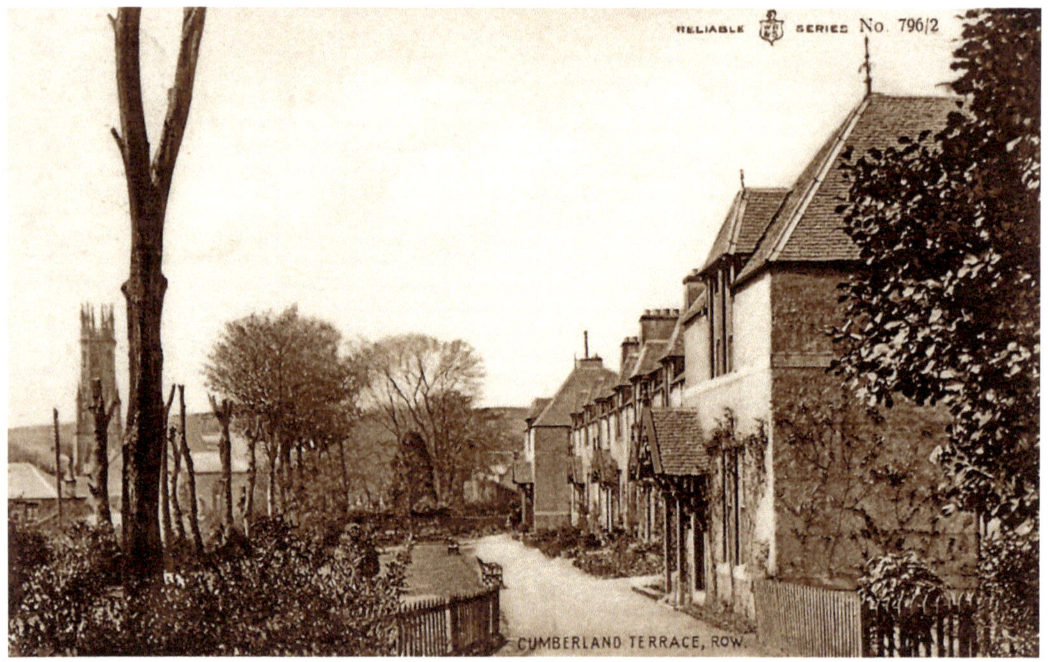

Cumberland Terrace

Named after a sail training ship, Cumberland Terrace in Rhu was built to house the ship's officers and a hospital. The *Cumberland* was anchored off Kidston Park from 1886 and was endowed by twelve prosperous Glasgow merchants to become a home for boys aged 12 to 14 at risk of being drawn into crime, until she burnt to the waterline in 1889.

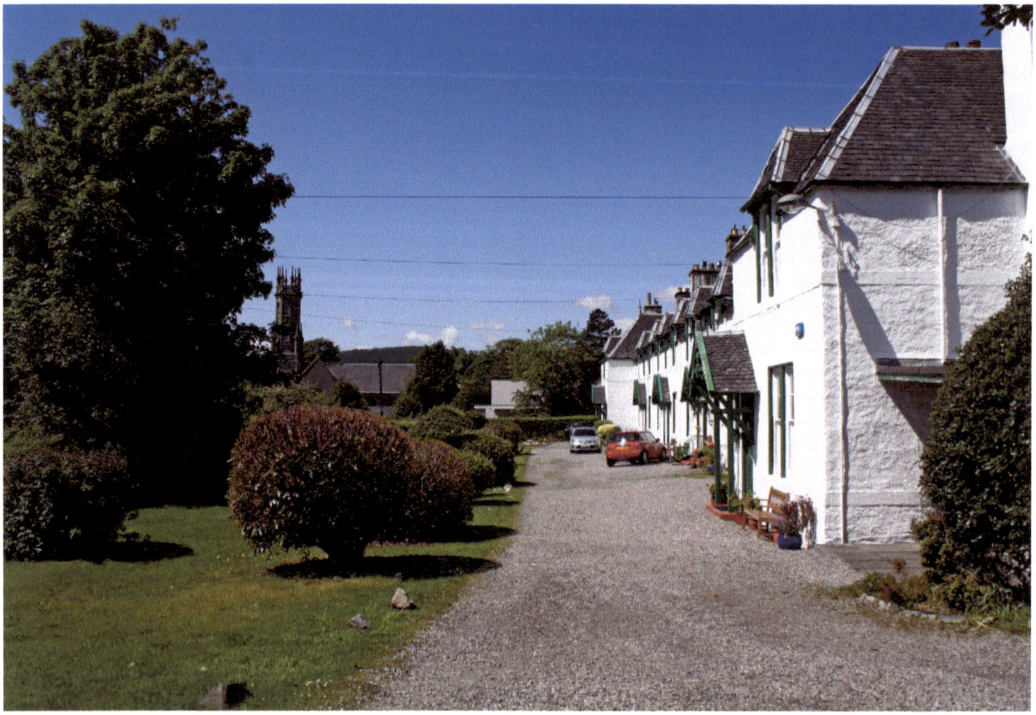

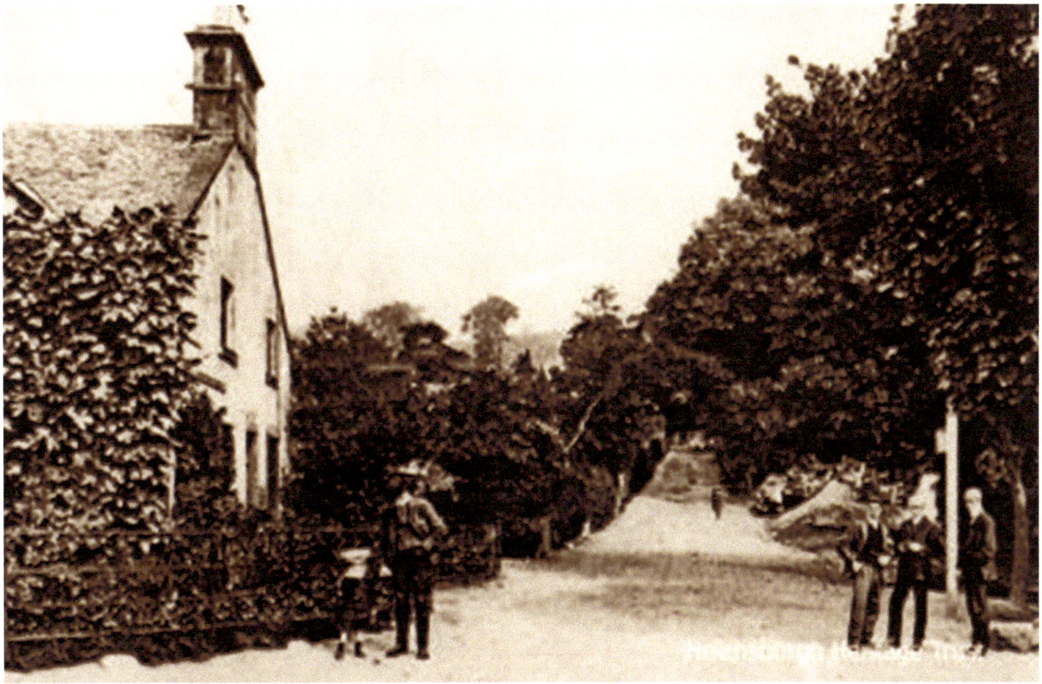

Manse Brae

An old image of what was then known as Post Office Road, Rhu, which is now Manse Brae.

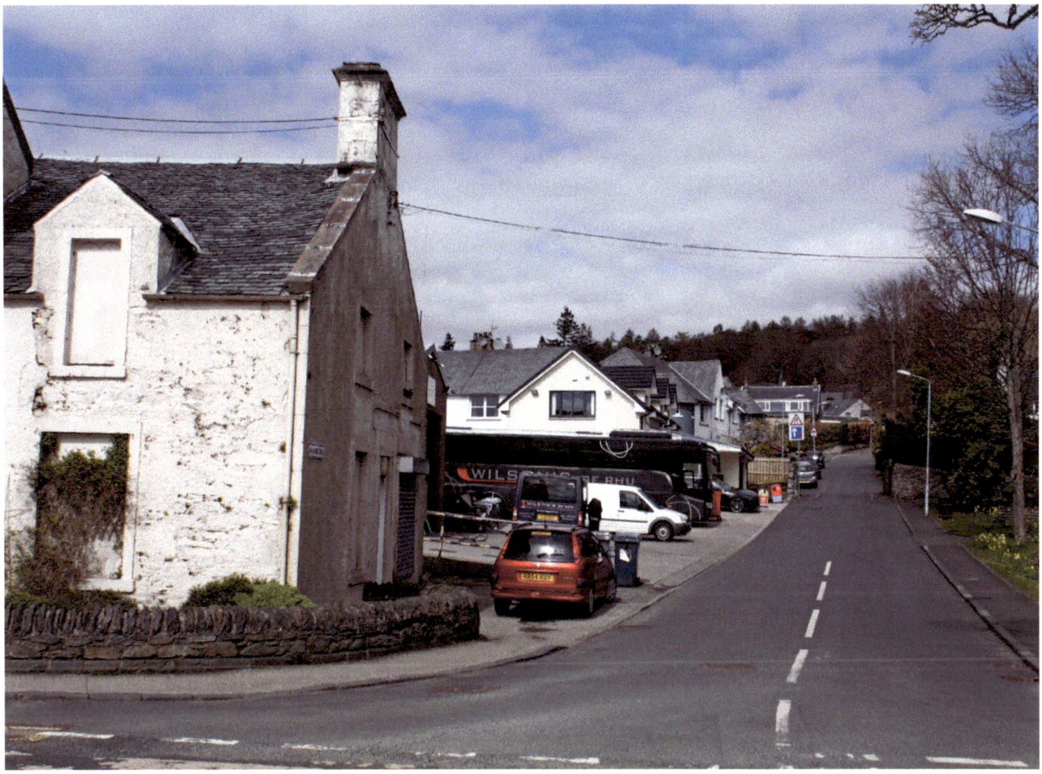

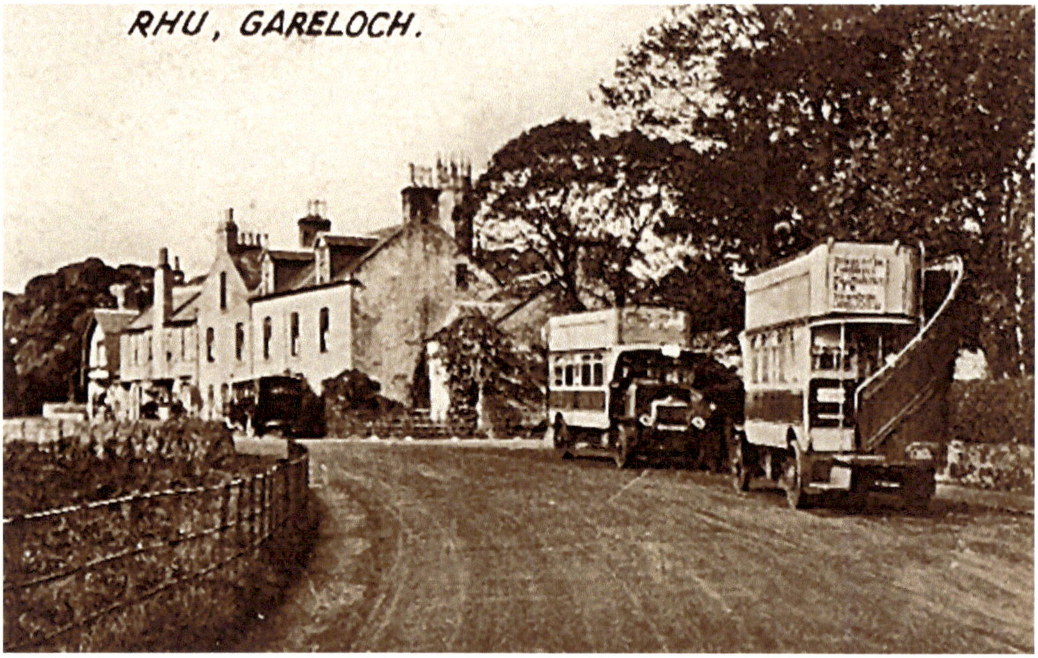

Bus Stop

Two buses wait in Rhu, probably in the 1920s. The bus stop remains, and the road leads to the major naval base at Faslane and beyond.

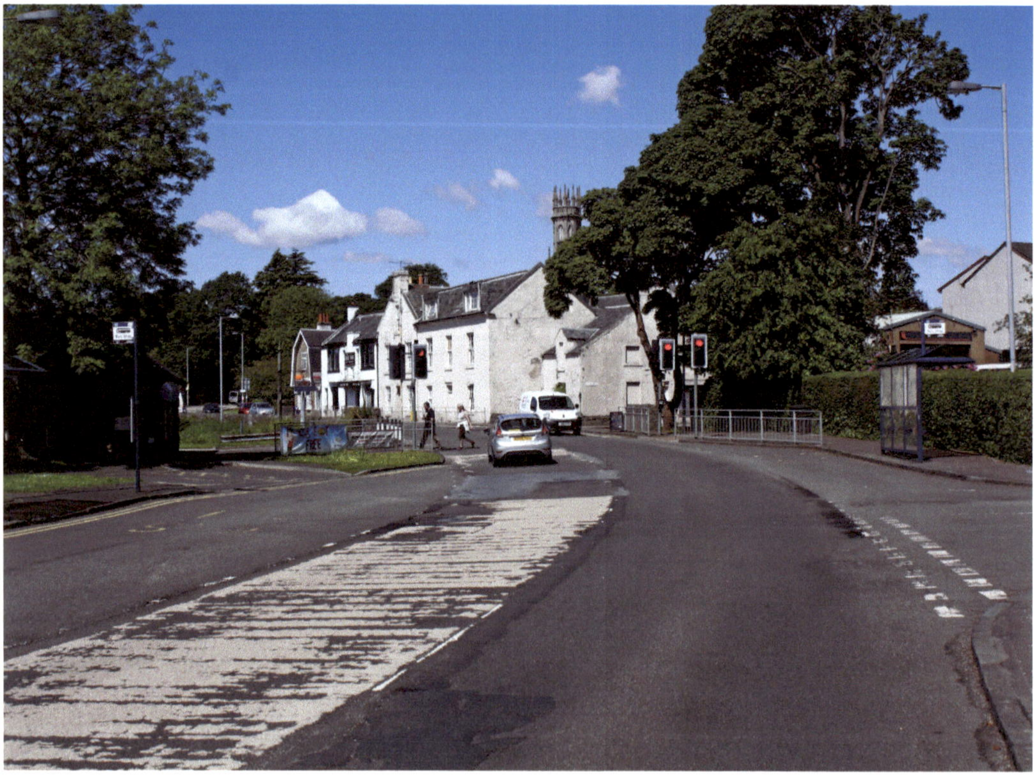

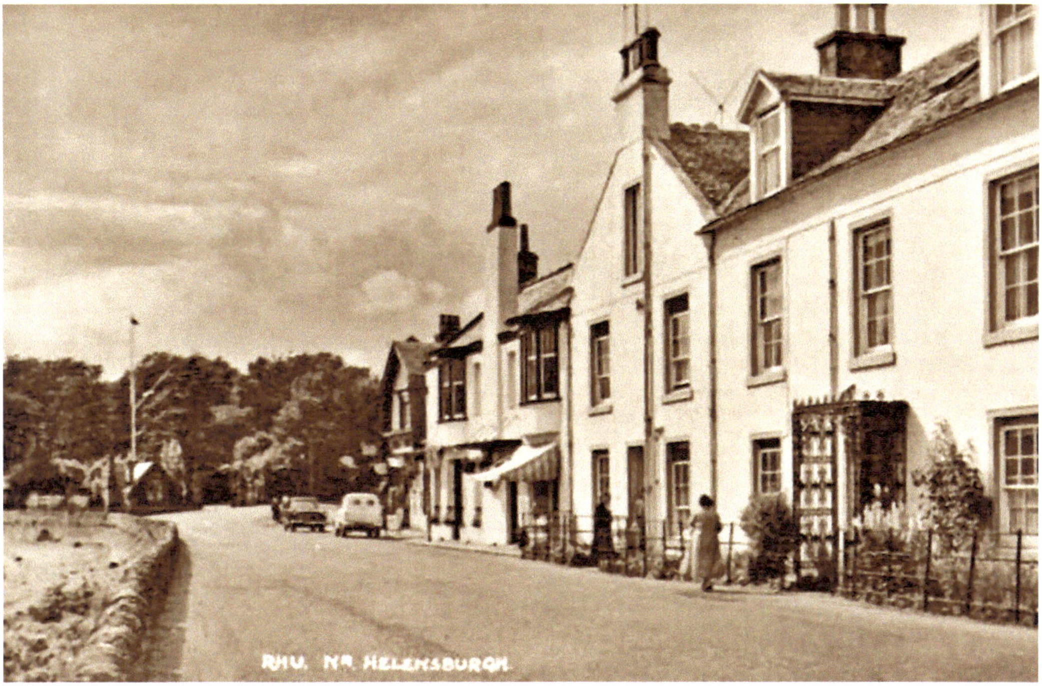

Rhu Inn and Post Office

The Colquhoun Inn, now the Rhu Inn, is in front of Rhu Post Office. David Winton left his job with the Post Office in Arbroath around 1910 as he was becoming blind, and he and his wife moved to Rhu where they were postmaster and postmistress until the mid-1950s.

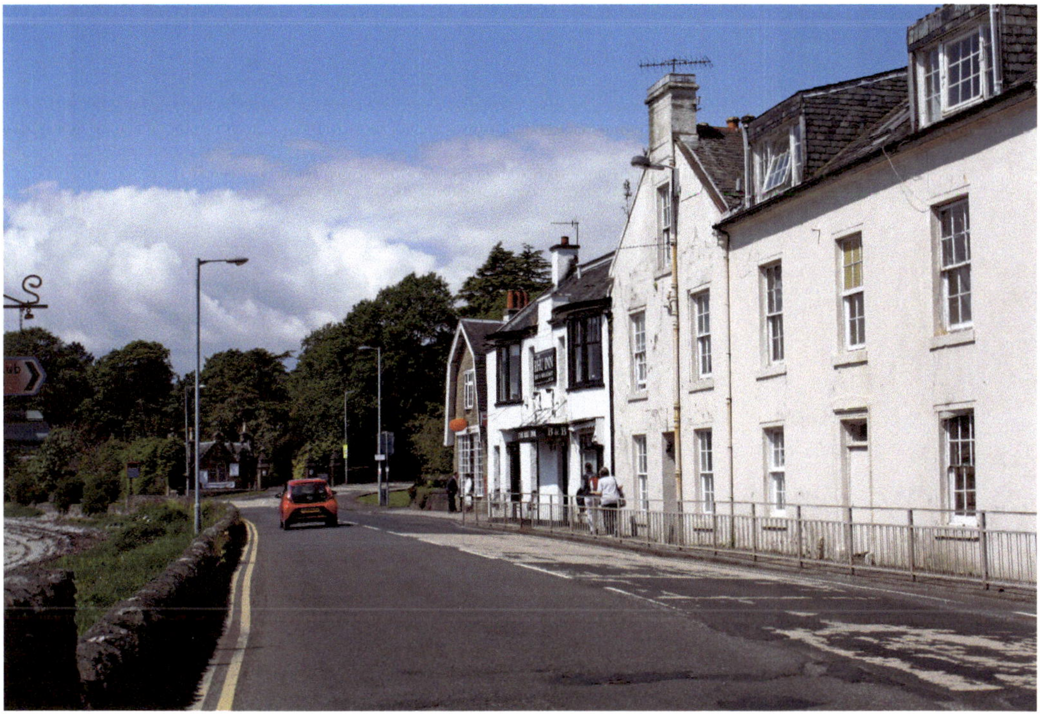

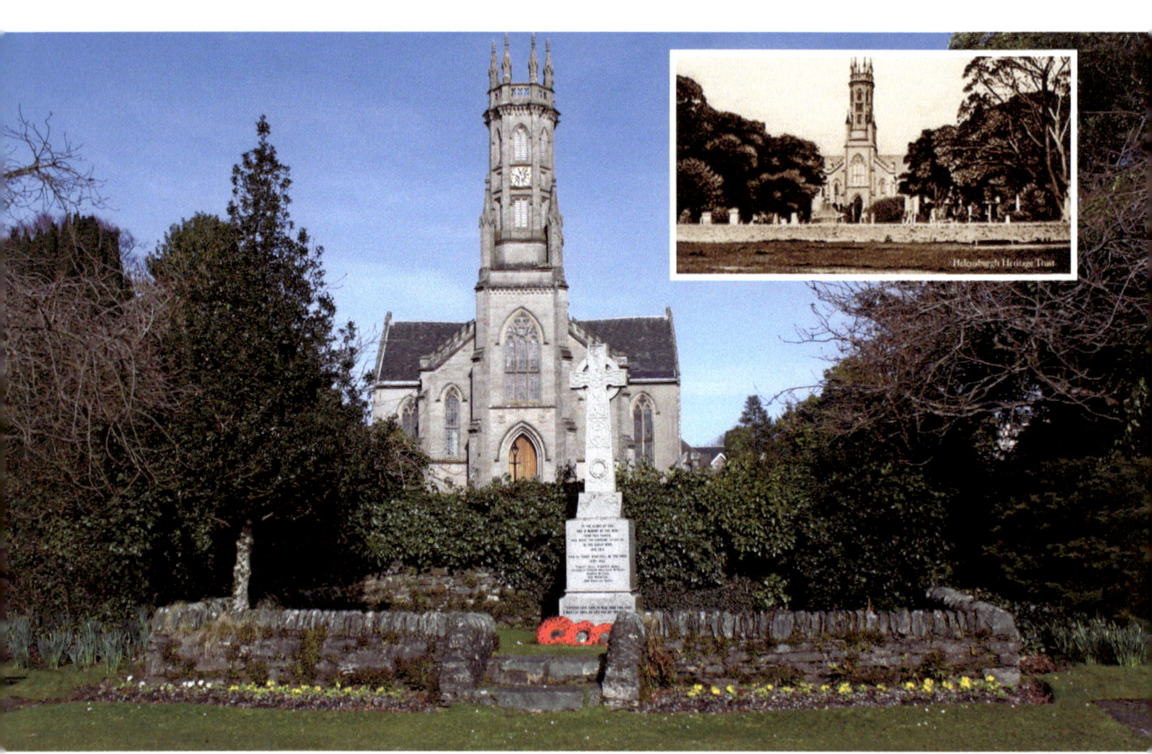

Rhu Parish Church

The third church on the site, built by architect William Spence in 1851, Row (now Rhu) Parish Church in 1906. The Parish of Row, including Helensburgh, was created in 1648 from lands belonging to the ancient parishes of Cardross and Rosneath, and the first church was completed the following year. The village war memorial was added in the 1920s.

Acknowledgements

The older images and text in this book depend on the work of Helensburgh Heritage Trust, especially Kenneth Crawford and Stuart Noble, who produced a comprehensive history of Helensburgh to mark its bicentenary in 2002, and Donald Fullerton, who runs the Trust's excellent website, which contains a vast amount of information and over 1,000 pictures. Fiona Baker, a local professional archaeologist, also provided very helpful advice.

Thanks are also due to Michael Curley of the Buffet Shop and Mike Thornley of Glenarn.

All the present-day photographs are the work of the author.

References
Noble, Stewart and Kenneth Crawford (eds.), *200 years of Helensburgh 1802–2002* (Argyle Publishing, 2002).
Walker, Frank Arneil, *The Buildings of Scotland: Argyll and Bute* (Penguin Books, 2000).
Helensburgh Heritage Trust website: www.helensburgh-heritage.co.uk.
Helensburgh Memories Facebook page.

About the Author

Chris Sanders was born in Aberystwyth in 1948, and moved to Scotland in 1973, and then to Helensburgh in 2006. Now retired after forty years of working in building research for a government laboratory and then Glasgow Caledonian University, he has been an enthusiastic photographer since his teenage years and has been a member of Helensburgh Photography Club, a very active local group, for several years.